WITNESS TO
WILDERNESS

WITNESS TO WILDERNESS

THE CLAYOQUOT SOUND
ANTHOLOGY

EDITED BY
HOWARD BREEN–NEEDHAM, SANDY FRANCES DUNCAN,
DEBORAH FERENS, PHYLLIS REEVE, SUSAN YATES

ARSENAL PULP PRESS
Vancouver

ARSENAL PULP PRESS
100-1062 Homer Street
Vancouver, B.C.
Canada V6B 2W9

Interior design by Gek-Bee Siow
Cover design by Nancy Pagé-Cuthbert/Blue Coyote Design
Cover photos by Mark Hobson and *(inset)* Adrian Dorst
Typeset by the Vancouver Desktop Publishing Centre
Printed on recycled acid-free paper
Printed and bound in Canada by Kromar Printing

CANADIAN CATALOGUING IN PUBLICATION DATA:
Main entry under title:
Witness to wilderness

ISBN 1-55152-009-5

1. Clayoquot Sound (B.C.)—Literary collections. 2. Canadian
literature (English)—British Columbia—Clayoquot Sound.* 3.
Canadian literature (English)—20th century.* I. Breen-Need-
ham, Howard.
PS8255.B7W757 1994   C810.8'0327112   C94-910470-1
PR9198.2.B72W57 1994

Table of Contents

Acknowledgements

The editorial collective wishes to thank:

Ted Reeve, for conveniently buying a new computer and then for learning more than he ever thought he wanted to know about formatting, and for opening bottles of wine at just the right time;

Phyllis Fafard, for keying in many seemingly unrelated bits and pieces;

Alan Wilson, for typesetting the original call for submissions;

Norman Abbey, for generously making available his scrapbooks of newspaper clippings about Clayoquot Sound;

Ron and Diana Mumford, for the use of their photocopier;

Vic Fafard, Cathy and Barrie Humphrey for their critical readings of the Introduction;

Glenn Olsen of North Island Custom Images for his photographic copy work;

Laurie McDonald, Doreen Milton, Phyllis and Wayne Lamb, Sue Vanderlee, and Sharon Dolan of the Gabriola Post Office for their cheerful handling of the increased volume of mail;

the writers, photographers, artists, and publishers who waived reprint fees;

all of our families and friends who enthusiastically supported this project.

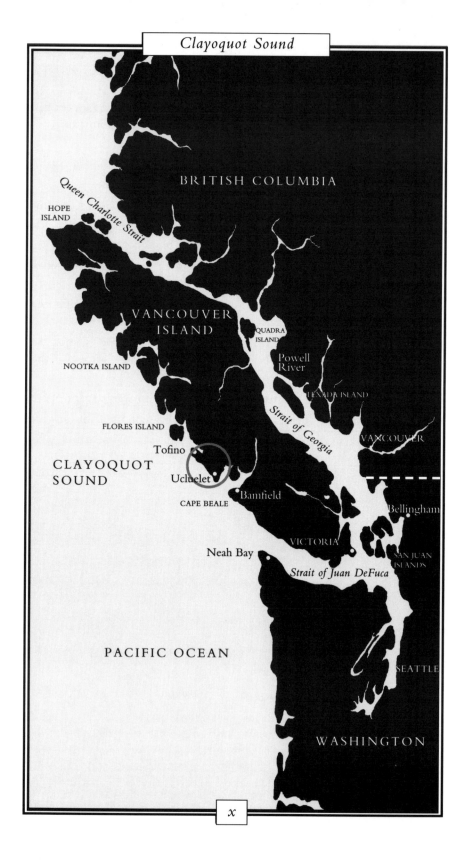

I think that I shall never see
A clearcut lovely as a tree
—*Winona Baker*

The misty, pre-dawn image of women and men and children holding hands in front of logging trucks at the Kennedy Lake bridge has circled the world. For months, television news ran the footage: self-appointed forest protectors, schooled in non-violent civil disobedience, singing or silent among banners, placards and friends, being led or carried away by Royal Canadian Mounted Police while MacMillan Bloedel video cameras whirred.

Who were these people? Why would they get up before dawn to confront logging trucks and the law? What would compel 859 people to be arrested in one summer? Were they just fanatics or could they be right? Are we really losing the last of our wilderness? What is wilderness, anyway?

These images and questions sparked a desire in the five of us to create an anthology. We hoped to explore the issues surrounding the daily blockade at the Kennedy Lake bridge and to decide for ourselves whether we wanted to join the protest and risk arrest, symbolically, if not physically.

We editors are, variously, a fiction writer, a visual artist, a bookseller, and two librarians. We are also a scuba diver, a peace activist, a resort-keeper, and an elected member of the Islands Trust. All of us are White, have children, and garden. We all live on Gabriola Island where a forest company, Weldwood of Canada, owns over one-quarter of the land.

In 1991, when company executives decided that periodic logging on Gabriola was no longer economically feasible, Weldwood offered to swap land for development rezoning. There began a long and arduous process, still not completed, at the end of which the community might receive 2,000 acres to keep undeveloped forever in exchange for a subdivision of about 360 houses.

The past few years have forced all Gabriolans to reconsider their ideas about logging practices, corporations, government and community on a deeply personal level. All 3,000 of us have been asking, one way or another, how we, as a community, deal with a multinational. Can we trust a forest company to keep its corporate word? And what about the land? Who looks after a forest if not a company? Should we let it look after itself? Where is our leadership? Why doesn't someone tell us what to do, or better yet, tell us what we want to hear?

Our Gabriola questions seemed similar to the questions the Commission on Resources and the Environment (CORE) was charged with answering about forest management changes needed all over British Columbia. CORE has been trying to accommodate the desires of communities, forest multinationals, government, and environmentalists. The process is painful. But is it the process that is at fault?

These questions, along with others about the rights of Native communities, justice and the judicial system, trees as members of ecosystems, nonviolent civil disobedience, and the mythic underpinnings of our changing society, intersected at the blockade in Clayoquot Sound. We have tried to weave them into Witness to Wilderness.

Before last August, we editors hadn't known each other well. Although we did not formally set out to do so, we have created this book by consensus; consensus is easier with five than 500, as some of the Peace Camp stories point out. Our styles of work, interests, and skills have complemented each other's so that we have been able to bring more to this project than we could have separately. We think this parallels how all the people have brought attention to Clayoquot Sound—to its trees and animals, and to the shifting values the struggle there signifies.

❖

Over the last fifteen years, Meares Island, the Carmanah, Walbran, lower Tsitika and Stein valleys, Lloyd, and south Moresby Islands have all had their moments in the media as protests over forest use have moved around Vancouver Island, Haida Gwaii (Queen Charlotte Islands), and the Lower Mainland. But no protest has been the size of the one in Clayoquot Sound in the summer of 1993, nor has garnered as much attention.

The settlers who felled the maple and white pine of Upper and Lower Canada in previous centuries probably assumed that forests went on forever. But Clayoquot Sound is the penultimate terminus of the European migration pattern on this continent. It is, literally and metaphorically, The End.

Of the sixty primary watersheds over 5,000 hectares (19 square miles) on Vancouver Island, the only seven that remain unlogged are in the Clayoquot Sound area. At 260,000 hectares (1,004 square miles, nearly half of Prince Edward Island), this area is the largest intact ancient temperate rainforest on Vancouver Island, and it is within easy driving distance of populated centres. It contains moss-hung giants of Sitka spruce, red and yellow cedar and Douglas fir, some of which may be 2,000 years old. As trees, they exist in a complex, diverse, and little understood ecosystem. As lumber, one of them can fetch up to $30,000.

Clayoquot Sound is not privately owned land (unlike tracts on eastern Vancouver Island and the Gulf Islands), but Crown land, popularly regarded as public land, much of it leased to forestry companies through Tree Farm Licenses.

Crown lands, in concept and in reality, are integral to Native land claim settlements. The bands comprising the Nuu-chah-nulth First Nations have considered this region their traditional lands for thousands of years, yet the government did not include them in the original "Clayoquot Compromise," announced April 13, 1993; only on March 19, 1994 was a joint Native and government Interim Measures Agreement signed. Still, some contributors to Witness to Wilderness, *both Native and White, question the government's and private sector's legal and moral rights to decide on any management plan while land claims are still outstanding.*

In the government's compromise, roughly one-third of Clayoquot Sound is protected; the rest is open for logging or limited logging in special management areas. Of the protected areas, nearly half is already part of a provincial or national park and other parts are bog and mountaintop which produce valueless lumber. The size of clearcuts is reduced to 40 hectares (0.15 square miles, about the size of downtown Victoria), but there is the problem of blowdowns at the edge of clearcuts, and of providing a corridor for animals. Under this compromise, as Cameron Young states, seventy-four of every 100 ancient temperate rainforest trees can be logged. Yet, extrapolating from figures provided by MacMillan Bloedel and the Council of B.C. Forest Industries, logging in Clayoquot Sound constitutes only about one percent of British Columbia's forest industry. So why not leave it intact, many contributors ask.

Much of the land on eastern Vancouver Island and the Gulf Islands in Georgia Strait was acquired by logging companies from land grants in the last century. Over time, parcels of land were amalgamated as companies which are now multinationals bought out smaller companies. Today, there are no unlogged watersheds on the east coast of Vancouver Island except the lower Tsitika, and British Columbia still has no legislation to regulate logging on privately-owned land. Moreover, people are only beginning to learn about old-growth forests and do not yet know if second or third growth will replicate them over time and if the displaced species will or can return.

As swede saws have evolved into feller-bunchers, and steam donkeys and A-frames into grapple-yarders, technology has allowed more efficient—some say rapacious— logging. Don Malcolm's overview details this evolution. As well, British Columbia has a history of governments too sympathetic to forest corporations; what few controls have been legislated have not been routinely enforced. And the IWA (International Woodworkers of America) has not complained much about the loss of 30,000 jobs in twenty years; they seem to have been busy negotiating higher wages for fewer workers. Everyone in the province is experiencing the effects of these legacies, when not outrightly suffering from them.

Having logged eastern Vancouver Island in the face of increasing protest about over-logging from citizens of all ages, some of the forestry companies are turning to real estate development. The population of southwestern British Columbia is swelling, due primarily to a wave of migration from the rest of Canada. The White residents of Vancouver Island and the Gulf Islands are feeling vulnerable, their lives subject to the whim of the forest companies. This experience somewhat parallels Native peoples' experiences of being confined or relocated at White whim and might be one factor in the Second Nation's increasing empathy with the First Nations over the last decade.

Canadians, and latterly British Columbians, have been saddled with the Eurocentric myth that Europe's colonists are looking after the wilderness. It is as if Charles G.D. Roberts' and Ernest Thompson Seton's descriptions in books of 100 years ago still exist, as if Native peoples are still "Red Indians," as if Europeans' wilderness is over here and is still plentiful. Paradoxically, this myth has been overlaid on the European pioneers' myth that trees are enemies which have to be chopped down so the land can be tamed. The heritage of a juxtaposition of "tree" and

"Indian" in colonial mentality is not to be disregarded when considering Clayoquot Sound.

Writing in Canada has always engaged the landscape; wilderness (a Eurocentric rather than Native concept as Chief Luther Standing Bear's statement points out) has always been "other" to Whites. As people have realized the damage being done to the planet, this concept of wilderness has shifted from something fearsome to something desirable. We are in danger of shifting too far: wilderness as destroyed; landscrape instead of landscape. Many pieces in this anthology celebrate wilderness, but do so from sorrow and loss.

As we sifted through submissions at editorial meetings, and discussed our background reading, we began to realize that there were more factors influencing the

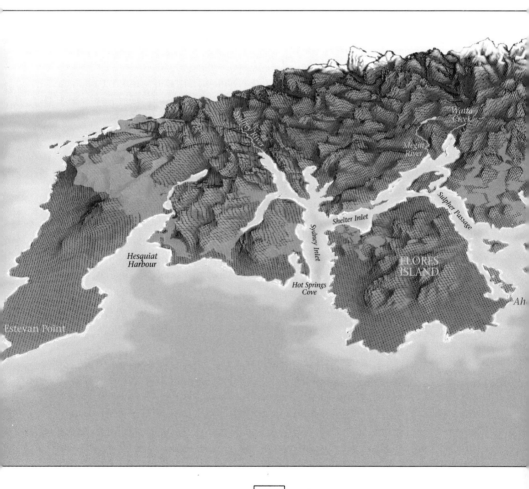

Clayoquot Sound blockade than we had previously considered. For example, there are now global technologies, instant information, and a world population of five billion increasing daily. In the last fifty years, Canada has produced the best-educated, best-fed, most secure generations ever. It is only when people's basic needs are met that values tend to shift from maintaining life to the quality of life.

As well, we Canadians have had two decades of looking at ourselves, our relationships, our needs, our self-esteem. We've tried to learn to be gentle (men), assertive (women), to set boundaries and break them down, and to expect attention and respect. We have been examining every value, braving taboos. Also, we have extended our identification to other species—in Clayoquot Sound, to trees.

Many contributors write about how spiritual their experiences were in Clayoquot

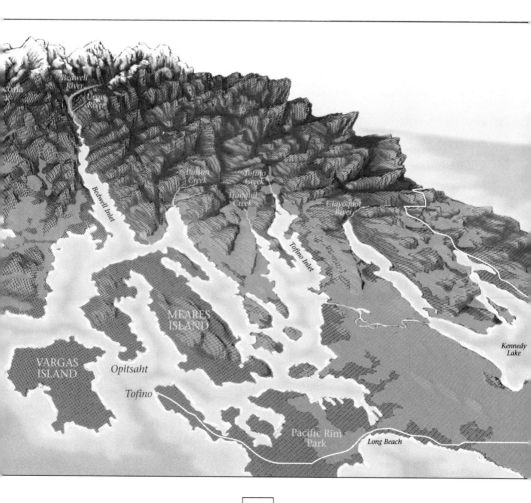

Sound, among the trees, in the Peace Camp, and on the blockade. God left the church in the sixties; in the nineties s/he's residing in the trees—a more accessible, comradely god, perhaps. Hugging a tree can be a friendly act or can, in our consumer society, signify metaphorical ownership; one can be closer to, and maybe even own, one's spiritual ecstasy. Are some people gaining a sense of celebration at being a part of (instead of apart from) this planet just as our species is threatening to destroy it?

We editors favour a forest industry, but on a different scale and with less destructive logging than the industry has used in British Columbia over the past few decades. We feel compassion for the forest workers and their families who have been losing jobs at an unprecedented rate in this industry, in this province. Joyce Nelson points out that the loss of jobs is due to increased technology of the sort that has put our species on the moon, and soon, according to Judith Merril, might put us on Mars. But loggers are losing more than jobs; now that Paul Bunyan has come to life as a feller-buncher, they are losing their professional heroes and dignity. SHARE BC, a group that belies its acronym, is not helping, as Des Kennedy, Stuart Lee, and others illustrate. We do not want ancient temperate forests in British Columbia to disappear like cod off the coast of Newfoundland; we fear they may. We believe it is better to lose jobs in the forest industry when there are still enough trees to support logging and remanufacturing than it is to lose jobs in fish processing because there are no fish.

We deplore the simplistic and frequently artificial polarization between environmentalists and forest industry workers. This polarization encourages an artificial division between nature and culture in which "dominion over" is played out in British Columbia as: we will cut these trees/you will not cut these trees. Allowing only two positions obscures complexities and by definition posits a winner and a loser—sometimes trees and always people. Until we as a society free ourselves from this model, nature, wild or tamed, will always be "other" to us. We must all ask: who is served by this model?

It is time to evolve new metaphors for our human selves on—and in—the land. A glimpse of ourselves as, say, organic gardeners instead of pioneers, colonists, industrialists, loggers, environmentalists, or elected officials—as members of the biosphere—might allow us some compassion for, and acceptance of, ourselves as we bumble through our landscape, as well as for our landscape itself. Can we not do better than stewardship? While an improvement on "dominion over," it still implies a separation and a right to look after. Perhaps it is ourselves we need to steward. The trees don't need us, as Phyllis Webb makes clear; we humans need the trees. There may be more metaphors to explore, but what is certain is that if we don't change our thinking, we won't change our behaviour. Nor, as Kim Goldberg points out in "Axed," is it productive to try to silence debate.

Our very first submission to this anthology was a scrawled note saying Clayoquot should "look like the moon" and "those hippy welfare scum" should "run for their lives." We braced ourselves for more hostility, but this note was unique; all of the other 300-plus submissions were concerned and thoughtful.

Witness to Wilderness is loosely structured around the events in Clayoquot Sound during the summer of 1993. It starts at the blockade on the Kennedy Lake bridge, moves through the Peace Camp set up in the clearcut black hole, then to the arrests, the trials, convictions, fines, and jail sentences. We've placed poems and articles and photos within this framework as we thought those on the blockade or following the daily news might have considered the issues the pieces raise or the memories they evoke.

We wanted to be as inclusive and representative as possible to parallel the variety and number of people who participated in the largest act of nonviolent civil disobedience in Canada's history. There are over 120 contributors, the youngest of whom is eight, the eldest eighty-five. Many were at the Peace Camp, and some arrested. Many are poets, novelists, journalists, playwrights, not just because this is a book, but because it is a writer's job to speak for and about the truths of the land, physical and symbolic.

We have not concentrated much on alternatives to the Clayoquot Sound dilemma, although at the outset we intended to. We read enough to realize that there are experts working on the specific problems of the forest industry. If we, the people, through our government, can implement some of these experts' ideas, we can have a sustainable forest industry and the ancient rainforest of Clayoquot Sound. We have included some of these books in The Editors' Idiosyncratic Annotated Bibliography: books and articles and organizations that we found relevant while we worked on Witness to Wilderness.

As press time loomed, we had to omit some excellent but previously published works; although the authors wanted them included, the publishers owned copyright and either demanded too high payment or delayed responding until too late.

We hope the voices in this anthology speak for the many points of view of those thousands of citizens who passed through the Peace Camp and stood at dawn on the Kennedy Lake bridge. We hope the voices provide insight into why so many people have risked liberty and reputation to save an ancient forest.

Sandy Frances Duncan, Howard Breen-Needham,
Deborah Ferens, Phyllis Reeve, Susan Yates
Gabriola, April 1994

"CLAYOQUOT"

The name of this Sound is derived from the tribe of Indians residing here, and was spelt by the early traders, dating from 1785, Clioquatt, Clayocuat, Klaooquat, and Klahoquat. In 1787 Captain Barkley, of the Imperial Eagle, *named it Wickaninnish's Sound, from the hereditary name of the principal chief residing here. Captain Meares spells this name* Wicananish, *and in his book gives a graphic account of a visit he paid this potentate on 14 June, 1788. Meares named a portion of the sound near the chief's village, Port Cox. . . . The number of Indians residing in the sound in 1788 is estimated at 4,000; their present number (census, 1904) is about five hundred, divided equally between the two villages of Clayoquot and Ahousat. . . . The name Clayoquot is derived from the "Tla-o" or "Cla-o," meaning another, or different. "Aht" means people or village, hence "Cla-o-quaht" means people different from what they used to be. There is a tradition to the effect that the inhabitants here were originally quiet and peaceful, later they became quarrelsome and treacherous; hence they were called by their neighbours "Cla-o-quat." (Rev. A.J. Brabant)*
—From *British Columbia Coast Names* by Capt. John T. Walbran (J.J. Douglas, 1971, 1st pub. 1906).

After the Clayoquot Indians, whose name has been given a remarkable range of translation. G.M. Sproat said it meant "another [i.e., different] people," while Dr. Brown thought it meant "other or strange house." The missionary Father Brabant told Captain Walbran that Clayoquot meant "people who are different from what they used to be," and noted a tradition that these Indians were originally quiet and peaceful, but later became quarrelsome and treacherous. A modern linguist, John A. Thomas of the Nitinats, says it means "people of the place where it becomes the same even when disturbed."

John Jewitt, at the beginning of the nineteenth century, described the "Klaa-oo-quates" as "fierce, bold and enterprising." Clayoquot was first known to the white men as "Port Cox," after John Henry Cox and Co., merchants of Canton who sent two ships to trade in the area in 1787.
—From *British Columbia Place Names* by G.V.P. and Helen B. Akrigg (Sono Nis Press, 1986).

WAITING BY THE BRIDGE

Sometimes one is aware of an aching tenderness, of love with a faint shadowing of pain, not only for the earth but for the entire universe. On Tuesday morning, September 14, at about 5 a.m., standing on a logging road near the Kennedy Lake bridge, waiting to set up a barricade against logging trucks, many people must have experienced this sense of awe, of quietness, of being with others and also of being alone under a vast sky filled with stars stretching, in one area, down to the horizon, stars as we never see them near city lights: enormous, pulsating constellations—giant dipper, Cassiopeia, the three brilliants making up Orion's dagger—and single stars, planets, particularly one, growing brighter as others fade, over the peak of low mountains emerging into day. That must have been the morning star, Venus, and there she hung, surrounded by a penumbra of light while the bright sliver-thin bow of the new moon rose close beside her, to her right.

As the light grew imperceptibly, the weather grew colder. Only those who kept this vigil morning after morning had brought warm enough clothes. The rest of us shivered and stuck our hands up our sleeves, but nothing would have dragged us away. Spokespeople told us the rules governing passive resistance, told us what to do when police and trucks arrived, never coerced us to risk arrest. We sang songs and some people held placards. A middle-aged man, bemused, said, "I feel as if I'm in a movie." And certainly that's what it felt like: unreal. In ghostly light, three or four hundred orderly people, a few children, all silent when they weren't singing, tired after a long, sleepless night, waiting for something to happen.

I used to go up to Long Beach, beyond Kennedy Lake, in the fifties with my three children and their father. When we first went, there was no road. We caught the *Uchuck*, a small ferry which held only one car, from Port Alberni, taking provisions from Woodward's because there was only one small and expensive store some distance from Singing Sands, where we stayed. Owned by Peggy Wittington, the little camp consisted of five or six cabins, furnished with wood stoves, bunk beds, sheets, blankets, towels, cooking utensils, and rented out for fifteen dollars a week. We took flour and made our own bread, took butter, eggs, a few vegetables. We dug razor-backed and butter clams, caught small white fish off the rocks, picked wild strawberries. Fishermen sometimes gave us salmon or trout if they had more than they could use.

We caught a bus in Ucluelet for Peg's place. I remember the first time asking when the bus would leave, and the driver looking at me in surprise and saying, "When everyone's here." We had no idea when that would be. He probably didn't either. Finally, he drove along a road towards Tofino, stopped at a gap in the trees, and let us off. Peg was there on the beach with her black Shetland pony attached to a cart which was to carry our suitcases and food along the beach to her clearing. The wide sand stretched to right and left as far as we could see and extended behind her to the curling surf; some distance behind the white line of waves, the sea crashed against a single island. The world smelled of blown salt and conifers and the faint iodine of seaweed. We had to raise our voices against the waves. Above the tide-line bleached silver logs piled one on the other, and the sand was hard-packed. People with cars could drive along it, and did, and sometimes waited too long; when the tide came in it sucked anything heavy down into the sand until it disappeared altogether. We passed an abandoned car with only its roof in view.

On some days the beach was hidden in mist. Eerie silence greeted the morning, and if we met someone coming the other way when we walked through it, we could see only feet, then calves and knees, and finally a ghostly person. But we seldom met anyone on the whole twelve miles of clean, pale sand. Sometimes it rained: water rushing down the windows of our cabin, clattering on the roof. A monsoon, but the water wasn't cold and we learned to go out in it, in shorts and bare feet, as Peg did, to squish between the trees which surrounded the cabins and grew helter-skelter throughout the small oasis which was her place. Her nearest neighbour was miles away up the beach.

Later the rough logging road was opened to the public and we drove up, passing Kennedy Lake, huge and dark with trees. More people knew of Long Beach now, but there had always been a few squatters there who lived off the land, eccentric characters who were at home nowhere else: an old man who kept goats in his shack and commissioned the bus to drop off a bottle at regular intervals; a man who panned for gold; an ex-navy officer who filled out government forms in a tiny shack in Tofino. His writing table was set near his stove which bore a pot of tea laced with gin. He drank it all day. Behind him, on the floor, were stacks and stacks of forms, never to be disturbed. His whitish sweater was so ancient all that remained of it was the ribbing and a few strands of cable stitch. If anyone was tactless enough to remark on it, he would pat his chest, look at his sleeves and say it probably was time he bought another one. As far as we knew, he never did. And there was Joe, part Native, who acted as unpaid guide, and showed us where all the best things were—the outlines in the sand of sunken Spanish galleons, the clutches of tiny shells, pockets of butter clams. He had a glass eye, not altogether comfortable, which he would sometimes remove and put on the table, so when you talked to him you weren't quite sure whether to look at the single eye in his head or the one that stared at you from the wooden planking. He'd once been a hunter, but stopped after he shot a wild goose on Kennedy Lake and its mate flew circling above his boat, crying, while he rowed, for miles it seemed, to shore. It was he who told me geese mate for life.

When the road was first opened there were slow changes. More cars on the beach and people—most appeared to be Americans—who came up in vans. They didn't rent one of Peg's cabins but slept inside their vehicles, locked away from stars and surf. They prepared themselves with propane stoves and canning equipment, and they dug gunnysacks of the razor-backed clams which nested in a line, about three feet wide, along the beach, and could be collected for chowder in a few minutes, there were so many, when the tide was right. Canning appeared to us an extraordinary way of spending a holiday, but these industrious individuals must have felt it was worthwhile to return over the border with a haul that would last them all winter.

The last summer we, a family of five with a dog in our Morris Minor, trailed off to Long Beach, there were no clams: even their exquisite oval, flat, mother-of-pearl shells had disappeared. And there were no green glass balls lying in the grass and vegetable garden and flower beds around Peg's cabins. She'd had about a hundred and fifty of them, of all sizes, retrieved from the sea after being swept across the Pacific from Japanese fishing boats. Tourists were buying them as curiosities, but one night some people in a van went off with every single one.

My daughter caught her first fish in Indian River. To reach the best fishing place, we had to walk over swampland. Once we misjudged the tide and had to wade back with water to our chests, children on our shoulders. Another time a fisherman took us back after he'd taken his limit of twelve trout in half an hour. After the swamp, we climbed up a path through trees. Enormous, they shut out the light. Impenetrable salal beneath them could grow along the ground for forty feet. The most noticeable thing was the quiet: no birds, only occasionally a squirrel. It was so darkly green and silent our own voices hushed. At the fishing place, we found a wooden bridge and my daughter caught her fish. When she unhooked it, it wriggled away, flopping, while she chased it desperately and we laughed, although we shouldn't have. It escaped over the side and swam away.

After the government made Long Beach part of a park (of course a wise move, but we hated it), Peggy Wittington was not permitted to remain. She'd lived there, renting out her cabins, since the war when her husband had drowned off the beach, swept out of a human chain trying to rescue men whose boat had, like so many others, foundered on rocks. He had taken part although he couldn't swim. Peg was now about seventy. No

money (and there was not a great deal) could compensate her for the trees, the singing sand, the wildness—alone during the winters, when she slept her hair was sometimes nibbled by deer mice, but she thought nothing of it—and the constant rhythm of the surf.

After that, we never went back as a family: the government campsite was too full, too noisy. Motels were springing up, stores appearing, restrictions being imposed, cars filling the roads, and black clearcuts suddenly shocking into view. I returned once, much later. Peg's cabins—stoves burning, the aroma of bread and clam chowder cooking, children coated with sand—were deserted, tumbling back into salal and conifers.

It was inevitable I should remember, painfully and gratefully, what it had once been like, while I stood on the road not far from the Peace Camp in its broken clearcut near the Kennedy Lake bridge. The demonstrators and their spokespeople were calm, well organized: they sang about their love for the earth, stood in the cold waiting for the day to begin, waiting, some of them, to be arrested. The police, when they arrived, were polite and pleasant. After the injunction was read by a man representing MacMillan Bloedel, most of us stepped off the road. Those who remained were taken away as criminals. The loggers—and, ironically, there were so few of them—drove by with their equipment, their eyes fixed straight ahead of them. Two mammoth boomtrailers attached to self-loading trucks passed; they would carry out the corpses. But it was the stars that defied description: unsullied, ecstatically beautiful—and beyond reach.

DISCOVERIES II

I can   paint   trees
like totems
limit my vocabulary
to a few strong strokes
identify all living things
as beaver   wolf   and   bear
chisel them into
the affirmation of
clefts and hollows
whose inverted simplicity
is stronger than the coastal mountains
place my own feet on
the cedar roots
and lock them into my
existence
and the dilettantes who anger all my
paintings
will see my own face
peering through the
leaves   hostile   wary   cunning
as the raven
my beak ready to
tear out their
pastel coloured
minds.

From HUNDREDS AND THOUSANDS

March 9th, 1934
Dear Mother Earth! I think I have always specially belonged to you. I have loved from babyhood to roll upon you, to lie with my face pressed right down on to you in my sorrows. I love the look of you and the smell of you and the feel of you. When I die I should like to be in you uncoffined, unshrouded, the petal of flowers against my flesh and you covering me up.

May 29th
I am circled by trees. They are full of chatter, the wind and the birds helping them. Through the sighing of the wind they tell me their sorrows. Through the chortle of the birds they tell me their joy. The birds are not so intimate here as down in the swamp. There they flew low and sought earth things and dug for worms. Here their concerns are in the high trees. My spirit has gone up with the birds. On the Flats it was too concerned with the mud. I hate to leave camp in the mornings, it is so delicious under the gracious great pines. In the afternoon, when the sun has dodged down and blares forth and gets glaring, red hot and bold, I like to get off into the calm woods. When he has gone, leaving just a trail of glory across the sky which the pines stand black against, it gets wonderful again and presently an enormous motherly moon comes out of the East and washes everything and all the sweet cool smells come out of things, not the sunshine smells of day that are like the perfumes and cosmetic smells of fine ladies but the after-bath smells, cleanliness, fine soap and powder of sweet, well-kept babies. And when you put out the van lamp and lie in the airy quiet, you want to think of lovely things.

June 16th
There's a torn and splintered ridge across the stumps I call the "screamers." These are the unsawn last bits, the cry of the tree's heart, wrenching and tearing apart just before she gives that sway and the dreadful groan of falling, that dreadful pause while her executioners step back with their saws and axes resting and watch. It's a horrible sight to see a tree felled, even now, though the stumps are grey and rotting. As you pass among them you see their screamers sticking up out of their own tombstones, as it were. They are their own tombstones and their own mourners.

There is no right and wrong way to paint except honestly or dishonestly. Honestly is trying for the bigger thing. Dishonestly is bluffing and getting through a smattering of surface representation with no meaning, made into a design to please the eye. Well, that's all right for those who just want eye work. It seems to satisfy most people, both doers and lookers.

September, 1935

Sketching in the big woods is wonderful. You go, find a space wide enough to sit in and clear enough so the undergrowth is not drowning you. Then, being elderly, you spread your camp stool and sit and look around. "Don't see much here." "Wait." Out comes a cigarette. The mosquitoes back away from the smoke. Everything is green. Everything is waiting and still. Slowly things begin to move, to slip into their places. Groups and masses and lines tie themselves together. Colours you had not noticed come out, timidly or boldly. In and out, in and out your eye passes. Nothing is crowded; there is living space for all. Air moves between each leaf. Sunlight plays and dances. Nothing is still now. Life is sweeping through the spaces. Everything is alive. The air is alive. The silence is full of sound. The green is full of colour. Light and darkness chase each other. Here is a picture, a complete thought, and there another and there. . . .

There are themes everywhere, something sublime, something ridiculous, or joyous, or calm, or mysterious. Tender youthfulness laughing at gnarled oldness. Moss and ferns, and leaves and twigs, light and air, depth and colour chattering, dancing a mad joy-dance, but only apparently tied up in stillness and silence. You must be still in order to hear and see.

—*From* Hundreds and Thousands: The Journals of Emily Carr *(Clark Irwin, 1966)*

CLAYOQUOT

100 miles west of here on the Pacific coast,
roads are cut into virgin forests
and the ancient trees fall, a sacrifice
to appease the bloated god of money.
In this religion, waste is a measure of success.
Natural resources are a sacred right.
The accumulation of wealth is a prerequisite for holiness.
Greed is a form of prayer.
Man is much wiser than nature.
Cutting down trees frees their spirits.
In this religion, people don't matter.
Politicians go to the highest bidder.
The poor, by definition, are all atheists.
Only a rich man can pass thru the gates of heaven.
The size of your paycheque is evidence of
the depth of your beliefs.
In this religion, the machine has to be fed.
Expediency is the highest virtue.
Do unto others before they do unto you.
Innocence is no excuse.
And don't worry, tomorrow never comes.

From THE ROYAL PROCLAMATION
OF OCTOBER 7, 1763

And whereas it is just and reasonable, and essential to our Interests, and the Security of our Colonies, that the several Nations or Tribes of Indians with whom We are connected, and who live under our Protection, should not be molested or disturbed in the Possession of such Parts of Dominions and Territories as, not having been ceded or purchased by Us, are reserved to them, or any of them, as their Hunting Grounds. . . .

And We do strictly forbid, on Pain of our Displeasure, all our loving Subjects from making any Purchases or Settlements whatever, or taking possession of any of the Lands above reserved, without our especial leave and Licence for that purpose first obtained.

And, We do further strictly enjoin and require all Persons whatever who have either wilfully or inadvertently seated themselves upon any Lands within the Countries above described, or upon any other Lands which, not having been ceded or purchased by Us, are still reserved to the said Indians as aforesaid, forth-with to remove themselves from such settlements.

CROWN LANDS

Crown land is commonly perceived to be public land managed by the elected provincial government for all citizens. In reality, Crown Lands were created by the British Parliament in 1839 out of all Indian lands not yet secured. The impetus (a Royal Commission) for the Crown Lands Protection Act can be seen as a well-intentioned but paternalistic desire to protect unsecured Native lands from the encroachment of White settlers, but because most Natives held land in common, this Act excluded them from the political rights arising from private ownership under the British system. Because of this, and other factors, when responsibility for Crown Lands was shifted to the provinces in 1930, there effectively became only two players in the British Columbia woods: the government and the forest companies.

THE SADNESS OF PONTIAC
(When the English Defeated the French: 1760)

Beneath the powdered wig, parched, sandy hair.
Beneath the flowered coat, the merchant's black.
He's known plumed nobles with a gay, free air;
But gallantry's in the grave with Frontenac.

Soldiers and nobles he can understand.
These kill with words, enslave with lines of ink.
Like puppets, spilled on earth from some Great Hand,
They strut about, consuming meat and drink.

Mean-souled they are: nobility's a joke;
Nobles mere beasts in woods round their new town.
The dagger hidden in the lawyer's cloak,
They lie in wait to pull their great ones down.

There is one earth for hunter and for chief.
The basswood slants above the long-grassed glade,
Red-budded, yellow-flowered, strong of leaf,
And bees build towns of sweetness in its shade.

There is one earth for peasant and for lord
(Wind-shaken poplars guard the soft-earthed farms);
One voice for living breath and uttered word;
In one sky lies the sun in the moon's arms.

But Fate, grown tired of humankind, decrees
An end to words infilled with human breath,
To glades, to wedded farms and royal trees.
The moon dries out; the sun's a drum of death.

On Abraham's Plain Montcalm and Wolfe are laid—
With them his world. All cut down with one stroke.
Mushrooming smoke-clouds darken Europe's glade.
He cannot bargain with these men of smoke.

ORIGIN OF THE DEPARTMENT OF
INDIAN AFFAIRS AND NORTHERN DEVELOPMENT

During the colonial wars, the French, the British, and the American colonies had all sought to win Indian support. This support was considered important enough for the British government in 1755 to form a special branch of the military to handle all dealings with the Indians. The main purpose of this Indian Branch was, of course, to win Indian support in the event of war. Among the means used to achieve this was the custom of distributing presents to the Indians each year as a sign of friendship. . . . This Indian Department continued to supervise Indian Affairs in Canada, and was the forerunner of the present Department of Indian Affairs.

—From Robert J. Surtees, *The Original People* (Holt, Rinehart & Winston, 1971).

CLAYOQUOT SILENCE:
WHO WILL SPEAK FOR THE TREES?

The first European settlers to venture onto Vancouver Island called it the back of the world. And even today we tend to think of the west coast of Vancouver Island as the back door of the continent.

But when you stand on the soft sands of Long Beach in the last light of the fragmenting sun—that same sun that is poised to announce the miracle of morning to the continent of Asia—you don't feel at the back door of anything. Here, where the water crashes against the land with a primal roar, and the land stands up to the sea like a defiant David staring down a restless Goliath—you feel like you are witnessing the perpetual big bang of Creation.

This is the wild side of Vancouver Island; the wild side of Canada. Here, the Nuu-chah-nulth evolved upon the land even as the land was evolving out of the last ice age. With the mysterious rainforest at their back they faced the powerful Pacific head on.

From out on the ocean the explosive sounds of humpback whales came drifting through the fog. Cougars, black bears and wolves prowled the shoreline, then merged back into the ancient forest. Salmon swarmed as thick as mosquitoes in the estuaries; the mudflats were carpeted in shore-birds.

This was a spectacular environment to be born into, and the Nuu-chah-nulth lived life on a grand scale. From Port Renfrew to Kyuquot, maybe 70,000 people from 100 different political groupings in hundreds of separate coastal villages spent their days living off—and with—the ocean and the forest.

The world's biggest whales, the blue whales and finbacks, cruised by offshore. Inland, some of the world's tallest and thickest trees, Sitka spruce and western red cedar, thrived in the valley bottoms. Among the spiral tops of solitary, leaning snags perched the all-seeing bald eagles.

The Nuu-chah-nulth built their longhouses with thick cedar posts and beams; they developed a cultural philosophy as subtle and complex as a delicately woven spruce root basket. The world of nature and the world of the supernatural was all one, and amidst the snowcapped domes and jagged peaks of the Vancouver Island mountains, the Thunderbird took wing, a killer whale clutched firmly in its talons.

The heart of this mythic west coast wilderness was—and is—Clayoquot Sound, ten mountainous river networks, each greater than 5,000 hectares. Lined up valley by wilderness valley, they stretch from Kennedy Lake in the south to the Hesquiat Peninsula in the north, overlapping one another and linking together a series of smaller watersheds and tributaries. Speaking aloud the names of the Clayoquot watercourses becomes a sort of holy chant: Clayoquot, Tofino, Bulson, Bedwell, Ursus, Moyeha, Megin, Sydney—

Nestled under Clayoquot's stark mountain peaks lie perfectly round lakes of shimmering turquoise. Like the first pure notes of a classical symphony, the crystalline water drips, then flows, then cascades down the mountainsides into steep and twisting secluded valleys. The pure mountain run-off ripples over the backs of salmon struggling upriver to spawn, and rushes down the valleys to spill into a maze of saltwater fiords. These fiords lead straight to the Pacific Ocean where the coastline and offshore islands, dominated by Meares, Vargas, and Flores, are rimmed with long slim beaches of deep soft sand.

Almost everywhere you look in Clayoquot Sound you see the ancient trees, the great green trees of the temperate rainforest. They fill up the offshore islands, they cling to the sides of steep-faced mountains, they hug the blustery ocean coast, and they erupt in magnificent profusion in the valleys and estuaries.

So you tend to forget that temperate rainforests are extremely rare, covering about 0.2 percent of the Earth's land area. About one-half of the world's temperate rainforests grow along the west coast of North America in a long narrow band from Alaska to northern California—but they take on their most luxuriant expression around the Olympic Peninsula of Washington and the southwest side of Vancouver Island.

This ancient temperate rainforest is arguably the most majestic forest ecosystem on the face of the Earth. Here, Douglas fir and Sitka spruce tower ninety-two metres (300 feet) towards the sky, roughly the height of a thirty-story skyscraper. There are cedar trees with more growth rings than there are years on the calendar. Dominated by lacy-needled western hemlock, this moss-draped, cloud-encased forest is built on ecological foundations that took 10,000 years to evolve.

The senior trees of the temperate rainforest are 300 to 800 years old, and many grow to be much older. In tropical rainforests, the oldest trees rarely make it to 500 years. The ancient temperate rainforest typically contains at least twice as much living tree and plant biomass as a tropical rainforest.

Age and mass are everything in the temperate rainforest, and it is not renewable in the human time frame. The ecosystem is as ancient as Greece and Rome, its monuments every bit as humbling.

When you leave the logging road and walk a muddy trail into the ancient forest, you leave behind everything you know. The air tastes fresh; sunlight squirts down on you from the oddest angles. The noise of the world seeps away and you feel obliged to whisper. The trail-side salal branches extend far above your head, obscuring everything. You can't understand, in this forest of giant trees, why you can't see even one tree clearly. And then you do, and you are overwhelmed.

A western red cedar fills the space before you like a church spire. First you are overwhelmed by its size, its mass, its texture, its shape. Then you are overwhelmed by its dignity and grace. You rub the bark for good luck and notice a hollow part near the ground, big enough for you to squeeze through. Suddenly you are inside a cavern of living wood. Then you hear a slight rustle overhead and in the inner gloom your eyes focus on a small bird's nest stuck to the tree wall. A winter wren lives here, inside the forest, inside the tree, secret and secure.

Diversity is the key to the ancient temperate rainforest, embracing all creatures great and small. From black bears to voles to bats, there are twenty-nine native species of mammals living on Vancouver Island; about eighty-five percent of these breed in the old growth forests.

Deer and elk seeking shelter from a heavy snow gather shoulder to shoulder under the protective canopy of big old trees—maybe 300 animals huddled within two square kilometres. The wind blows the wispy lichen off the trees; it drops lightly on top of the snow. This lichen, which sustains the animals through hard times, only grows on old trees.

But the most biologically rich region of the ancient temperate rainforest is not found above ground, but in the forest soil, where some 8,000 species of arthropods (tiny insects, spiders, centipedes, and millipedes) play a crucial role in decomposing wood and recycling nutrients. This dynamic environment also gives life to over 3,000 species of mushrooms, making the Pacific Northwest the epicentre for fungal and lichen diversity on Earth.

And like the species-rich forest soil, the shadowy canopy of the old-growth temperate rainforest is its own crucible of life, home to an estimated 2,000 species of beetles, butterflies, moths, bees, ants, flies, and collembola—pencil-point sized "springtails" that thrive in the mats of rich green moss covering the branches high in the old-growth canopy.

This tree-top environment is a world flowing with mysterious lichens, a world flowering with unknown epiphytes. Above all, it cradles the tiny, elusive nests of the tiny, elusive seabird, the marbled murrelet. Feeding all day on the open ocean, then flying more than twenty kilometres to its home in the ancient forest canopy, the marbled murrelet traces a direct link between land and sea.

The complexity, the majesty, the beauty and mystery of North America's temperate rainforests have been shattered by more than a century of logging.

Virtually all the rainforest in Washington has been logged; only one-third of Vancouver Island's original rainforest is still standing. Despite the intensity of the debate over the state of Vancouver Island's wilderness rainforests, less than five percent has been protected.

The recent decision by the Commission on Resources and the Environment (CORE) to protect thirteen percent of Vancouver Island's total land area falls far short of protecting thirteen per cent of the Island's ancient temperate rainforest. The CORE plan would protect less than an additional two percent of the ancient forest, bringing the total amount of protected ancient rainforest on Vancouver Island to roughly six percent of the original forest cover.

There may be twenty years left before the rest of Vancouver Island's old-growth rainforest is liquidated. In many Island regions the grand forest heritage has all but vanished completely.

But in Clayoquot Sound close to eighty percent of the ancient rainforest is still intact. This is the largest single tract of ancient temperate rainforest remaining on Vancouver Island—and one of the largest anywhere in the world. For many people, that is more than enough reason to try to protect it.

The struggle to save Clayoquot Sound began with Meares Island, its heart and soul. Wrapping itself around Lemmens Inlet, this massive wall of ancient forest is anchored at each end of its horseshoe curve by the twin volcanic peaks of Mt. Colnett and Lone Cone. As you stand on the Tofino dock and stare out across the water, Meares stares back from almost every direction.

In 1979 MacMillan Bloedel (MB) made clear its plans to clearcut about half of Meares Island. Local residents reacted by forming the Friends of Clayoquot Sound. They lobbied hard to save Meares, and the word began to spread to the cities. But five years and several government-appointed planning teams later, MB sailed into Heelboom Bay to start clearcutting. They were met by a flotilla of protesters from the Friends of Clayoquot Sound, and by emissaries from the Tla-o-qui-aht people.

The Tla-o-qui-aht are one of fifteen First Nations that today make up the Nuu-chah-nulth; they have lived among the cedar rich forests of Meares Island for thousands of years. Together with the neighbouring Ahousaht people, the Tla-o-qui-aht undertook to protect Meares by declaring it a Tribal Park. They welcomed MacMillan Bloedel to the island, but cautioned them against logging. To this day the chain saws have stayed silent. The issue of Aboriginal rights to the forests of Meares is a matter that courts and governments are still wrestling with.

The second time the Friends of Clayoquot Sound mobilized to save their ancient forest was the summer of 1988. At issue was a logging road

Fletcher Challenge was building into an unlogged region called Sulphur Pass. Behind it lies the pure forest wilderness of Shelter Inlet and the Megin Valley. Every day the company's dynamite crew came to blast more rock for the road bed. Every day the protesters placed themselves inside the blast safety zone. Injunctions were issued, arrests were made, and by fall, some thirty-five people were sent to jail for as long as forty-five days for impeding the progress of the road. By now the news of Clayoquot Sound had spread across Canada.

Fletcher Challenge ultimately abandoned work on the logging road at Sulphur Pass. They built a different road instead, farther back in the mountains, out of view from the water. But what is clearly visible today are the clearcuts scarring the slopes of Shelter Inlet.

Sulphur Pass is not a stranger to gunpowder. In 1864 the Victoria-based gun ship *Devastation* sailed through on its way to bombard nearby Ahousaht villages. Missionaries and land commissioners soon followed, wasting little time in outlawing Native traditions and assigning all Nuu-chah-nulth peoples to small, scattered reserves. Much of Clayoquot Sound then became Crown land.

In the mid-1950s, the B.C. government gave most of the wilderness rainforests of Clayoquot Sound to MacMillan Bloedel and British Columbia Forest Products (BCFP) in long-term forest licences. This was a corrupt time in B.C. politics and the circumstances under which BCFP got its share of Clayoquot Sound were particularly corrupt: the province's forests minister was jailed for taking a bribe as part of the deal. BCFP subsequently was taken over by Fletcher Challenge which, in turn, has sold its Clayoquot licence to International Forest Products (Interfor).

The protest the Friends of Clayoquot Sound mounted at Sulphur Pass helped to launch several more years of discussions on the future of Clayoquot Sound—by yet another round of government-appointed committees. Everyone was now talking about sustainable development. Finally, in April 1993, the B.C. government made its Clayoquot decision, which in effect allows for the logging of seventy-four out of every 100 old-growth trees. Protected in its entirety are the magnificent wilderness forests in and around the Megin Valley.

In reaction to the government plan, the Friends of Clayoquot Sound organized a summer long campaign of non-violent civil disobedience. Every morning before sun-up, several hundred people gathered by the Kennedy Lake bridge on a gravel road leading into Clayoquot Sound, waiting for MB's logging trucks to come rumbling through. And every morning a select group of protesters would stand, sit or lie down in the middle of the road.

The logging trucks would come to a stop—their motors racing—as RCMP

constables escorted or carried the protesters to an old school bus that was waiting to take them to jail. Then the caravan of trucks would rev up and head into the rainforest.

The people who gathered by the river every morning to place themselves between the logging trucks and the rainforest came to Clayoquot Sound from all over the world. Ultimately, the judicial system condemned as criminals over 800 of them, for conscientiously opposing an injunction the court had granted to MB to let the company's logging trucks keep on rolling down the road.

The short-term fallout from the 1993 summer of protest has been international condemnation of B.C.'s logging policies in general, especially in Clayoquot Sound. In the long run, ordinary people with nothing material to gain, will continue their struggle to save the ancient temperate rainforest of Clayoquot Sound. This rare and remarkable ecosystem is a gift to humanity that comes once in the lifetime of the planet. It must never be compromised.

SULPHUR PASSAGE

The first Clayoquot logging blockade took place in 1988 at Sulphur Passage. Someone hung a banner high in the trees quoting the Republican rallying cry from the Spanish Civil War: no pasaran—they shall not pass.

Come you bold men of Clayoquot,
Come you bold women.
There is a fire burning on the mountain,
The sting of smoke blowin' in the wind.
Hear the blast of the whistle,
Hear the snarl of the chain,
Hear the cracking in the heartwood,
Hear it again and again and again.

No pasaran, Megin River
No pasaran, Clayoquot River
No pasaran, Sulphur Passage

There is a valley torn asunder,
There is a mountain stripped to bone,
Grove of spruce, stand of cedar,
The ancient garden sacked and burned.
Hear the blast of the whistle,
Hear the snarl of the chain,
Hear the cracking in the heartwood,
Hear it again and again and again.

Come you bold men of Clayoquot,
Come you bold women
There is a cry deep within the forest,
Hear the whisper in the wind.
Hear the breath in the cedars,
The sighing in the salal,
The beating deep within the forest,
The grouse, the thrush, the great horned owl.

We'll stand with these cedars,
Stand with these balsam groves,
Stand with the heron, the cougar, the otter,
Like the tree by the water, we shall not move.

Come you bold men of Clayoquot,
Come you bold women.
There is a fire burning in the mountain,
The sting of smoke blowin' in the wind.
Hear the blast of the whistle,
Hear the snarl of the chain,
Hear the cracking in the heartwood,
Hear it again and again and again.

HOW FAR IT RUNS

That morning you took your stand
on the road—did you notice
how it stretched from the bridge
over the thin-waisted lake,
how it widened and greened
onto Parliament lawns?
In the summer dawn you can see
the outline of fairy lights, the wedges
of pansy and salvia. The woodcutter
walks in the forest with his axe
and high leather boots. He meets
an elf, a hag, a creature
with powers. There's a road
here too, the way the story
moves along. Brambles,
a door, and somebody's bound
to wake up. Look how
the real road bends
through the halls of the Company.
Such a shine on the parquet
floor! The Company smiles.
They've planted trees in Georgia.
When the last wood here is finished
those yellow pines will tower
and hold the balance. Now
the road twists
among courtroom alleys, tall
gates guarded by lions. The sun
rises in the storybook
picture. In this province
clearcuts hide
beyond mountains, off
the highway and away from town.
A family's dirty secret shoved
into a cupboard under the stairs.
Though you've been given three
or seven tasks, and keys
by the pocketful, this is no fable.
There is a closet door, and hag
or elf, you've opened it.

TO STAND ON THE ROAD

We know we must be getting there when we see neatly lettered slogans on the cement guard rails along the snaking road to Ucluelet and Tofino: ECO-FORESTRY = MORE JOBS and CORPORATE $CAM. When steep mountains give way to a flat plateau of huge, charred stumps with small cedar saplings starting from square one again, and a sign says CLAYOQUOT SOUND INFO BOOTH AHEAD, we know the four-and-a-half hour journey is nearly over. And when we see a string of assorted national flags flapping beside a wooden structure full of maps, photos, signs, posters, and people, we know we have arrived at the Peace Camp.

We check in at the information booth also called The Gate. "We" are ten residents of Quadra Island—adults, babies, and children—in three vehicles. Not a large contingency, true, but all that could be scraped up with one day's notice. Because the Peace Camp is about to close, this is our last chance to physically protest the destruction of Clayoquot's mighty and ancient rainforest.

We park our vehicles wherever we can and walk the long, rough road into camp. The road is lined on both sides with a motley assortment of cars, vans, trucks, campers, and a yellow school bus, all covered in dust. Licence plates range from "Beautiful" British Columbia to Washington, Idaho, and Florida. We come to the Fire Circle: a conical plastic canopy about thirty feet in diameter supported by an arrangement of poles. There is a stained smoke hole at the apex. The floor is liberally spread with clean, dry straw; rough-hewn benches and planks on log butts circle the outer edge, with rocks creating a central hearth. A dog, a small puppy, and a kitten romp in the straw. To one side of the Fire Circle is the kitchen area, tarpaulin covered, complete with all the necessities for the volunteer cooks (anyone can volunteer) to make three meals a day for everyone in camp—today, about one hundred people.

We join a circle of newcomers sitting in the straw listening to Jean, a white-haired Raging Granny who has been at the camp three months. She explains camp organization and etiquette, the consensus system by which everything is done; she instructs us in non-violent confrontation and other procedures and we discuss attitudes and concerns or questions we have.

Dinner at 6:30 p.m. is a well balanced vegetarian meal—no charge, but there is a donation can on the table. We wash our own dishes and leave them on a rack to dry. Then there is a gathering at the Fire Circle for open discussion and comments. A further briefing by two Peacekeepers ensures that we are prepared for tomorrow, but it does little to lessen my apprehension.

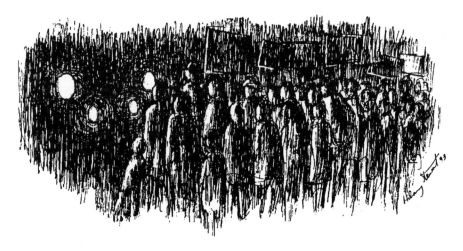

As night cools the air after a hot day, a thick fog settles over the camp, blotting the full moon's brightness into a dull glow. I think of my friends on Quadra Island who, right now, are drumming up the moon by a fire on the beach. I have set my tent at the edge of the camp road, in a small space between three vehicles. There are some tent spaces up the hill, but bears have been a problem, ripping one tent to shreds. Most people sleep in their vehicles. With extreme tiredness I crawl, fully clothed, into my sleeping bag without washing or cleaning my teeth. There are no shower or washing facilities, only a plastic shielded biffy amid the charred stumps and rubble reached by a rough trail. It has a real seat, rolls of recycled toilet paper, and a can of lime for after use. The wide open view is of more clearcut mountains.

It is 10:15 p.m. I close my eyes but sleep is denied as voices and laughter alternate with the crunch of feet on gravel, cars, singing, and intermittent applause from the Fire Circle. When at last sleep takes over, it is soon shattered by the wake-up call: someone with an accordion walking the road playing "Roll out the barrel, we'll have a barrel of fun—yeah!" It's 3:45 a.m. I haul myself out of my sleeping bag, push my feet into shoes, fall out of the tent, and almost off the edge of the road into darkness clutched by thick, damp fog. No morning shower, not even a face wash, and teeth still unbrushed. Groggy from lack of sleep I stumble my way to the van.

Vehicles leave camp and line up on the shoulder of the main road. Those with space for people needing a ride leave their hazard lights flashing until the vehicle is full; several pile into the back of the van I am in. 4:30 a.m. Everyone has a ride. The Peacekeepers' lead truck pulls out and the convoy pushes its way through the foggy darkness eventually turning onto a logging road. There is little talk in the van—an occasional comment, a question that goes unanswered. And there is tension. Each has his or her own reason for doing this. We are from all occupations, all ages and backgrounds. . . .

Four-fifty-five a.m. One by one vehicles pull over into an area cleared of trees, with rock and gravel fill. A Peacekeeper with a glowing red baton directs the parking so that all vehicles become a gridlock mass. I help to unload protest banners and signs from the camp's truck and these are set up with a speed which obviously comes from repetition. The shaft of each is wedged between rocks already in place along the road's edge. One says SAVE THE SOUND, another TREES FOR CLAYOQUOT and SHEAR B.C.—about a dozen in all. A large cloth banner is stretched across the entrance to the Kennedy Lake bridge.

The full moon barely pierces the fog with a fuzzy glow; soft silhouettes of conifers and the spiked trunks of dead trees seem veiled in muslin. Fires are lit in two stone hearths, a few chunks of wood become seating and people huddle around the orange warmth while two men play drums. Water is put on to boil and soon there is tea and coffee and apples from a box.

Six a.m. About a hundred people form a huge elongated circle on the logging road. A Peacekeeper gives a final rundown of the procedure, what will happen, what we are to do, what we must *not* do. Non-violence is stressed; no angry words, nor even a gesture, nothing but a peaceful response to whatever might come our way. Those who wish to risk arrest are asked to step forward. Eight people do, each to become an "arrestee" within an hour. That word is new to me. It sounds harmless enough, like "absentee," but it is fraught with meaning and the uncertainty of how the courts will deal with these deeply committed people. The circle breaks up and people go back to the fires. Beating drums continue in the tense fogbound silence and we wait. I have made the decision not to get arrested, yet doubts begin to invade my mind. I have a mug of coffee and then a cold, crisp red apple that makes my teeth feel clean.

Six thirty a.m. Still dark, our small world still wrapped in fog, the drums continue the same repetitive beat, and we wait. Suddenly a Peacekeeper calls out, "Here they come—everybody on the road!" I think, this is it. We cross over the ditch and spread out facing the oncoming trucks, our backs to the bridge the loggers must cross. The Quadra group finds itself at the front of the crowd. Two women cradle babies and hold small children by the hands. In the distance are headlights blurred by fog, it seems like four of them, and slowly they advance. No sound, just the lights growing bigger and getting closer and I am reminded of *Close Encounters of the Third Kind*. We stand in total silence, the lights piercing the fog, crawling closer—closer. What if they just keep coming? All I can do is stare as though I am hypnotized. I hold a firm stance, feet apart, arms down, hands clasped. I feel my head high, eyes just staring at the advancing lights. Standing on the road, together with these diverse people who share a single purpose and the belief that the magnificence of Clayoquot Sound is worth protecting. I feel powerful. I am proud to be here. Adrenalin runs high.

The vehicles stop maybe twenty feet away. As well as headlights, two floodlights beam into the dark, the fog, and onto us. A man with a video camera and a spotlight mounted above it slowly sweeps the group with his lens. This is for possible use in court, we have been told, and the brightness fills my eyes as he passes by. A man with a loud-hailer leans over the cab of the front truck. He announces that due to continuing hot weather the forest is closed for logging, and a great cheer breaks the tension. However, they have to go in to do some clean-up work, he says. An RCMP officer reads the official court injunction, a detailed and complex piece of legalese that seems to go on interminably. When he finishes, we are asked to clear the road or we will be arrested. We move off to both sides, crossing the ditch to the safety zone. I turn and look back at the road and there in front of the bridge are eight people—like a group sculpture, like statues cemented to the ground, motionless, solid, staring straight ahead. Three stand upright, rigid. In front of them, five sit cross- legged on the rough road, all rooted in determination, empowered by their decision. Floodlit against darkness, they somehow seem to glow from within. The image burns itself into my mind and for a moment I want to jump the ditch and join them. But I stand immobile, tears in my eyes.

Five RCMP officers appear, seemingly out of nowhere. One places a hand on the shoulder of a woman sitting and tells her she is under arrest. Two officers carefully lift her by her shoulders and ankles and, amid applause, carry her off into the dark, into a waiting bus that I cannot even see. Then the next. And the next. Those sitting have decided to be carried away and they go limp in turn. Those standing have decided to be in charge of their own bodies and walk beside the policeman into the darkness and the bus. There is singing from the Peace Camp crowd and applause for each arrestee. The total number of people arrested is now 782. This morning's eight will be taken to the police station in Ucluelet, officially charged, and let go. A bus from the Peace Camp will take them boxed breakfasts and bring them back to camp.

When all the vehicles are gone, many of us return to the road. As though imbued with fresh energy and with the tension gone, we dance wildly on the road to the drumming until daylight finds its way through the fog. Then somebody says, "Let's have one big OHM!" and in a huge, tight, warm-bunched hug we "OHMMMM" in varying keys and intensities for several minutes. It's over.

7:30 a.m. I walk onto the Kennedy Lake bridge—it's a lot longer than I had thought; the far end disappears into the shroud of thick, white fog that envelopes and nurtures the giant trees of the westcoast rainforest.

We untangle the cars and return to the Peace Camp for breakfast.

AXED

How the Vancouver Sun *Became a Black Hole for Environmental Reporting*

It's been called the biggest environmental story in North America. British Columbia's ancient hemlock, spruce, and cedar are dropping faster than you can say "grapple yarder" as transnational logging companies race to liquidate this province's irreplaceable temperate rainforest while they have a shareholding government on their side.

But just about the only way those trees will turn up in the pages of B.C.'s largest and most influential newspaper is as pulp. And a New York-based public relations firm, famous for whitewashing corporations and governments from James Bay to Argentina, is implicated in the *Vancouver Sun*'s virtual purge of industry-negative copy.

In 1991, amid threats of a European boycott of their clearcut timber products, B.C. logging companies hired Burson-Marsteller to concoct and run a pseudo-populist, industry-funded pressure group called the B.C. Forest Alliance, with a start-up budget of $1 million. With more than sixty offices in twenty-nine countries, Burson-Marsteller is the largest independent public relations firm on the planet. The same company was called in by the Mexican government to help fast-track the North American Free Trade Agreement, by Hydro Quebec to peddle the James Bay II hydro-electric project, by Union Carbide after the company's Bhopal gas disaster in India, by Exxon after the Exxon Valdez oil spill, and by Argentina's military dictatorship in the seventies to lure foreign investment.

British Columbia's timber magnates were in good hands—the hands of a skilled media surgeon who knew that once negative coverage was expunged from the province's paper of record, all other media would fall in line or become irrelevant. Before long, delegations from the Forest Alliance and the companies funding it were a common sight in the editorial offices of the biggest newsroom in the province.

"It seemed like for a while almost every week there was another group coming in from some forest company," says senior reporter Mark Hume, who has covered many forestry and environmental issues in his ten years with the paper. "I bet you the chief executive officers of every major forest company in B.C. have been in to meet with the editors," he adds. "Usually a team of executives would come in. That's tapered off in the last little while. They haven't had any need to complain."

Prior to the launch of the Forest Alliance in April 1991, the *Sun* had five full-time reporters dedicated to forestry, fisheries, Native affairs, energy and mines, and the environment. Today only the environment beat remains, and *Sun* management has instructed environment reporter Glenn Bohn to concentrate on Greater Vancouver and the Lower Mainland—an area conveniently free of large tracts of old-growth forest. The other environmental beats have been collapsed into a catch-all called "resources" and handed over to a couple of business reporters who juggle them along with the rest of their story assignments for the business pages, commonly located behind sports.

"A couple of years ago the *Vancouver Sun* was a leading voice in covering the environment," Hume says of the west coast flagship for the Southam newspaper empire. "That has completely vanished. The *Vancouver Sun* has pretty much turned a blind eye to the biggest environmental story in North America, which is happening right here in its backyard, and that's the termination of the temperate rainforest."

David Suzuki's environmental column was axed (senior editors claimed it was boring and repetitive) the same day the *Sun* retained Burson-Marsteller to boost the paper's sagging circulation. Meanwhile, Hume and other reporters who persistently told the truth about Burson-Marsteller, the Forest Alliance or B.C.'s SHARE movement—the logging industry's frontline troops battling environmentalists in the woods and in rural communities— were targeted with fierce complaints, shoved to the back of the paper, and even summoned into the editor's office to be grilled by industry representives.

One SHARE leader, angered by Hume's articles linking B.C.'s SHARE groups to the right-wing U.S. "Wise Use" movement and Reverend Sun Myung Moon's Unification Church, tried unsuccessfully to drag Hume before the B.C. Press Council. The council rejected the complaint, but in response to a related industry tantrum Hume was hauled into his editor's office where a MacMillan Bloedel representative and a SHARE supporter interrogated him for over an hour. Managing editor Scott Honeyman observed the kangaroo court.

"It told me that clearly there was no support for me coming from management," says Hume. "Nobody has come to me and said don't write about clearcut logging, don't write about SHARE. But the message gets through. They don't want you breaking stories on these issues. And when you do write about them, the stories generally sit in overset for a long time, and they run very truncated versions." Hume admits he has largely given up fighting for his coverage of forestry issues because he just "got worn down by the battle," and because "it was so incredibly frustrating to not be able to tell the truth."

The *Sun*'s former forestry reporter knows all about frustration. Ben Parfitt, who had covered forestry for the paper since 1989, was pulled off the beat last year because of a revealing article he sold to the *Georgia Straight*

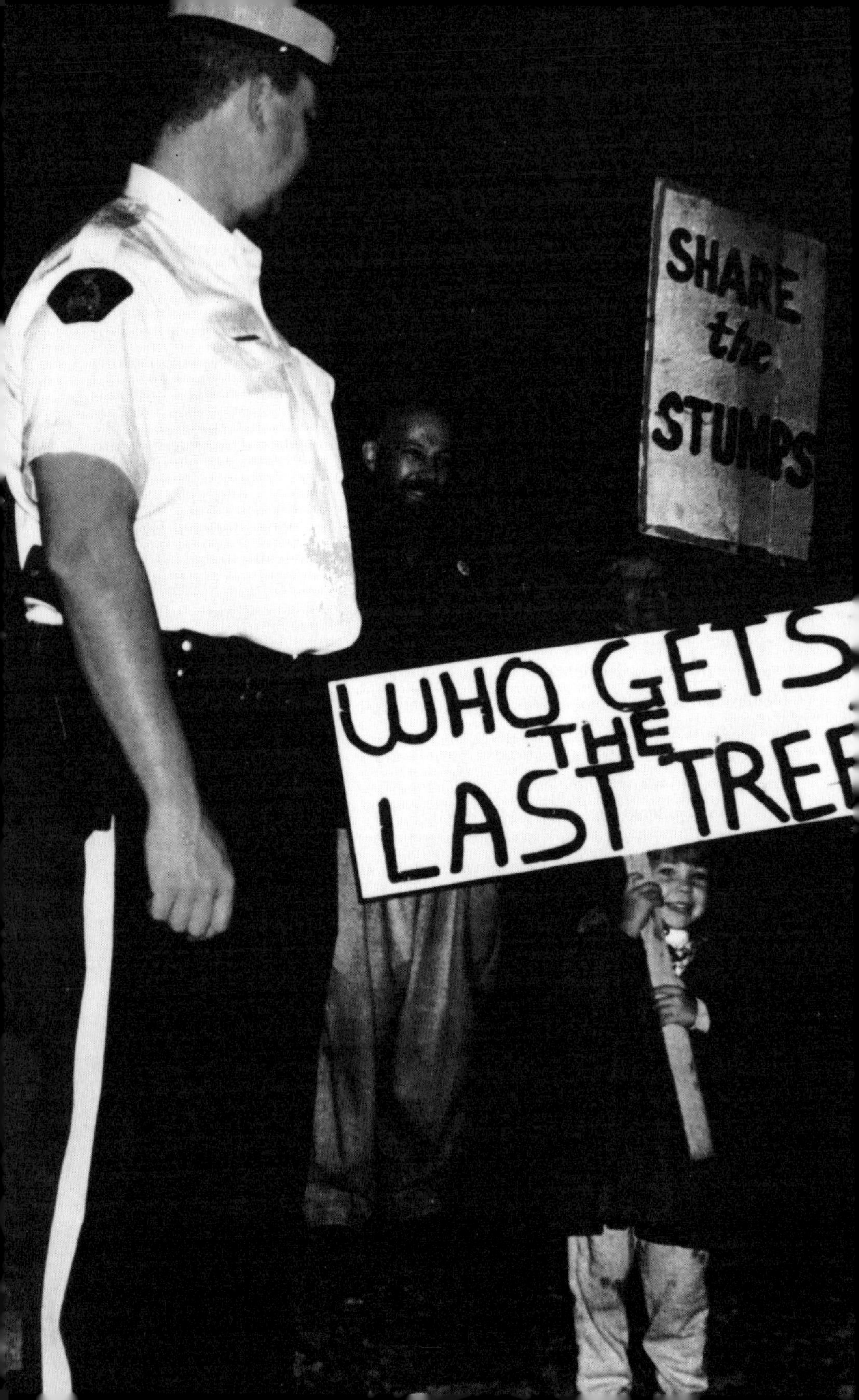
SHARE the STUMPS
WHO GETS THE LAST TREE

(after his own paper whittled it down to almost nothing) on Burson-Marsteller and the Forest Alliance. Among other things, Parfitt identified senior Burson-Marsteller employee and Forest Alliance consultant Ken Rietz as a key figure in Richard Nixon's scandal-ridden 1972 re-election campaign.

"I was told that by writing that piece I had compromised my ability to cover forestry for the *Sun*," says Parfitt, who heard the news first from Honeyman, then from editor-in-chief Ian Haysom. In Honeyman's words, Parfitt "was declaring himself not a dispassionate reporter" with his *Georgia Straight* article. Disillusioned and defeated, Parfitt left the *Sun* earlier this year, along with former Native affairs reporter Terry Glavin.

The pressure the logging industry applied to *Sun* management and certain reporters throughout 1991 and 1992 turned the newsroom into "a bloody war zone," according to Glavin. "Every time we touched on a story that in any way cast doubt on the ability or the intent of B.C.'s major forest companies to provide secure, stable, safe jobs to working people, and to provide a viable, environmentally sound, well-managed forest industry on public lands in British Columbia, the amount of grief that would result was—well, it was pretty hard," Glavin recalls.

The *Sun*'s self-censorship finally hit bottom in the summer of 1992, when scores of environmentalists were arrested for blockading MacMillan Bloedel's logging operations in Vancouver Island's Clayoquot Sound, one of the world's last great temperate rainforests. But no news of this contretemps would soil the pages of the logging-friendly *Sun*. When reporters in the newsroom caught the radio reports announcing the standoff in the woods and the mounting arrests, they asked their editors what their paper was doing on it. "The response was: 'We're simply not covering it,'" Glavin recalls.

In defending this decision and similar examples of *Sun* silence on B.C.'s war in the woods, Honeyman reportedly said: "My feeling was we were not dealing with urban environmental problems in our own backyard at all. Instead, we were covering sexy block-a-road protests, and some of them were just becoming photo opportunities."

In late 1992 and early 1993, the Clayoquot arrestees stood trial, with thirteen defendants receiving jail sentences. The trials dragged on for days while numerous defendants testified about shoddy and illegal logging operations, even calling expert witnesses and showing slides in one case. But the *Sun*'s 500,000 readers were spared the unflattering details. The paper merely ran a three-inch wire story announcing the combined verdicts for two trials and no story on the third trial, even though Victoria and Nanaimo newspapers were filing daily courthouse coverage on the Canadian Press wire service.

By March, the *Sun*'s virtual blackout on the escalating Clayoquot controversy had become so conspicuous that other media were commenting on it. So *Sun* management sent its environment reporter, Glenn Bohn, into the bush to get the goods on the spectacularly beautiful 260,000-hectare network of mountains, forests, and rivers disappearing beneath MacMillan Bloedel's buzzsaw.

Bohn, whose reports have seldom incensed the logging industry, came back with a four-part series that read like an advertising feature for the Forest Alliance. Environmental groups seeking total preservation of the Clayoquot were portrayed as unreasonable extremists. The industry viewpoint was represented by a personable, small-business mill owner who had already lost two sawmills to preservation.

The sole argument for preservation Bohn allowed in his series came from Native artist Roy Vickers, who, for sentimental reasons, hoped the Megin River, one of the Clayoquot's ten watersheds, would not be logged. Bohn neglected to mention that all parties in the dispute had already informally agreed the Megin was off-limits.

And in the final installment, a *Sun* photographer shot a patch of second-growth forest, which the paper identified as the Black Hole (a massive, eight-year-old clearcut stretching from mountaintop to valley floor), but which local environmentalists insist is outside the horrific Black Hole. To add insult to confusion, the photo was shot from an extreme low angle and with a wide-angle lens, magically transforming the once-blighted landscape into an emerging Eden. While the headline read "Forester slams scarred practices," the accompanying photo was a virtual paean to large-scale clearcuts and their mythic ability to regenerate.

One month later, in an unsuccessful attempt to dodge environmentalists, Premier Mike Harcourt and a press corps were air-lifted to a secret mountaintop in the Clayoquot (at a cost of $30,000 to the taxpayer) where Harcourt delivered his government's long-awaited announcement on the fate of the rainforest: two-thirds could be logged, one-third would be preserved.

To the chagrin of B.C.'s NDP government, Les Leyne, an enterprising reporter at the *Victoria Times-Colonist*, had uncovered the disturbing fact three weeks earlier that the provincial government was now the largest shareholder in MacMillan Bloedel, the logging company with the biggest holdings in the Clayoquot Sound. But the *Sun* saw no need to harp on this embarrassing detail in its coverage of the government's logging plan for the Clayoquot—not even when MB's stock value shot up after the plan was announced.

BCTV saw fit to report that MB's shares were selling at seventeen dollars in mid-February just before the government picked up an additional 2.1 million of them, climbing to twenty-one dollars in late April one week after Harcourt announced the Clayoquot logging plan. But the only way you'd glean that information from the *Vancouver Sun* was if you took a magnifying glass to the stock listings on the business pages and plotted the graph yourself.

With the *Sun*'s most aggressive environmental reporters gagged or gone, there was no one left to investigate, analyse, or interpret the government's Clayoquot decision and apparent conflict of interest. So from the pens of government public-relations flacks to the pages of the *Vancouver Sun*, the press releases spilled forth. The *Sun* faithfully repeated Harcourt's declaration that he was preserving one-third of the Clayoquot, without bothering to note that most of that land was either already protected as park, or has been logged, or is marginal forest and alpine rock.

To his credit, *Sun* columnist Stephen Hume, brother of Mark Hume and target of numerous complaints from the logging industry, exposed the "statistical flim flam" by calculating that the government had really sentenced eighty-five percent of the Clayoquot's productive forest to logging, not the usually quoted two-thirds. But his was a lone voice in the soon-to-be-levelled wilderness.

In May the *Vancouver Sun*'s increasingly obvious mutation from watchdog to lapdog on environmental reporting prompted Simon Fraser University's communications department to hold a symposium entitled "Take Back the News: Media, the Environment, and the Public's Right to Know."

When asked to justify his paper's declining environmental coverage, Honeyman tried to convince the audience of more than 700 activists, academics, and journalists that the elimination of specific environmental beats would lead to better coverage because reporters could employ a "team approach" when different issues overlap. "I believe strongly and have said many times in the newsroom that we need to all be environmental reporters," said Honeyman, who served as the *Sun*'s environmental reporter between 1967 and 1972 before spending nineteen years at the *Ottawa Citizen*.

When asked if the *Sun* has been editorially constrained by its business relationship with Burson-Marsteller, he replied, "I don't believe so." On the same panel, Ben Parfitt bluntly stated, "My personal experience in trying to cut through the deceit surrounding Burson-Marsteller was not greeted with favour by the paper."

Even with the aid of the formidable Burson-Marsteller, the forest industry's overwhelming influence on *Sun* editorial policy is, at first glance, difficult to explain. Logging companies account for very little of the *Sun*'s

advertising revenue. Environmentalists are quick to cite the presence of Noranda boss Adam Zimmerman and Canfor director Ronald Cliff on Southam's board of directors. But the connection between industry-linked Southam directors and muzzled reporters is not a direct one, according to Parfitt.

"I don't think Adam Zimmerman has any direct control over what appears [in the *Sun*]," says Parfitt. "But the people who control Southam share a corporate philosophy that is similar to Noranda's," he adds. "Why else would you choose to have Adam Zimmerman on your board of directors unless you shared similar values?"

And what is that shared corporate philosophy? According to Terry Glavin: "It seems as though the only role of the *Vancouver Sun* that has been identified from the top is to increase the circulation. The whole overarching ideology is: 'Fuck the rural areas, to hell with our resource economy, who cares who's getting arrested over at Clayoquot Sound, never mind if the mills are shutting down. . . . ' The ideology is we have no memory anymore." And when a paper loses its memory, says Glavin, its stories have no continuity, no history, no larger context.

But who needs memory when you can have fun instead? When Scott Honeyman's appointment as managing editor was announced in 1991, Honeyman had this to say: "It's a great opportunity to come back and have some fun. The readers want to have some fun and we should have some fun making a product that readers will enjoy."

When asked at the May media symposium if he still believed the purpose of putting out a newspaper was to have fun, Honeyman told the audience: "My concern at that time was that journalism in general and the *Vancouver Sun* in particular were overwhelming themselves with seriousness and were not giving readers what they wanted."

It's a dream come true for corporate executives and their spin doctors: a pace-setting media outlet whose editorial motto is "all the news that's fun to print."

This article first appeared in This Magazine, *August 1993.*

In March 1994, as a result of this article, Goldberg was invited to appear on CBC Newsworld's "Media" show for a segment on how media cover the environment and whether they are subject to manipulation by activists and public relations companies. But once the interview was in progress, host Trish Wood promptly terminated discussion of the forest industry's pressure on the Vancouver Sun, *saying it was unfair to pursue the topic when the industry was not there to defend itself. Consequently Burson-Marsteller went unmentioned throughout the half-hour segment.*

clayoquot dreaming

. . . . clayoquot . . . .
. . . . clayoquot . . . .

What?
. . . . clayoquot . . . .
. . . . Do you hear that?

hear what?

That sound! Like branches clacking. Or frogs croaking.
. . . . clayoquot . . . . . clack . . . clack . . . clackwhat . . .
There! There it is again.

No! Where am I going to hear frogs clacking? We're in the middle of the
city!

Stop and listen for a minute. It's there. It's something.

I always thought you were a little off, but what the hell, I got a minute.

. . . .
. . . .
. . . .

O.K. Time's . . . clackwhat . . .
up.

There! There it is again! You heard it that time, right?!

Hear what, you moron! You mean that, over there? That's just a guy
puttin' up a fence. You and your damn crickets. Let's go!

No, not crickets . . . frogs! But not frogs, crickets, or anything like that
exactly. It just sounds like that. It's something
. . . . clayoquot . . . . . .
else. There! there it is again! C'mon! You gotta hear it now!

Look! I don't "got to" hear nothing when there's nothing there.
Lighten up! Listen, tell me what you hear besides that guy
whackin' at a fence.

O.K! It's . . . (like I said) . . . it's branches clacking. But real soft. And it's
frogs croaking, or maybe just a frog, now and then.
It's also like . . . like water, dripping a drop at a time into a pond. It's like
chickens in a barnyard on a hot day, kind of
murmuring as they peck through the grass. It's sort of like all that, and
more.
. . . . . clack . . . . what . . . . clackwhat . . . . clayoquot . . . . .
Are you *sure* you can't hear that?

Listen, you know what I hear? I hear that lumber [. . . clack, clack,
clackwhat . . .] being hammered together. I hear that guy snapping
his newspaper [. . . clayoquot . . .] when he turns the page. I hear those
train wheels clacking, the one pulling all those logs
[. . . clackwhat, clayoquot, clayoquot . . .] Hell, I even hear the chopsticks
[. . . clayoquot . . .] from that Chinese restaurant.
What I *don't* hear is frogs in a pond or crickets in the grass. There is no
clackwhat, except in your head. There's just all this
around you, and it's only the sounds of the city.

There is no clackwhat . . . clack . . . what . . . clayoquot.

WITNESS TO WILDERNESS

The great and small whales cry out when they are harpooned; they moan with the pain of the hot sun and the fear of death when they are stranded on a beach. Science eventually informs us of things that we have known all along—that an animal's pain is as painful as ours, that its depression and loneliness and need to be loved are like ours. Not long ago the belief swept our continent that plants and trees respond to kindness and can distinguish between Mozart and Rock 'n Roll. We talked gently to our house plants and played beautiful music to them and, whether or not it helped them, it sharpened our attention to living beings.

In our time more and more human beings are learning reverence for life through the anguish of seeing it extinguished. An orgy of deforestation has been going on for centuries; innumerable animal, insect and plant species have already become extinct, but we know at last that if the destruction of life continues, the legacy will be a dead planet. Those people who suffer from this knowledge have an irresistible desire to save, to talk to and caress other living creatures and beg them to stay alive in spite of the crimes committed against them. Sometimes we stretch our arms around a millennial tree and lay our faces against its armoured skin. We sit in the cradles made by the roots that buttress it, or we draw the movement of its branches, as Emily Carr did, dancing in figure-eights and spirals. Now we grieve for the fate of a red cedar which has stood for centuries with the elders of the rainforest in their monumental dignity. It is on a list, scheduled for amputation soon by a chainsaw that will scream through its heart. The sky above it will empty when the tree begins a slow descent to earth, still hinged near the base of its trunk. The hinge bears the last drops of the tree's life; it will be severed with a rending cry, followed by the cacophony of the tree as it settles its length along the ground. The empty sky above, the ravaged space on the forest floor will bear witness.

THE FOREST WEST OF OUR HOUSE

The forest west of our house began behind Southlands School at the end of 38th Avenue when I was nine years old in Vancouver in 1954. This forest went on to the edge of the sea, and contained deer, frogs, and darkness, all of which I had seen for myself.

But the woods to the south, around Eddy's Nursery on Marine Drive, belonged entirely to older boys. Their travellers' tales of Tin Can Creek, the Musqueam village and the Fraser River thickened and deepened the brush and shadows in the southern woods.

East of Dunbar and below 41st Avenue, Collingwood bush disappeared sometime in Grade Seven. I didn't know where its secrets had gone. Now and then still, I drive down Dunbar Street and look east to find the woods which once were there.

The blurred mass of trees on the mountains north of the city flowed on to the end of the world when I was a child. The distant, crowded darkness of the forest took shape in the far reaches of my mind as a refuge. I, or anyone else who wanted harder and more honourable ways, could go to the woods, I thought, when we came to the end of our strength out here. The forest would wait for us forever, I believed.

THE SOULS OF ANIMALS

If animals have no souls
it's because they do not need them.
There is something forever about their time
on earth, whether they move on wing, paw or hoof,
or slide with huge, cold bodies
across the blue-green worlds.
Wherever they dwell, their gaze
when they look at you
comes from a great height—
the yellow of hawk or leopard eye—
or so close up
they've slipped under the leaves
of your eyelids and stare from the inside out.

In spite of theology and metaphor,
a cat placing its back paws
precisely where the front have been
it simply walking as a cat must walk
across the snow. A dog winding himself
like a pocket watch into dream
is doing what a dog must do. Still,
in books of the dead the human soul
transmogrifies, becomes bird or butterfly,
or soft-pawed, graceful thing.

Grant animals a soul: might they not leave
their bodies in the shape of ours,
assume the best of us, the high forehead,
the shapely arms, the exactitude of
thumb on index finger.
That's what those bright ones are,
those people with a glow about them,
an ecstasy. The souls of animals
crossing from one country to another,
pausing among us
only to rise in glory,
beasts again.

THE WHITE ONES

They filled me with the frozen sperm with the cold deliberation and anonymity of a rapist. I suppose I had to be thankful it was a needleless hypodermic that was raping me, instead of other forms of torture they might have employed. I am very uncooperative, and they have done their best to change that. Legs and arms in restraints, mind sedated, flat on my back, I will remain for hours on end, leaking thawed ejaculate. I will never meet my donor-lover. He's probably frozen like his semen.

It wasn't as if I don't have just cause, being so uncooperative, a "mean bitch" as my captors call me. I am not interested in what they have in store for me. After all, they dragged my family from our home, murdered my grandfather when he tried to resist, and imprisoned us here, until we finally died off one by one. All but me—I am the last. I alone mourn for the dead and the destruction of our forest home.

The White Ones try everything to bring out my maternal instincts. They want children—my children—to continue their experimentation. If the White Ones thought I was going to make it easy for them, I had other ideas. It pains me to my very depths to deliberately lose each child-seed they implant. They've long since removed anything from my cell which I might use to abort with, leaving me to resort to beating my swollen belly with my fists. Vengeance consoles me.

I have been in solitary confinement for eight years now. The only company I have are the roaches that find their way into my cell. I leave the compound only to be subjected to experimentation and new implants. Before the others passed away, I was permitted the occasional "conjugal visit" with another prisoner I had come to know and love. But when I refused to carry his child to term, they even denied me his company.

Recently, the White Ones have taken to projecting films of my childhood into my cell to spur me into motherhood for loneliness' sake. I pretend to pay them no notice, but yesterday's imagery haunts me as I lie on this table, strapped in, alone and vulnerable to my only belongings—my past. Damn them.

I'm in the nursery rumpus room with my older brothers and sister. The room has indoor trees and oversized constructions for toys, and exercise. I watch myself intently, finger-playing with my sister. My brothers tease us and I watch my young self chase them to their hideaway. I am tempted to wrestle with them, but I'm too young to win. I kick my largest brother's backside with a small bare foot and run off, tripping and somersaulting as he catches me. I see myself look around triumphantly and holler with glee when I slip from his grasp.

I watch myself and siblings play, sadly wishing they were here today to comfort me. To make me laugh again.

A sound at my back causes me to glance over my shoulder to see our cell door open. A White One enters. We run off in fear. I hasten after myself and finally I look up over my head, and there I am frozen with fear, perched on a limb of a tree, unsure of my balance. The White One takes my sister screaming from our cell. I can hear my sick father banging on the adjoining cell wall. My mother's voice penetrates the rock wall, trying to console us. The danger past, I see myself scurry off, hand over hand, into the arms of my eldest brother. I wish I had the power to see through walls.

I never see my sister again.

The White Ones return me to my cell.

When the sedation wears off, I walk over and peer into the two-way wall mirror, reflecting on the beginnings of life implanted within me. I smile at myself, knowing the White Ones can't read my thoughts.

By killing us off, their destiny is sealed. Soon, their planet will be no longer fit for habitation.

I squat down on my haunches to eat the meal they have left behind, my tail comfortingly curled between my legs.

ALLIGATOR SONG

my shoes want to be alligators
& pick their teeth in the closet

my shoes want to return to the mud
to invade the earth of the swamp

shuffle on you shoes   shuffle on
feet that are blind

feet that belong to an oak tree
shoes moving on their bellies
across the white sand

shoes that lie on their backs
welcoming secretary birds to pick
the scraps of rotting meat

from rows of teeth   blue cornflower eyes
gape at the clouds   alligator shoes

hum alligator tunes   dududu   dudu

shoes amble home to the mudflats
below the gems of an alligator heaven

my shoes snap at moths
shoes aching for high polish

move on tired feet before the alligators eat
your corns your dirty toenails

alligators love mud

ENDANGERED SPECIES

Breathless but ahead
she turns and waits
to fight the hunters

    drops

licks blood from wounds
leans back into the vines
that mingle with her hair

    dreams

thinks of others dead or caged
since so few like her are left
why this need to hunt her down

    stirs

presses down ferns in front
wishes that she had some help
well they won't take her alive

    listens

HIS MOTHER WEST
poem for my granddaughter

Your great-great-grandfather rode
his mother west on the backs
of Chinese railroad slaves and became
the first white male born in Vancouver.
He opened his infant lips and sucked—
cedar, ash, hemlock.
Sophie, your grandmother is a poet,
who inks herself up,
covers her ink-stained body with paper
composed of details she tells you about
in her poems—seeds, singing birds,
animal lust, racoons mating in branches,
shaking the trees, but also,
clearcut, shrieking saws and animal panic.
she swallows the story of trees,
vowel and consonant. Digests and swells.
Stands in this window, this moment,
wants you to listen, think
the thing inside her is also her child,
or child of her child,
several if you believe she's a cat
and will land on her feet,
her breasts leaking secret ink you might later
read in the dark with a candle.
She wants to tell you she once
swallowed the blade of an axe and lived.
What you see running down this stone wall,
these stone steps, onto the lawns and open
drains and the open mouths of spectators,
waiting for her to jump,
is her prayer for you.

TO BE BLIND LIKE A SALAMANDER

To be blind like a salamander
Son of a dragon,
To steal sight from the ground with a sticky skin.

Home is the clay street streaked with grey
The village of root and rock, the rotted log
Where the blood of the salamander king runs cold.

And stiff-toed and ancient, slow he moves
He walks secure in his palace of fire
Free of the dark night, free of the hurricane
And blind to care and woe.

And when at last the floods come down he digs
Down, down in the deep brown mud.
To the layer of limestone gem and gold
To warm his heart by earth's sweet furnace
And wait for the thousandth spring to pass

To dream of a winged awakening
Armour-crusted, iron-tailed
Heart of fire, Shoulder swinging
Mightier than men.

THE WILD WEST

"We did not think of the great open plains, beautiful rolling hills and the winding streams with tangled growth as 'wild.' Only to the white man was nature a 'wilderness' and only to him was the land 'infested' with 'wild' animals and 'savage' people.

"To us it was tame. Earth was bountiful and we were surrounded with the blessings of the Great Mystery—when the very animals of the forests and fields began fleeing from the approach of the settlers, then it was that for us the 'Wild West' began."

Chief Luther Standing Bear, ca. 1829-1908, quoted in High Country News, *March 9, 1992. Standing Bear's real name was Mo-chu-no-zhi. He was a member of the Poncas.*

WILDERNESS 1948-1994

In the vacant lot at 15th and Tolmie in Vancouver's Point Grey the grass is as high as my chin. I am six. I can tunnel into the middle of the lot on hands and knees, smelling the warm dirt, watching the grassy tips above cut the sky. I know I'm invisible and that, if I sit very still, no one will ever find me. Or I can stand up and run in ever-widening circles, falling on the grass, trampling it, grappling out handfuls and flinging them in the air, until all the grass lies flat, subdued, and I'm King of the Castle.

The forest behind our next house in North Vancouver marches up the mountain and, I'm told, down the other side. "What's behind the mountain?" "More mountains," my mother says. I try to imagine the other side. The bear went over the mountain—but all that he could see was the other side of the mountain. I imagine trees marching like bears.

Now I am nine I am given a hatchet and told to go play in "the bush." I, and my friends, the boys next door, chop down small cedars and firs and alders to make forts, leaving miniature clearcuts as if training to be loggers. We hack chunks out of trees to blaze trails so we won't get lost, pretending to be the pioneers our parents had been. The forest is our domain and refuge. Only a few yards into it and our houses disappear. Just as we call the ocean the *chuck*, we call the forest the *bush*, that familiarity removing terror, dominating it, cutting it down to size.

Ecological damage. Environmental concern. No such phrases then. Just trees, marching up one side and down the other, mountain after mountain.

Does one ever recognize wilderness when one is in it? I think of wilderness as something far away, something in the Bible: Jesus, wandering for seven years. Pictures of him in a rock-strewn desert; that is wilderness. We can't wander in our bush, there are too many trees. We have to clamber over blowdowns, zigzag around trunks and crouch to avoid branches. Wilderness is a dangerous place, inhabited by lions and tigers and serpents that strike from behind rocks. It is also exciting; consider opening a closet door and finding the wilderness of Narnia. But my friends and I feel safe in our predictable bush; we ignore the possibility of cougars or bears or disease-causing ticks that drop from trees. Our greatest danger lies in fights with each other or in our parents' punishment. Therefore, can our bush be wilderness?

At thirty-eight, I cast myself out of my home, my family, and my marriage and am consigned to wander through my interior bewilderedness for five years. Here there are serpents under psychic rocks, bears that peer out of black holes, vines that trip me up and prickle. I wish someone—even I—would find me. Each time the ground seems steady or I climb a rise of land that allows a larger view, my next step stumbles or I have to cross an avalanche of mud. Eventually I stagger forth onto calmer, drier land, as if out of the blazed bush of my childhood toward home. I have wandered far; I have seen the other side of my mountain.

Now, at fifty-two, I live in a house surrounded by trees. I can lean against a cedar and listen to the towhees in the salmonberry tangle. I can look out my back window at the bush and accept my bewildered wandering of a decade ago as a step in getting here. The bush is thinner now and there are fewer vacant lots. The sound of chainsaws on a Saturday morning is louder than the sound of lawnmowers. I, too, garden now, behind a deer-proof fence, digging beds, moving flowers and shrubs about—trying, perhaps, to create a new and miniature wilderness, one under my control?

Our species, like beaver and ants, seems to need to work, to move this from here to there, to take down that and put up something else. We have clearcut the sides of many mountains: a wilderness of charred slash and stumps. We have felled, bunched, and yarded off in ever-widening circles. But have we grappled with what it means to leave no dank, secret, unkempt places waiting to have their wild life honoured?

TREES ARE RENEWABLE, BUT FORESTS ARE NOT

A few seasons ago, I sailed with three friends around Vancouver Island, a 600-mile journey along some of the intertidal world's most wondrous coastline. An unforgettable incident during that voyage was gliding, late one Sunday evening, into a tiny cove past Meares Island on Clayoquot Sound.

We were exhausted from the day's long sail, clutching our mugs of tepid coffee as if they were crusaders' chalices, anxious to drop anchor and be done for the day. I remember standing on the sloop's cabin top, trying to judge depths and distances through the darkness, reaching out to touch my boat's shivering mast with a lover's hand—tenderly, yet loosely, feeling reciprocated confidence. There were birds everywhere, gulls being wafted up in the nocturnal wind while cormorants flew overhead in long trailing echelons. The four of us felt as if we had drifted into a cloistered cathedral.

Until the next morning, that is. Dawn revealed that the shores of the cove we had so gently entered in darkness the previous evening, had been clearcut. Our cathedral had been desecrated. We found ourselves anchored in a barren, ugly place that resembled nothing so much as the cone of a burned-out volcano.

It is from this highly subjective viewpoint that I judge the current controversy about the forestry companies being permitted to cut trees in Clayoquot Sound. They should on no account be allowed to touch a single tree.

The dispute is not, as MacMillan Bloedel would have us believe, about cutting old-growth to provide wood for the construction industry. This dispute is about values. What kind of society do we want to perpetuate in these northen latitudes? Is the short-term gain of harvesting wood for profit worth interfering massively with the essential function of rainforests in the earth's breathing mechanism? It all depends on your point of view. Like most city-dwellers, I never gave trees a second thought until I moved to British Columbia a dozen years ago.

It was only when I witnessed the devastation of clearcutting firsthand— it's not like giving the landscape a crewcut; it's more like deliberately devastating it to shoot a First World War film about trench warfare—that I realized what was involved. A tree is not a vertical stick with green fuzz at the top, it's part of a local and regional ecosystem whose value is beyond calculation. The pulp-and-paper firms and their lobbyists maintain that that's a stupid attitude, because trees are a renewable resource. They plant millions of saplings every year and take countless TV pictures of the tiny, perfect plants becoming less tiny, perfect trees to prove it. The B.C. government's compromise of harvesting part of the Clayoquot timber with special harvesting techniques satisfies nobody. It still wrecks the forest, and turns the available trees into the world's most expensive lumber.

They're wrong for one simple but telling reason. Trees are renewable. Forests are not.

It takes literally centuries for bunches of trees to turn themselves into a fully integrated forest. The process involves not just trees, but the quality of the underbrush, natural ponds and the animals that make the forest their habitat. Nature's few original rainforests still remaining on this earth are a precious, highly finite commodity.

B.C. environmentalist Cameron Young has predicted that unless we stop clearcutting immediately, the Pacific coast's temperate rain forests will disappear by 2010. He estimates that they are now being ravaged at the rate of twenty-six million cubic metres a year so that within seventeen years, the original growth will all be gone. Companies dedicated to cutting these venerable plantations maintain that ancient trees die from natural causes and that they are merely managing the forests. Not so. The forests are being liquidated.

The environmentalists out there on the front lines of Clayoquot are reviled for being radical tree huggers. If defending the ecosystem is judged a radical act, then we're all in deep doo-doo. But yes, they're tree huggers. And so am I.

There is nothing quite so glorious as hugging one of those first-growth giants that still stand tall in the dwindling pockets of British Columbia's untouched forests. When we sailed to the Queen Charlotte Islands two years after our Clayoquot adventure, I recall being part of a human chain at the edge of an unnamed inlet on the east side of Moresby Island, and it took seventeen of us, hands joined, to surround this big mother of a tree. Old-timers like that deserve all the hugs they can get. Bill Reid, the great Haida sculptor, caught that feeling when he wrote, "I would like to think that the people who call these bountiful islands their home will have more than nostalgic memories of how it used to be, upon which to build their own vision of the past. I would like to know they can go to at least one sacred place that has not been crushed by the juggernaut of the subduers to create their own myths of a living culture."

Old trees even contain their own music. I remember hanging out with a Vancouver musician named Michael Dunn who shapes guitars out of weathered logs. "You need old-growth for the soundboards," he told me, "because the grain is tighter and the chemical composition stronger." He added, "In the ancient forests, trees had to fight for survival under fairly harsh conditions. The newer, commercially grown trees mature under ideal

conditions, producing more growth rings, but they don't have the strength, quality or consistency."

Loving forests is very much within the Canadian tradition. The wild land's moods, seasons, and weathers were the original chronometer by which we measured our lives. We first laid claim to our citizenship by planting settlements on the shoulders of our shores, the elbows of rivers, and the laps of our mountains—testing nature rather than trying to conquer it.

It has always been the land—which really means its forests—that has anchored our sense of who we are and what we want to become. The shape and growth of our landscape has been the most potent influence on formation of the Canadian character. Let's not flatten it.

FOREST

Here is the dance of the forest; here is the clearcut tune.

You take a tree that has stood for a thousand years, and in one morning you chainsaw it down. Then slice it into a thousand guitars. Sitka spruce, they say, is an ideal wood for sounding boards. How many guitars can you make from the Carmanah Valley? How many musicians then to play on them, singing and composing songs of protest, songs that deplore the cutting down of trees?

To get there, you must drive through the hectares of clearcut logging, through the wreckage of a landscape. The scar on the forest is a scar on your heart: it will show up on your cardiograms. bill bissett once wrote, "if we are here for anything at all, it is to take care of the earth." What have we done with this duty? Who even dares to catalogue its cost?

You take a tree that has stood for a thousand years, and you link your hands around it. It will need fourteen of you to reach that far. Hold on to each other's hands: this is the dance of the forest. This is the breathing of the planet's atmosphere. This is the music of every guitar that ever was carved. Don't let go.

PHOTOGRAPH: THE FOREST FOR THE TREES

Just after the Gulf War was declared, I found myself on a B.C. Ferry travelling from Nanaimo to Horseshoe Bay. I remember standing at the black railing on the white deck, leaning out into the Pacific wind, watching the small Gulf Islands slip by in the mist. At first, when their size bulked up, they'd appear as perfect islands, their trees glistening abstractly in the haze. Then, as the ferry drew up close to some of them, I could see the real texture of each, real trees now, pushing up out of the rocks and bramble, real people living in real houses that had been built over time on these places.

Of course, my mind was full of omens and portents, caught up in the impossibility of war, and it occurred to me that for us, for North Americans, even though we charted each Scud missile's course over Jordan, the war itself was distant, abstract, and that these qualities almost allowed it to happen, almost granted it a strange kind of permission. It seemed to me that if we had to draw up to it as closely as the ferry had brushed against these islands, we'd have to acknowledge how horrifying our abstractions of it were in the long run, and admitting that might save us in the end, or, at least, prevent some wars.

I caught myself seeing in this way and I thought, I do this all the time. This is how I see. I abstract things into a great, ideal movie of me seeing them instead of simply sight itself, and that when I saw like that, I distanced myself perfectly from the things themselves. I realized with a clarity that vanished as soon as I felt it, that this distance protected me from myself and everything around me so I could impose my movie on the earth instead of living on it. It was the real texture of things, including myself, that I was going to avoid if I could, and it occured to me suddenly that this texture could save me where the movie never could.

The movie was short-term, immediate; it rescued me from myself and the things I had done. The texture was forever. I promised myself I would remember this, then lost it to the image of a man leaning forward, squinting into the mist, thinking: we have to begin to see things more closely, and stop hiding behind a dangerous, limited kind of sight.

THE SUBVERSIVES

You have abstracted from me
    an abstraction of your likeness
piled bouquets of approval at my feet

You made me a uniform
        a place in line
           stick me in the dictionary
legitimize your understanding

I exist as a definition
                  intransitive verb in a line
                      I break from your sentence

                      write a paragraph of my own

                         create new forms

                  space

dig lane ways
                    jump your ratrace rides
turn gutters into trenches

Ida is a higgler in the marketplace
Rita a drummer in the band
Heather is part of the Incite collective
Sheila a woman identified woman

You have taken my abstractions
broken my images
carved images-of-broken on my mirror
data process needs
package dreams on TV
separate me from self

race   gender
    history

We who create   space
who transform what you say   is
          send you scurrying
          scurrying to the dictionary
to add   new words

We, we are the subversives
We, we are the underground

From COMING OF AGE

Coming of Age is structured as a spiralling series of small stories, each reflecting a significant moment in women's lives at seven-year intervals. The performance style is based on a technique called "authentic movement" in which the actors offer each other non-judgmental, silent support as they open the secret chambers of their lives. This episode was inspired by the women I have encountered who have moved beyond anger without losing the heart to bear witness to values that grow out of a lifetime's experience.

Young Woman: You said something before, about tapping into the power over . . .

Old Woman: Not power over. Power with.

Middle-aged Woman: Like being *in* love, we can't be out of it.

Old Woman: It's not a matter of *doing* anything, exactly.

Young Woman: Do you mind getting a bit more specific?

Middle-aged Woman [to Old Woman]: Show us seventy.

Old Woman: I am standing in the middle of the road, facing the bulldozers. I look past the drivers of all this earthmoving machinery, to the distant board of directors. I know what I am doing here: I am standing in the way of your profits. Just for a moment, while they read the law to me, I'd like you to see me, a seventy-year-old woman who has very little money.

And you, the politician with the power to remove me from the road, I'm standing in your way, the way you have chosen to maintain your power. Just for a moment, while your hired men explain that I am under arrest, I would like you to see yourself reflected in the eyes of a seventy-year-old woman, standing in the road. Just for a moment.

[Middle-aged Woman and Young Woman join her for a moment. Young Woman breaks away.]

Young Woman: But nobody listens, nobody cares if we stand up for ourselves, it doesn't change anything.

Middle-aged Woman: It changes us.

Young Woman: Is that enough?

Old Woman: It's all there is.

From CLAYOQUOT SUMMER

We are the people
The force that lies behind
Every campaign
The people of the earth
The people who have stood
In the path of destruction
Time and time again
To save
A dying planet
And we will not go away.
Stop, this is not fair
I am standing before the trucks
Because you cannot do this
You cannot do this to the earth
And you cannot do this to my children.

And Michael Harcourt told them:
Yes,
I can
And I will
Forever
And there is nothing
Nothing that you can ever do
To stop me.

Thousands came
From the ends of the earth
From the four corners of the world
From the farthest outreaches of time and history
To live at the peace camp

Hundreds stood on the road
And they did not move to the side
When the injunction was read

They stood there,
And they did not flinch
When the police took them away

To Ucluelet
To jail
Like criminals

As though they had not only been trying to
Save the last remnants
Of a dying planet
Before SHARE BC and MacMillan Bloedel
Moved in
To destroy a magical land
Of Trees
And power
And beauty
That never belonged to them
At all.

The mass trials began
Fifty-one people
Tried at once
Without lawyers

Stop!
The people of the world said
You cannot do this
This is our earth
This is our world
This is our planet
And you are taking it away from us
And it is ours.

You cannot log Clayoquot Sound.
This is the lost,
The oldest,
The most precious watershed of all.
This is the home of the giant cedars,
The abode of the spirits
That live.
Randomly
In the mossy, fern-covered wheels of time.
You cannot log this place.

Yes,
Michael Harcourt answered
From his plush office far away
In Victoria, worlds removed
From the living reality
Of Clayoquot Sound
Of the Peace Camp
Of the sound of the branches of the fallen trees
Creaking mournfully
In the summer wind.
Yes, I am
And nothing that you do will stop me
Ever.

And that year,
A thousand people were arrested
At Clayoquot Sound
And every day,
The trucks moved forward.

THE BLACK HOLE PEACE CAMP—
CLAYOQUOT SUMMER 1993

The History of Summer 1993
Learning compassionate activism
Non–violent civil disobedience
Communication skills

Circle of smiling faces
Nighttime singing around the fire
Honouring the four directions
Our roots go down into the earth

Marmite sandwiches with
Organic Earl Grey tea
Peanut butter cake with apple topping
Made by a shiny-eyed young man

At home in this community
Living on the wounded land
Fighting for the rainforest
Sisters, brothers, elders, children

Hope for the future
Hope for nature
Hope for the coming generations
Without selfishness and greed

THOUGHT

"Get a life and get a job," an irate logger shouted at me, while I was standing on the side of the road during a blockade. Even in the sadness of the moment, as I stood there clutching my camera, I had time to reflect. This is my job. I am a writer, photographer, and traveller and I record events. I am beginning to see that as a writer I may use up too much paper, but I always use the other side when I mess up, and I recycle every tiny bit. I think I have a good life and a good job.

THE EQUINOX, SEPTEMBER 24, 1993

"What was that?"

Clair leaps up beside me in the van, we are chattering from the cold. The windows are foggy from icy drops. Everything in complete darkness except the blue gleam of headlights streaming past. It has been night forever.

We listen as some truck streaming through the night blasts its horn. We are told if we hear a whistle to gather at a certain location because there have been attacks at night on the camp. The RCMP, who will arrest people on the blockade in the morning, will not come tonight.

I lie awake, not moving, hoping my stillness will generate warmth in this rocky place.

Should I get arrested? Should I do it—commit a crime, an act punishable by law, a wicked or forbidden act? I'm afraid; I don't want to be in the system, I'm afraid of the computer, afraid I won't get work, afraid of the record, afraid of the government, afraid of the police, afraid of what my colleagues will say, afraid for my children, afraid of the hassle, afraid I'll be kicked out of the country, afraid of the fine, afraid no one will support me, afraid of the courtroom, afraid of being blacklisted, afraid MacBlo will sue, afraid I'll lose my property, afraid of how much it will cost, afraid of crossing the border. Afraid.

Finally I fall asleep. I dream of this land calling, pulling me awake. I see into another world where some thin blue shadow leads me up out of this black hole into Clayoquot still living.

Woman should not allow her dreams to be corrected by reality.

All of a sudden, voices. Lights shine through the fog on the windows. It is pitch black. "Get up and at it. Come, let's go."

I don't like this—this standing in a circle in the middle of some logging road in the middle of the night, singing. I'm not in my body, only thinking that since it's happening, I might as well be some kind of example.

There's something magnificent about the way all those logging trucks are a parade of light up this road in the middle of the night, but now dawn is just about here. It is happening fast—they have got to get these beasts up over the Kennedy Lake bridge and into Tranquility Creek *now!*

A man stands on top of the cab of a truck. There are lights above that shine into our faces. Hundreds of people off to the side of the road stand watching. Someone with a loudspeaker shouts something about the injunction and everything that was full of sound is now quiet.

"Leave the road."

That's right, go the other way, start with the woman over there, let me be the last one here. Out of somewhere I don't know because I have turned to face Casey—she is afraid, I hold on tight. There are three or four men with cameras and very bright lights. The cameras are in our faces bigger than the men in police uniforms who are going from one person to another saying something. I can't hear because of the roar of the trucks and the sound of our singing and the people standing but thinking so loud, this has got to *stop*. And then the big cameras take the first of the circle away and we move closer together, we want the cameras and the lights and the men to be in the centre, but I cannot reach the last part of the circle. It starts to calm down about when my friend Mitzka is asked if she understands the order of the injunction. The look she gives the officer, the only one of us tall enough to look him in the face, is the gaze of a deer caught on the road by headlights. We think deer are afraid, but they're not, they're only amazed. And on it goes as this group of lights and cameras and big men get closer. And then I am the only one left standing. Oh yeah, what was it I was supposed to sing?

The cameras are now here shooting pictures and the RCMP officer asks me my name, then hands me a piece of paper that cannot be read in the dark, only it is not dark because the lights in my eyes are so bright. He then walks me over to the bus that is parked so conveniently to the side of the road. And then I am no longer little me standing in the middle of the road with eighteen other shaky souls.

I'm in some larger place. The dawn has cast a murk up this gravel road, the bridge is to our backs, the fires burn by the side of the road, the spill from the camera lights illuminates the faces of the almost 200 people at the sides of the road. Behind them, as far as I can see, a line of logging trucks, waiting. And I am beyond the script that says you get up in the morning and do what you're supposed to do, no matter what. I've walked the path in my dream that leads from the black hole to Clayoquot. And said *no*. This roar in the wilderness has to stop!

And for one moment it did.

And then the cameras are following me as I climb into the bus that will take us to jail. In the movies, doesn't the heroine, just before she is taken away, turn and wave to everyone to show she is not afraid any more?

And she wasn't.

GETTING ARRESTED:
CLAYOQUOT PROTESTER HAS NO REGRETS

I was arrested on Friday morning, August 20, for failing to observe the injunction of July 16 and physically impeding the movement of logging trucks from MacMillan Bloedel on the Kennedy Lake road in the Clayoquot Sound area of British Columbia. With our group of eighteen, the number arrested to date is over 500.

I am not a shrubbie. I am not unemployed. I am not on welfare. I am a self-employed editor, a fifty-eight-year-old woman with a grown family and a busy schedule.

Did I want to jump to the side of the road when the RCMP officer laid his hand on my shoulder and made the arrest? Was I remorseful when I saw, below my photograph, a set of large white numbers against a bold black band? Did I regret my decision the next day back at home? Are my children aghast? No—on all counts, no.

The serious personal risk I have undertaken in being arrested is a protest against the destructive logging techniques practised by MacMillan Bloedel and other logging companies in B.C. at a time when environmentally protective alternatives exist, and against the NDP government of B.C. for failing to use the opportunity available last spring to protect all of Clayoquot Sound as one of the few remaining viable areas of ancient temperate rainforest.

My arrest is contributing to the largest non-violent civil disobedience protest Canada has ever seen. It is bound to succeed.

ERYSICHTHON

Erysichthon scorned the Gods, never sacrificed or bowed.
He scorned the laws, defied what Codes allowed,
And logged the grove of Ceres, which, they say,
Continued, undiminished and unhacked, until that day.
Within the holy woods stood a knotty, old-growth Oak,
A forest in itself, hung with testimonials which spoke
Vows and thanks for answered prayers and hearts' desires.
Here the Wood Nymphs frisked and sang, a lyric choir,
And oftentimes, danced hand in hand a joyful round
About the trunk, which measured, of timber good and sound,
Full thirty feet around. Other trees within the wood besides
Compared to this, were puny weeds, so far it did them hide.
Yet Erysichthon could not be moved to hold,
But bade his crew to cut it down. And when he did behold
Them balk at his command, he snatched an axe with furious mood
From one of them, and wickedly declared: 'Although this wood
Not only were the darling of the Goddess, but also
Goddess of the Earth herself; yet I would make her ere I go
Kiss ground with her top branch that flaunts and mocks me so.'
This spoken, as he swung his axe aside to fetch his blow,
The menaced Oak quaked and sighed, the Acorns that did grow
Thereon, and the green branches, boughs and leaves
Shrank in for fear, and paled like one who grieves.
As soon as his cursed hand had wounded once the tree,
The blood came spinning from the wound, as freshly as you see
It issue from a Bullock's neck whose throat has just been cut
Before the altar, when his flesh to sacrifice is cut.
The Horror! Everyone recoiled, and one among them all
Dared step in front and 'drop the hatchet!' call.
Erysichthon, obscene, confronted him: 'Take thou here to thee
The Bleeding-heart's reward.' And turning from the tree,
Chopped off the fellow's head. Which done, he turned again
To hack the wounded Oak. Straight from amid the tree then
Came such a mourning sound as this: 'Within this tree dwell I
A Nymph beloved of Ceres, and now before I die,
In consolation and revenge, I warn thee thou shalt buy
Thy doing dear within a while.' He proceeded wilfully
Still thorough with his wickedness, until at length the Oak,

Pulled partly by the force of ropes, and cut with axe's stroke,
Fell. And with its weight the smaller trees bent low and broke.

—*From* Metamorphoses, Book VIII. *Adapted from Arthur Golding's translation (1567) by Phyllis Reeve.*

MAGNA CARTA:
AN EARLY FOREST PRACTICES CODE

Forest management issues were as perplexing to thirteenth century legislators in England as they are to legislators today in British Columbia. Did forests exist for the King's pleasure? For the barons' economic prosperity? For the peasant's sustenance? For Robin Hood?

These problems were addressed in the Magna Carta of 1215. King John, who, as A.A. Milne taught us, "was not a good man," agreed to the following reforms:

> All the forests that have been afforested [i.e. converted into forest or hunting ground] in our time, shall instantly be disafforested [i.e. returned to the status of ordinary land]; in like manner be it of rivers, that in our time and by us have been put in defence.

and

> All evil customs of forests and warrens, and of foresters and warreners, of sheriffs and their ministers, of rivers and of guarding them, shall forthwith be inquired of in every county by twelve knights sworn of in the same county, who must be chosen by the good men of the same county. And within forty days after they have made such inquisition, the said evil customs shall be utterly abolished, by those same knights, so as never to be revived; provided they be first made known to us, or to our chief justice if we be out of the realm.

The first Charter of the Forests in 1217 continued the correction of abuses: abuse of the rights of access to and use of the forests. No one asked if the forests themselves were abused.

FORESTS OF THE MEDIEVAL WORLD

Forests of the medieval world, that's
where her mind will wander
the three dissertation years, lucky girl—
Forest of Bleu, which crowded around
the walls of Paris and stretched 10,000 leagues
in every direction; the great Hercynian forests
of East Prussia, from which each year
334 drovers bore the logs for the fires
in the Grand Duke's castles of Rostock,
of Danzig and, furthest east of all, guarding
the borders towards the Polish marshes,
Greifswald and Wolgast. I'm so sad
I could die, you said as you left, but
my children, how could I bear it—
and I know, I know there are ways
of losing children, of seeing them stray off
among the trees even now, especially now!
Every fleet needed for its construction
the razing of an entire forest—
lost forests meeting on the tilting hills
of the Caspian, the Baltic, the Black Sea,
over the mountains of water the file of forests
comes. Your face is a mobile mischief,
do you know? Your eyes mocked before
they entreated, your lips rendered
both comedy and its dark twin
in microseconds, and your tongue
harried my mouth's bays and inlets.
The *Oberforstmeister* of Kurland promised
the King 'at least half-fabulous' beasts
for the hunt, his forest measured
140,000 *arpents* and even on the swiftest mounts
horsemen could not traverse it
in a month. My mind runs fast
down its *arpents* and leafy corridors,
seeing no one, I should slash
tree-trunks to procure my safe return
but I can't stop. My mind is running
on pure grief and pure love, I want you

to know this. The Forest of Othe
was so still you could hear a shadow
cross a face at 60 leagues distance—
it had linked the Lyons Massif with
the Woods of Gisors but after a hurricane
levelled a million trees in 1519 the diligent
peasants moved in with plows and those forest
were never reunited. And
the forests of Finland, have you thought of those?
All the way to Archangel and the White Sea?
They can show you how you were
before these excuses. What can you do
about this, your exigent look said
in the doorway, I am going do you realize
I am going? And that both of us will survive this?
When the Swedes needed cash they cut down
the Forests of Pomerania, the result in
many cases is sand-dunes. This for day-trippers
is nice, in your rented *Strandkorb* there is room
for everybody, also for dressing and undressing
when the beach is crowded. In the forest of Morois
Tristan lies with Iseult, they are waiting
for the King her husband who will tell history
they were only sleeping. In
the Black Forest dwarf trees and greenheart
still flourish—as for the Rominter Heide
it was so huge that most of its lakes
and forests were 'held in reserve',
not listed or even mentioned, so for generations
all that those lakes and forests could do was
grow uncontrollably in the imagination. I
would take you with me into the Rominter Heide
if you would come: there
each child we must not hurt will
wear a rose in sign of her ardent, forbearing
heart, in sign of his calm-eyed ascent through
our extreme necessary years.

WOOD
for Naoko Matsubara

There is nothing that cannot be
wood-spoken,

lettered in wood
and spelled out strongly by wood,

the language knurled and gnarled
by years of trees,

The syllables a sway
of leaves and boughs,

the thought a dark thought
dipping through the root

to chills of water
hidden deep within

the fundamen, the dream
a shining dream

shaking its leaf to sky
and sky on sky.

There is nothing that cannot
be wood music,

nothing, nothing, nothing;
smoothed and carved

and blessed and healed,
wood builds us, holds us, names us,

guards us, keeps us,
leads us through the doors.

Woodman, spare that tree!
    Touch not a single bough!
In youth it sheltered me,
    And I'll protect it now.
                —*George P. Morris (1802-1864)*

From EARLY VANCOUVER (1932)

August, 1931

A tall, ragged remnant of a forest monarch, a black monument, hollow and jagged, of a bygone day, stood before us today as we watched the noisy steam shovel, huge grunting groaning leviathan, ripping up earth, stones, bushes, and rubbish, as it tore its way out of what has been for so many years a primeval oasis in the centre of a densely populated city; they are making the approach from Cedar Street to the new Burrard Street Bridge; north of First Avenue West is the Indian Reserve, once a forest, but now very largely covered, where not utilized already, for industries, with small trees, salmon berries, mountain ash, willows, maples, and wild cherries.

The old black stump, a great sliver reaching perhaps seventy-five or a hundred feet into the sky, is a memorial of the once great forest which covered Vancouver; the only remaining, and last, relic within the old, the first, city limits; sole survivor of the silent vacuum of our unknown past.

Soon they will chop down the black old fragment, the last of many thousands of forest monarchs out of whose dark and mighty depths grew this magic city.

December 30th, 1931

I notice it has gone.

WHO OWNS BRITISH COLUMBIA FORESTS?

Who does own our forests? We, the people of British Columbia, do, yet we continue to allow multinational companies and government to clearcut our forests at an alarming rate. It is time we became informed and involved. It is time we take responsibility. To do this we first must educate ourselves.

There are no watersheds remaining intact on the east coast of Vancouver Island. MacMillan Bloedel would like to log further into the lower Tsitika Valley, which is a proposed protected area and the site of the world famous killer whale rubbing beaches. There is no conclusive evidence that logging is not a threat to the killer whales of Robson Bight, which is on the estuary of the Tsitika River.

There are sixty primary watersheds on Vancouver Island larger than 5,000 hectares. Of these, only seven are unlogged, all of which are located between Clayoquot Sound and Brooks Peninsula on the west coast of Vancouver Island: Megin, Moyeha, Sydney, Power, Nasparli, East, and Klaskish. Remember these names. They are the last.

In 1992, the B.C. Ministry of Environment hired D. Tripp Biological Consultants to study the application and effectiveness of the Coastal Fisheries-Forestry Guidelines. Twenty-one logged cut blocks were selected on Vancouver Island: twelve on the west coast and nine on the east coast. The Tripp report concluded that compliance with fisheries-forestry guidelines and government agency site prescriptions were generally poor. On average, there was one major or moderate impact on one stream in every cut block inspected. The report recommended education for people who work in the forest industry and enforcement of fisheries-forestry guidelines.

The Carnation Creek Experimental Watershed Project is a long-term research project to measure the impact of forestry practises on a small watershed, located near Bamfield on the west coast of Vancouver Island. Carnation Creek is now the longest running fisheries-forestry research project in North America. This project has produced evidence of increased sedimentation and gravel movement, which entombs developing salmon embryos, and decreases spawning and rearing habitat and fish size; that the streamside removal of trees causes increased water temperatures and changes in fish cycles; that the loss of instream woody debris decreases fish habitat and bank stability; and that steep hillslope logging increases risk of landslides into fish bearing streams. The project has also shown increases in water run-off and water table levels. Carnation Creek has been in operation for twenty years, yet we have much more to learn from long-term forestry research.

In order to have sustainable forests, we need to know exactly what makes a forest, but at present, that knowledge is very limited. Nature designed

old-growth forests to live from 500 to 1,500 years; today, our forests are rarely allowed to live to 100. Preserving a handful of the once majestic old-growth forests as intact watersheds is imperative. These living laboratories are blueprints of the biological diversity of a healthy living world.

We are no longer the pioneer society of our conquering ancestors. Do we need to take all the land? What of the creatures of the forest? What of our children? We must look at forests wholistically, not as a commodity to be consumed until it is gone. Forests challenge all people to understand and reassume a more humble and sustaining place in the world. The forests of British Columbia belong to the people of British Columbia. We need to become involved and take responsibility. The time to act is now.

THE RIDGE TREES

Distantly on stone ridges
the highest trees lean wearily
like old men
in Oriental paintings
shuffling eternally before the wind

Helicopter clacks down the valley
chopper preceding the choppers
airborne timber tallier
counting the moneyherds
of the untouched conifers

Next year we will practice havoc
in that green trench—
the saws will yammer their nagging dirge—
the donkeys will gather the corpses—
the land will be hammered to stumps and ruin

And when our depredations are done
only the twisted ridge trees will stand
above the brown carnage
like meditative old men
shuffling eternally before the wind.

ALL THE LITTLE DEATHS AT CLAYOQUOT

Someone's sitting on the stump off to my left. A stranger, so I throttle down the engine and turn. Sure enough, there he is—an old-timer from a Pete Trower poem, stagged pants, corks, the works. He gives me the high sign so I go back to my levers and he sits, sucking on a cold pipe, watching us snake logs out of the creek. When we stop for a smoke the stranger joins us. He's a woods push for a local logging company.

"You fellows have a pretty good show going," he says, looking over our two-drum donkey and the short tight line we're using to break open a log jam. "It gives me an idea that might interest my people."

Johnny and I were working at Kootowis Creek. As streams go, it wasn't much. It starts in the middle of nowhere and a few hours later debouches into Grice Bay. Find Long Beach on your map and Grice Bay is on the other side of the highway. The first time I was there we called it Indian River; a decade later it was Kootowis Creek.

Unlike others in the area that spring, we're not interested in trees; at least not live trees. Anyhow, the spruce and hemlock along the creek were humdrum, pretty much what you'd find in any area that's been burned and logged repeatedly. But as I say, trees weren't on our agenda, salmon were. That spring we were involved in what may have been one of the final chapters in what appears to be the least-known environmental project in British Columbia—stream clearance. On most jobs our boss was Stephen Zablosky, a field technician with Fisheries Canada.

Kootowis Creek was the Alpha and Omega of my career with that outfit. Between my first trip there and the last, we completed jobs at a score of places between Bella Coola and the Fraser River. All the projects had one purpose: to enable salmon to get upstream and spawn.

Some of these projects lasted days, others went on for weeks in bitterly difficult conditions. The work was always hard, eighteen-hour days, seven days a week, but the pay was good; so was the country. And the company: Steve was a man to ride the trail with, and Johnny, a huge, laughing slab of a boy who showed up one day and stayed, couldn't be daunted. When the record was written up every fall, there was a sense of satisfaction: we'd done the jobs right.

You see, the salmon we were helping weren't just any salmon. They were our salmon. Sometimes they swam alongside us as we worked our way upstream. We got to know these fish. If the job went slower than expected, in the evenings we carried the fish over the debris and set them free.

Years later when my newborn son was handed to me and let out his first squall, I remembered a ten-pound coho flicking its tail as it darted into the dark, fast-running water. That's how close we lived to our work.

In 1968 or so I spent the winter at Ocean Falls and didn't go back to work with Steve until the following spring. What had been Fisheries Canada was now Environment Canada and everything about our work seemed out of kilter.

For one thing there was more paperwork. For another, everywhere we looked there were engineers. A city-bred bunch, insofar as I could tell, they were not interested in the environment or in salmon; good Joes for the most part, these guys loved being engineers and collecting paycheques. Only trouble was, if it wasn't in their book it couldn't be done. And they'd not read Steve's book.

We encountered them first while doing cosmetic blasting on the site near the soon-to-be-built fish hatchery at the base of the Cleveland Dam in Capilano Canyon. That's where I met the man who came to be known up and down the coast as Nerves. This was the guy who said we couldn't go to work at 5 a.m. because he didn't get up that early.

About this same time, retiring field technicians began to be replaced by another bunch of retirees—sergeants. The technicians were bush-smart characters who had learned their jobs the hard way and loved their way of life. The new men, mostly in their forties, were twenty-five-year men who had retired when the armed forces unified. Salmon meant nothing to them and they liked the bush even less than did the engineers.

We spent most of the next year out of town. Our last job was a long misery north of Bella Bella, back at the head of an inlet deep in the Coast Mountains. You don't know what a long misery is? It's weeks in a tent camp eating a terminally stupid cook's food and being hounded by incessant rain. It was a great place to get sick or hurt, and one by one the crew had to be flown home. Finally it was Johnny, me, and a lot of bear.

The job was hell. But my worst memory is the afternoon the engineer flew in to approve our work. To our disgust the man crawling out of the Cessna was Nerves, The-Man-Who-Sees-Bear-Everywhere, according to other field crews. Nerves had surveyed one job from the air, saying later he'd seen too many bear to land. It didn't matter that an unarmed field crew had worked there for three weeks on *his* project. We weren't so lucky. That afternoon our grizzlies were sleeping off lunch.

He remained about five minutes. "Is that all?" Johnny asked as Nerves scrambled through the berry tangle to his waiting plane.

"That's it."

"What did he say?"

"It's going to rain."

It was April before Johnny and I found ourselves back in Zablosky's cramped office, waiting orders.

"Remember Indian River, Red?" I sure did. It was blocked by massive log jams that no fish were getting through. "The honchos are going to let us clean it up."

"It's about time," I replied. Steve didn't respond. Behind his glasses his eyes had the clouded faraway look I'd seen so many times. He was thinking of our last trip to Kootowis and the circling salmon with nowhere to go.

That's why we're at Kootowis Creek, me and Johnny. Steve isn't with us, but had he been, nothing would have changed much.

"I'll come by tomorrow and we can talk," said the woods boss. "First, I've got a couple things to do."

Next day he is back, his pipe's smoking this time. "Okay, how about this? You've got a working proposition here. My people will pay your wages and expenses, if you'll stay here and clean up some of the other streams here in the Clayoquot."

Johnny and I nod. It will keep us working. Steve hadn't sounded optimistic about the outlook for the summer. Every creek we'd seen in the area needed attention, I didn't think anyone would argue that.

"You've got to talk to your company. You do that and let me know. There's no hurry; some of these jams have been here since World War II."

So we've discovered. Under one moss-covered log pile we uncovered a dam built for a nearby military installation. This explained the stubs of piling we'd found on one side of the creek. They'd supported a boardwalk.

Next morning I phone Vancouver, but it isn't going to be my day. No how. The deck's stacked against us—Nerves has replaced Steve's boss as project engineer and Nerves doesn't believe in stream clearance. Fish hatcheries are the answer. He's told me this repeatedly. Carefully, politely even, I explain about the creeks and the log jams and the fish.

"Log jams float, Lillard," he snorts. "Shit, even you must know that. Fish swim right through them; always have, always will."

That's that. A year later I'm reading in my office at the University of Victoria when the phone rings. Johnny. It turns out he's now a welder in a Vancouver shipyard. That makes two of us who didn't go back to Environment Canada. Steve and I keep in touch and he puts up the good fight for a few more years then retires—to spend his time battling to save what remains of 6,000-acre Burns Bog in Delta.

Some nights I feel the cat moving against my legs. Half awake, my first thought is of salmon swimming against my legs in the dark water. Then I open my eyes. Those creeks we flushed are dead again, the dark water is black water, stagnant water. There are no salmon shoaling in the eddies, flashing silver and red as they move upstream into the clear and steady current.

THE GREAT BEAR CONSTELLATION
for Allan Safarik

Bear reached up and swallowed
a white silk sun,
its white burning,
locked in his belly.

And now the darkness world is our home.

Bear cub on the road.   Dirt
                and dusty road.
   He clowns for cookies and garbage thrown
from tourist cars.   Under the night cedar, the silent
      dark shape is a she-bear.

      Dark

         world.

Her fur matted with blood and dirt / bear-mother
      screams.
Red milk flows from her scarred breasts.
      The paws
 lash at invisible   salmon in the air,
teeth snapping,   choked with fur
   she has ripped from the wound.
Two stars drawn from the night sky
      fill her eyes;
the blood in her throat,
         a flame.

The hunter carries in his rifle
      the bawling of a bear cub,
the surprised
   cry of a bear-mother as she whirls,
tearing at her spurting haunch.

      Bear slept in the briars,
      one eye turned
      to his shadow

and he slept not at all.

Bear slept in the briars,
The cold contained him
and he slept not at all.

Bear slept in the briars
and his shadow bruised him.

She's dead. She's dead. A bundle of fur
    beside the road.
        Noon. Sun. Heat.
The mist rising still from the underbrush.
    She does not move / will not move,
    the dark world in her belly—

       white maggots.

From A DAY AT THE PEACE CAMP

I watch the faces of the men in the trucks as they rumble by. Many look straight ahead, avoiding our eyes. Some stare down at us, their eyes full of anger, fear, and frustration. Some wave. One morning when we lit candles, a few of the loggers flicked their lighters in support, and my heart glowed. I cannot blame the loggers. Like the fishermen of the east coast, they have been led down a highway of obscured or non-existent off-ramps, and they now find themselves far along what seems to be a No Through Road. Perhaps if I were in their shoes, I too would leap at any excuse to behave as if the road continued, despite all indications to the contrary.

"How did it come to this?" I wonder. How did this gaping impasse develop between two usually reasonable, honest, law-abiding groups of people? As I watch the big rubber tires turn and the exhaust fumes rise up I realize that this is about something bigger, much bigger. The conflict surrounding this stand of old-growth giants, as vital as it may be, merely cracks open the window looking out (in?) to a Big Picture—a picture of the power of multinational corporations. It is also about government compliance; it is about the power of the media; and ultimately, it is about the role and the responsibility of you and me, the consumers, the citizens, the voters.

I feel small and ignorant and powerless and lazy. Sometimes I just want to crawl into a hole and disappear, to escape the responsibility that was dealt to me the moment I was born a member of this destructive species. But then I look around at all the extraordinary people who surround me—the two chefs who came for a day and stayed for over two months to run the camp kitchen; the Raging Granny, arrested nine times in the past for standing firm for what she believes in, who shares her knowledge and experiences through the extensive civil disobedience workshops; the ex-logger who coordinates the training of the peacekeepers and nearly always ends up with the graveyard gatekeeper shift (the gates of the camp require twenty-four-hour vigils due to very real security concerns); and the many, many others who have sacrificed in some way in order to be here, to stand and be counted. I am shamed and proud and uncertain and inspired, alternately and all at the same time.

This article is about one little experience in the life of one little person trying to keep from drowning in a sea of (mis)information and despair. Some nights I go to bed hoping that I won't wake up in the morning. But I do wake up, and I must face the day and consider my existence and my place in this system, as well as the responsibilities that go with it. I am

not telling you what you should do. By printing this essay on a paper product, I am supporting the forest industry. I am not against logging—I am against unsustainable logging practises. We receive wild and conflicting "facts" from both sides of the issue. Everyday we are reminded that there is so much in our lives over which we have no control. Such is life. But there is one thing I know that I as an individual *can* do, and that is choose how I wish to live with myself. And that choice is mine, and mine alone, to make.

ON A SHARE BLOCKADE

"Where you from? Why are you fucking us around here, man? This is my land. My father made his living off of this land. This is my land, guy. Why don't you just go back to your city? Why don't you just go home? Go home. Go home!"

I just looked at him and turned away, slowly, to keep it from being an act of fear or defiance, which would have just provoked more nastiness. He wore a yellow arm band. I was in a crowd of people wearing yellow arm bands, and baseball hats, and trucking outfit nylon jackets, horizontally striped shirts, fleece pullovers in baby blue. Chubby incensed women with long hair, bangs from hell, big curls.

The crowd was crammed at the junction of the Kennedy Lake logging road and Highway 4. The logging trucks did not go through today, a massive blockade, too many protesters to arrest. This crowd, though, had gathered to lock the protesters in, to keep them from returning to the Peace Camp. The police got called in and one by one, the protesters' vehicles crawled through the mass. One by one, car after car, for an hour at least. And there were still 500 at the blockade.

A crowd cursing at people they'd never met, banging on their cars, tying yellow flagging tape around the vehicles' mirrors, antennae, door handles— jeering at the drivers "Litterbug! Litterbug!" if they ripped the tape off in disgust.

"Fucking bum—get a haircut. Yeah, you. Get a job."

"Oh, you're not looking so happy now, are you? So now you know what it feels like to be on the other side of a blockade. Doesn't feel so good, does it?"

"Fuckin' shrubs—we pay your welfare, bums."

"Nice hair, buddy, why don't you get a haircut. Come over here, I'll chop it off for you."

I wore a pink arm band. I was a peacekeeper. Why was I there, in the middle of that mosh? Someone had told me peacekeepers were needed up front. The SHARE people were getting nasty. So I went there. My participation, my contribution to peace on the blockade. I stood there in a sea of people for forty-five minutes, was called names, called scum of the earth.

I'd heard the stories—people getting beat up with baseball bats, protesters getting kicked in the mud, thrown off cliffs. I'd heard the stories, I'd seen some vandalism—but today, I got a taste of what it was all about. Yep, one wrong word, wrong stance, inappropriate gesture even, and the angry men would've been on me. Fear and loathing ran amok through the crowd— mothers' shrill voices as they stuck their fingers through a man's open window right into his face and started screaming at him. Words coming out like a jet of steam from a whistling kettle—screeching resulting from an immense pressure inside. "Those people are evil," my friend Janet had warned me. But in the moments between abuses, I looked at them, and I saw the people I grew up with in Edmonton. The people at the hockey rinks and community league barbecues. I saw the Herzogs, the Barabases, the Puhfalls, the Kuzyks. They'd me over for supper, fed me lunch after Sunday morning street hockey. I saw all those good people, infuriated that a group of city-bred strangers, and foreigners even, could come into their home and take the food off their table. These were the same people whose yards I ran through, who I'd delivered papers and sold chocolate-covered almonds to. Here, I stood amongst them, a symbol of everything they despised. Yes, I'm from the city. No, I have never worked in a mill. No, I do not know these hills like the back of my hand.

But those details, the exact wind and flow of the rivers, the precise slope of the ridges, are really just the details. They are of course important, but the exact land at stake is not the point. The point is, we fail to acknowledge the power of the quiet, the thing that does not try to defend itself. I see the forested ridge, undulation in the series of sharp rock folds that are the west coast of this island, the fog creeping through the huge, scarred, unique cedars and fir and hemlock, and there is a power and beauty in the land, resting, breathing, living—a mighty power, the force of repetition over time of fog and rain, ceaseless upon the land. A relationship honed, growing, adjusting for over 10,000 years. Powerful, silent. Needs no drums, no war pipes. Still and sentinel.

And next to the stand—shorn, naked, rocky burn stumps clinging by black roots to rocks—lay the hills, "harvested," "deforested," clearcut. "It's a rape," said Serena. "I've been raped before; I know it when I see it."

This power, this presence has no fury, exacts no immediate revenge, cannot defend itself—and now depends for its existence only on our ability to respect it—to perceive and respect it.

And that is the point. People taking care of the silence, and what it grows. Honouring the rhythms in women's bodies, the talents of the "beautiful losers," the cries of hungry children—anyone's hungry children. That is the point—allowing joy and irregularity and power and vulnerability through each one of us. Recognizing, acknowledging our impact on others, our impact, through our very being, on life all around us. That is the point—compassion, balance, wisdom.

"Why don't you just go home!" he screamed at me. He didn't have to, I was only two feet away. He seemed like a good guy. I'd have drunk beer with him down at the Strath, or at the Commercial in Edmonton.

But here I was, frightening him so much by my mere presence, he had to scream and threaten violence. God, here I was, Mr. Compassion, Mr. Peacekeeper, intimidating someone so thoroughly by simply standing there. I did nothing to ease his pain. I did not respond to him. I just turned away.

I represented people actively working towards destroying his way of life. I had to look at this young man and know that. And today, the trucks did not come through. Today, we had destroyed his way of life. Peace, brother, peace.

Out there on that cloudy, cool Thursday morning, with that man shouting in my face, I learned about the effects of our actions, the rocks and dirt behind our rallies and plans and letters of protest. Someone's going to get dumped on big time, and it's not going to be me. The consequences of our actions, however well-intentioned, will be terrible. People will be driven to the bottle. Couples will break up, children will lose parents. And that's just the short term.

Changes? Alternatives? Sure we can offer them, but who's to say what will happen? How can we predict market whims? How can we foresee how Japan will fill its storehouse of logs? And in the new paradigm of community forestry, who's going to do all the work? Not me, man, I'll be up in the coffeehouses, or out hiking through newly protected wilderness. And who's going to invest their lives away in small companies with uncertain futures? Not me, man, I'll be living in the information industry, safely seated in the lap of technology.

This understanding changes things. If I am to continue along this course of action, my actions need to be well thought out, comprehensive. A vision of "Stop!" "No!" "Erase!" is as barren as a Clayoquot clearcut. "Models," "paradigms," and "alternatives" are as wishful thinking as tree planting and herbicides. The task demands fully swimming with the sharks. We need to depart from ideological raving, and act out of a strength of purpose, a nobility of process, building, co-operating, fighting, erecting something new, something better than before. We cannot leave a community in ruins and just walk away. That's what MacBlo does.

It's all about respect and responsibility. If we "win" this conflict, it's going to get worse before it gets better, and I *don't* mean worse for me. I must respect that. My people deserve it.

THE NURSELOG *

These are my children
these are my grandchildren
they have green hair
their bones grow from my bones
when rain comes they drink the sky
I am their mother and grandmother
I am their past
their memory is my thousand years
of growing and waiting for them

Four hundred rings past
in my body count
there was fire
it touched me and I glowed
with blue fire from the sky
the sky was so close
it hissed and shimmered in me
then rain fell
Three hundred and fifty rings
past there was no rain
for many growing times
but when it came I heard
the forest talking together
How great a time ago
is lost but I remember
long-necked animals eating me
one great-jawed creature eating them
everything consumed everything else
and wondered if living was eating
Then the birds came
but strange birds like reptiles
with broad leathery wings
flapping and crashing through me
they changed to specks of blue
and orange and green and yellow
little suns sleeping in me
I remember this in a dream
when we all dreamed
as if I were an old repeated story

once told to me that I retell
And now the little green ones
nesting cleverly in a row
some love the shade and some the sun
another is growing crookedly
but she will straighten given time
one grows more slowly than the others
and has my own special affection
They are so different these small ones
their green hair shines
they lift their bodies high in light
they droop in rain and move in unison
toward some lost remembered place
we came from like a question
like a question and the answer
nobody remembers now
no one can remember—

★ *When a fallen log in the British Columbia rainforest begins to decay, it becomes a nursery for hundreds of tiny seedlings.*

STAMP FALLS

The Stamp Falls parking lot is crowded. In the shadow of a dusty half-ton, a young man steps out of his hip waders. It is mid-afternoon and the light is softening. Drawing near, I ask how his luck has been. "Got my limit, Pops." He folds the waders over his arm, smiling broadly, showing off his white, even teeth. His cockiness irritates me. "No problem," he continues. "Where's your gear? Or are you a tourist?"

I suppose I am, though I've been here before and have a cabin on Gabriola, an hour and a half away. But I don't like being taken for a tourist. "No. I've come for a walk. The salmon are running?" Beyond the trees at the bottom of the parking lot, I can see fishers like knots in a ragged string across the rushing water. I wonder how they keep their lines from tangling and recall the rod and reel in my crawlspace. It has been years since I have dangled a hook in the water, suspending my mind so it floats like a kite in the clouds.

"You bet, same as ever. I haven't missed a run in years. No fishing allowed below the falls now, though. Goddam government." The young man turns away, his truck door slams. He waves as I pass him on my way to the path which skirts the river, but I don't acknowledge him.

The roar of the rapids swells and then I can see one, two rods bending double from the weight of striking fish. I press on, anxious to reach the pool which lies at the bottom of a gorge. On a previous visit I watched a troupe of boys leap from a cliff, screams of excitement trailing them like ribbons as they plummeted toward the water. The pool is fed by several streams, plus the Stamp River of course, which also empties it, meandering away over more gentle terrain on the far side.

Breathing through my teeth in a vain attempt to screen out the odour of rotting fish, I climb the trail alongside the river. I stop frequently to look for eagles but the sky is empty. At the lock which has been installed to assist the salmon in their climb upstream, a young man wearing a bright red peaked cap hunches over a metal grate. A clumsy orange tarpaulin is pitched nearby. I assume he is from the local band office and is counting the fish; he does not look up so I pass in silence. At the next grate, I climb out over the lock so I can look through it. The smell is worse here. The water is turbulent; the battered corpses of fish are jammed against concrete protuberances.

Farther up, the trail follows the edge of the cliff. Moss trails like hair from overhanging branches. There is a short balcony of rock, the edges cordoned off with strong wire mesh. The noise is tremendous. Below me the torrent is maculated by jagged black rocks. A salmon leaps at the wall of water and is hurled back. Again and again the big fish arch like sickles and strain for purchase. Below the falls the fish crowd together, exhausted, heads into the current. There are great patches of white on many.

To reach the pool they have to tack away from the edge of the gorge. It is cool among the trees and the scent of fir and cedar is fresh. The path drops abruptly and I slide toward a pebbly beach, duck beneath an overhanging cedar bough and gaze out over the shimmering surface. Not fifty feet away, a large blue heron stands motionless on a rock. I sense movement at my feet: a school of sockeye nudging the shore. They are waiting for rain perhaps before they struggle up one of the shallow streams to spawn. The bigger fish which were fighting the falls are Chinooks and rest in deeper waters. The bodies of many of the sockeye are bright red; fungus, abetted by the warmth of the fresh water here, sprouts in patches on their dark, misshapen heads.

The heron flaps heavily away. A high ringing sound makes me think of the bell I jangled at mass when I was an altar boy. Two dark birds on the far shore—dippers, who bob up and down like sandpipers but also walk underwater and forage on the bottoms of streams.

Clambering along the base of the cliff, I step in a decaying mass of roe. The water is deep here; below me long shadows slide among huge rocks. Across the pool a salmon leaps repeatedly, finally slapping back onto the surface and wriggling on her side toward the far shore. She dies before she reaches land, her abdomen still distended with eggs.

I climb onto a flattened boulder, open a bottle of beer from my knapsack and light a cigar. Through a cloud of smoke I catch a movement in the bushes. A glossy black bear has ambled down to the pool; he dips a paw into the shallows, pulls in a floppy fish which he seizes in his jaws and carries off into the forest. He does not look up and I remind myself to collect pebbles to rattle on the trail back to the parking lot. You don't want to surprise an animal like that.

Except for a small flock of twittering juncos, the darkening woods are silent when I leave the pool. I repeatedly indulge in the thought of the bear reaching into the water for his dinner. It irritates me that the image progressively loses its uniqueness and dissolves into memories of scenes from television nature shows. Near the parking lot the fishers are silhouettes on the twilit river and I watch from the bank. One of the men whoops as he lifts a still struggling fish from the black water. The lure, which hangs from the side of the victim's mouth, flashes like a knife as the man labours with heavy pliers to remove it.

Later I meet a biologist friend in Port Alberni. He works at the Tseshaht Band's hatchery seven miles upriver from the falls and tells me the police had to be called to break up a melee at the park last week. The run was peaking and there were far too many fishermen for the banks where angling is still permitted. A fight broke out and people were hurt. "The limit is two fish but they compete to see how many they can catch. Sometimes they'll bring in as many as forty, which they have to let go. Once the run starts, the salmon don't eat; they strike at the lures out of instinct. The ones those bozos release are too exhausted to fight the current and are swept back over the falls."

Driving back to catch the last ferry to Gabriola I settle into a blue funk which persists until I crawl into bed and fall asleep. The next morning I am awakened by the sun and the familiar scream of a pileated woodpecker who lives in a deadhead on the other side of the meadow. A squirrel is scolding an intruder somewhere in the surrounding forest. As I crawl out of bed I replay my friend's story about the annual ritual at the hatchery upstream from Stamp Falls. One night every spring the fish culturists there get drunk on rye whisky and swallow salmon fry live. My friend, however, insists on biting their heads off first so they won't feel the stomach acid which awaits them.

TECHNOLOGY, NOT ENVIRONMENTALISM, CUTS FOREST JOBS

On May 29 [1993], former International Woodworkers of America (IWA) President Jack Munro (now president of the corporate-sponsored B.C. Forest Alliance) gave a speech in Port McNeil that was by turns rousing and heart-rending. Addressing a community audience of some 240 people, Munro recounted stories about U.S. forest workers losing their jobs and living in pickup trucks, while their wives gave birth to malnourished babies. Munro warned that, in order to keep such horror stories from becoming commonplace in B.C., people have to "get involved" and "protect your way of life." "We'll win this scrap because we're right!" roared Munro, winding up his speech, but neglecting to identify just whom he meant by "we."

Barely a week later, on June 7, Bruce Vincent—a spokesman for the U.S. industry-funded "wise use" movement—addressed an audience of 200 in Port Alberni. Sponsored by the local chapter of Share Our Resources, Vincent called environmentalism "the Big Lie" and characterized it as "an attack" on the communities that built North America. Claiming that U.S. environmental legislation has been based on "fake science" and has caused "unbelievable social disruption," Vincent reproached environmentalists for what he called "callous disregard" for people who live and work in rural communities.

By July 21, IWA Local 1-80 President Bill Routley was telling the local press that loggers in the Cowichan and Chemainus valleys will protest any NDP reversal of the Clayoquot Sound decision. Claiming that reductions in provincial annual allowable cuts have cost logging jobs in the Alberni Valley, Routley stated: "A lot of our [IWA] members want to do something to help loggers in Port Alberni. If the government gives in on the Clayoquot, I'd encourage our members to blow apart."

Just what Routley means by "blow apart" isn't clear, but the thought of frustrated men with chainsaws is not reassuring. As the rhetoric heats up daily—especially through that divide-and-conquer public-relations strategy of pitting workers against environmentalists—the public deserves some answers to a couple of key questions in this dispute.

Over the past three decades, the annual volume of timber logged in B.C. has approximately *tripled*: rising from some thirty million cubic metres per year in 1961 to roughly ninety million cubic metres in 1989. Over the same period, however, the number of direct forestry jobs per thousand cubic metres logged has been *cut in half*. Obviously, the increasing volume of timber logged has (paradoxically) not generated work in B.C.'s forest industry. The reason is simple, but it is never mentioned by those who like to scapegoat the environmental movement.

Throughout the 1970s and 1980s, the big multinational timber corporations (who control ninety percent of the forest base in B.C.) introduced a series of new technologies which massively replaced human workers, both in the forests and at the mills. Historically there were two key moments, 1974-75 and 1983-84, in which such high-tech innovation decimated the labour sector. So far, those jobs have never been recovered, despite the rebound in volume of timber logged.

The first instance of "labour-shedding" (as it's called in the corporate boardrooms) was the result of the decision to bring in grapple-yarders for clearcutting the forests, while in the mills extensive automation (including mechanical wood-sorting on the green chain) replaced workers by the thousands.

Less than a decade later, in the early 1980s, a second round of technological innovation—including giant feller-bunchers in the interior and electronic end-dogging systems in the mills—again decimated the labour sector. *The Globe and Mail* (May 22) estimates that in Port Alberni alone, the forest job losses that can be directly attributed to the 1980s high-tech innovations number at least 3,000.

The question that arises is this: Why didn't the forestry workers and/or their unions vehemently resist these labour-shedding schemes and mount massive protests at the time? Undoubtedly, they would have been widely supported by the general public, especially in B.C. where so many people care deeply about primary-sector workers and their communities.

I talked with four different forestry experts, each of them fully knowledgeable about the industry and its history in this province, and all of them told me that over the past thirty years there has never been any significant protest by organized labour against technological replacement of forestry workers. Indeed, in talking with these sources, I have come to understand that the IWA itself "cut a deal" with the corporate bosses, agreeing to massive and permanent job losses in exchange for higher pay to the few remaining human skills. If this is so, again the question is why? To me, this sounds like shafting your fellow-workers for the sake of your own higher paycheque.

When Jack Munro reminds his audience about the importance of "the first buck" generated in this province by the forest industry, I agree. And when he complains, "How is it that we have allowed ourselves as a province to know more about cholesterol and designer jeans and what the most popular TV show is, and we don't have a damn clue about how the economy works," again I have to agree. But what both Jack Munro and Bruce

Vincent leave out of their analysis is the fact that over the past thirty years the North American economy has become almost entirely dominated by multinational corporations whose operating buzzword is "jobless growth."

This overall corporate strategy has not only devastated the environment, it has affected workers in every sector of primary industry. For example, between 1979 and 1986, automation helped U.S. Steel to reduce its workforce (and thus its labour costs) from 28,000 to 9,000 people. If anyone has caused "unbelievable social disruption" in our society, it is the multi-nationals whose bottom line is shareholder profits. The attempts to blame the environmentalists for job losses reveal just how cynical and manipulative corporate public-relations has become.

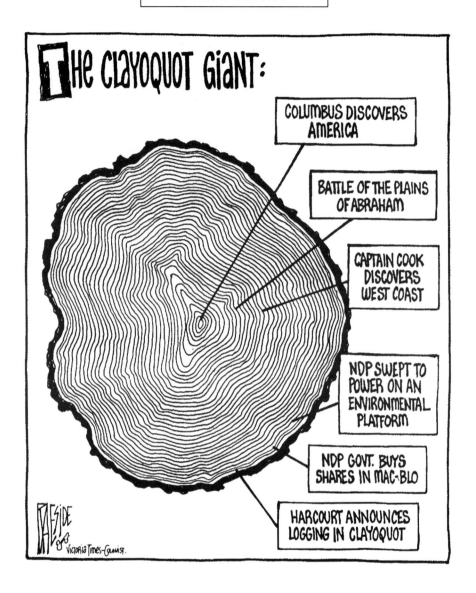

LOGGING POSSIBLE WITHOUT DESTRUCTION
Letter to Parksville-Qualicum Beach News

Editor,

Fifteen years ago a group of women and myself purchased a forty-acre cedar timber lease on a large lake in the Cariboo region of B.C. The Ministry of Forestry set the rules for our logging activities. The only machine we were allowed to have in the woods was a chainsaw with an attachment for making lumber. The rest of our equipment were hand tools—froes, mallets, axes, and a hand-operated strapping machine. We were required to selectively clear trees—had to use the whole tree then cut off the branches and scatter them on the forest floor where they would compost. We had to work at least 400 feet away from all streams to protect the sensitive wild fish stock. We used the bark to make pathways over swampy areas. The trimmings from the shakes were bundled and sold as kindling. To transport the wood products out of the forest, we chose to use a draught horse and stone boat. We would then barge our products down the lake where they were loaded onto a truck then taken to town and sold. The second season we logged, some of the men convinced the forestry ministry to allow them to use rubber-tired vehicles in the bush. The men spent much idle down-time because of having to wait for parts. We never lost a day's work with our horse and all it took was a little bit of hay and some loving care. We logged our property for three years and all we left behind was pristine wilderness and a few trails for future nature lovers to stroll on. We only worked late spring, summer, and early fall and made plenty of money to live on year round without collecting unemployment insurance or welfare. So you see, the forestry ministry does know how to enforce environmentally sound logging rules. But they only do so for small-time operators. A couple of years after we finished, the ministry allowed big-time logging companies to clearcut the same area we had worked so hard to keep in harmony with nature. I haven't been able to go back there to see the destruction and violent rape of the land. I've only heard the sad story.

Namaste
Wild Iris Dragonwomon
Coombs

OUR CIVILIZATION

There is no forest
never was a forest
forests are a rumour
There are trees
(here and there)
but they shun each other
never get together
because they're aware
should they ever
we'll cut them down
our civilization

From CEDAR

Before felling a cedar in the forest, a Kwakiutl man beseeched the spirit of the tree, with ritual, for the trunk to fall in the right direction. He chiselled into the heartwood and picked up four chips. Throwing the first where he wanted the tree to fall, he said:

O Supernatural One!
Now follow your supernatural power!

He threw down a second chip in the same place and said:

O friend, now you see your leader
who says that you shall turn your head
and fall there also.

He then threw down the third piece in the same place and added:

O Life Giver! Now you have seen which way
your supernatural powers went,
now go the same way.

When he threw the fourth chip in the same spot, he ended his plea:

O Friend, now you will go
where your heartwood goes.
you will lie on your face
at the same place.

Answering for the tree with the assurance he sought, the tree faller said:

Yes, I shall fall with my top there.

PAUL BUNYAN AND BABE

The myth of Paul Bunyan and Babe, his enormous blue ox, originated in the nineteenth-century lumber camps of Quebec or Acadian New Brunswick and spread west as logging did. By swinging his axe around him, Paul could cut down a whole valley of trees at a single blow. His voice was like a clap of thunder and he could clear a mountaintop in one stride. Babe lay down and rolled over and when he got up, there was Lake Superior. He put out a forest fire by swallowing a mouthful of fog and breathing inland. Paul and Babe's exploits were first published in 1910 or 1914, and as the tales grew wilder, these two eventually became credited with inventing logging and felling the timber of a continent.

LOGGERS: THE GLORY DAYS

Throughout the islands and inlets at the northern end of the Strait of Georgia, there exists a visible record of logging from its beginning more than a hundred years ago in British Columbia. Stands of hundred-year-old, naturally regenerated, second-growth evergreens mark the locations of the earliest timber extraction in the area. Here can be seen the massive stumps with the notches cut to accommodate the springboards on which the fallers stood to do the hours of chopping and sawing required to bring the giant trees crashing to the ground.

Getting above the taper of the root bulge, common to the large trees of the Pacific rainforest, was an attractive incentive when the felling was done with a hand-pulled, eleven-foot, crosscut saw, the men plagued by mosquitoes and blackflies, while the friction of the saw pulled back and forth created just enough heat to cause the tree's pitch to gum up the saw. When it became harder and harder to pull, the fellow on the other end tried to help out by pushing a little, and each push caused his end of the saw to dig in, until his partner on the other end would call out, "Get off the saw; you're ridin' it; let's oil," and from a glass vinegar bottle, with a hole burned through the cork, worn on a leather thong tied to a belt loop, they splashed on coal oil to dissolve the pitch and make the saw run free again. After the oiling, a few drops always ran down the pant leg on the thigh where the bottle hung so that the skin underneath was blistered there, but it was the only place the blackflies didn't bite.

After the undercut was finished the sawyers turned around to the opposite side of the tree and, with the sharp teeth of the saw passing back and forth about a half-inch from the flesh of their legs, they began the backcut. Finally, at the shout "Timber," or "Let 'er go," they threw the saw straight back out of the cut, scrambled down from the springboard and watched, apprehensive and awestruck, the death of an ancient giant.

The trees were cut into log length where they fell, and with oxen or horses, were skidded to salt water where they were boomed up for delivery to market.

The areas where that first logging occurred are now well on the way to natural restoration. In the order of their natural appointment, berries and brush, maple and alder, and other deciduous plants indigenous to the location, filled up the holes in the forest left by the loggers. Each, in its time, protected and restored the soil, and provided shade and nutrition for its successor, until the evergreens pushed up through the cover, overshadowing the competition and decline of the pioneer species.

It's unlikely that those early loggers could have treated any aspect of their chosen calling with nonchalance. They were applying, to a new location and a vastly different topography, methods and lessons learned in the logging of the eastern part of the continent, in a different type of forest. Changes had to be made. They learned as they worked.

Around their fires they shared experiences and exchanged ideas. From those discussions came the legends that would fire the imaginations of young men for the next century. Heroes were made who would challenge those young men to live up to, and outdo, their reputations.

In the beginning, logging was restricted to those areas easily accessible by water. From the developing centres on the Strait of Georgia, the water-borne waves of adventurers floated their hopes and makeshift camps and equipment to the islands, bays, and inlets of that great sheltered body of water.

In 1890, Canada had suffered through three decades of depression. Many of those early loggers were unsettled, unattached drifters. If an operation went broke the drifters simply moved on to what might amount to room and board at some other job. After thirty years of depression, it's likely their expectations were somewhat lowered. Those who were married with a family faced an entirely different prospect. They went home with nothing to show for their hard work and weeks of separation, disappointed and destined to do it all over again if nothing better came along. Unheralded and unsung was the heroism of wives, left to tend the home and family while they worried for the safety of their husbands.

In the first three to four decades of logging in the coastal areas the surface was barely scratched. Only the very best trees were taken. Any wood other than number one cedar and fir was left in the bush. Hemlock was considered worthless.

During the fifteen years of Wilfrid Laurier's government (1896-1911), two million people came to Canada to take up free homesteads. The spectacular development of the prairies triggered a surge in growth and prosperity throughout the country. Railways were expanded, homes, barns, and grain elevators were built. Coincident with the arrival of the immigrants, the pulp and paper industry began and flourished. Great changes were in store for the primeval forests.

In the last quarter of the nineteenth century, crude steam machinery made its appearance in the Georgia Basin. Arrival of the steam engines would eliminate the expense and labour of transporting oxen, horses, and great amounts of feed to remote logging shows. Steam engines didn't eat and free fuel was available in abundance. The teamsters would soon be leaving the coastal rainforest. The squeak of hames on horse collars, accompanied by the jingling of heel chains, would be replaced by the puffing, banging, and whistling of steam.

Those first machines were little more than steam powered capstans with a single drum from which a cable was pulled out to the felled timber by a "line horse." There men attached chokers to the logs, sought out a safe place clear of the rigging, and signalled to the engine man, or "donkey puncher," as he soon became known in logging language. At the signal, the donkey puncher opened the throttle which set the drum to turning, reeling in the large cable, with as many logs attached as the machine could pull. When the logs were unhooked at the landing, the horse pulled the rigging back out to the timber. A hundred years later the scars from these operations would still be visible. Great ditches were torn in the forest floor by the logs as they were skidded to the landing. Small trees were torn out by the roots, snags were toppled, or chokers broke if a log jammed against a stump. Men learned to keep well clear of moving rigging.

With the advent of logging railways, the very best of the ancient forests became available to the rapidly expanding timber industry. So rich were the valley bottoms, so dense the stands of Canada's largest trees, it must have seemed the reach of the railhead would always exceed the insatiable corporate grasp.

With the full utilization of steam, logging operations became more and more efficient. Logs were swung aboard flatcars right at the high lead landings. Soon, eastern manufacturers began supplying truck sets, four wheels and a bunk to a set, each set connected by an adjustable reach. Flatcars were virtually eliminated, the payload itself becoming part of the strengthening backbone of the train.

With each new mechanical design, and every new system innovated by the workers themselves, the pace quickened. Men worked to the speed of the machines and they pushed the machines to the limit. The increased speed and efficiency of yarding and hauling the felled timber nipped like an irritating dog at the heels of the fallers who had not yet realized any benefits from mechanization.

The byword in the bush was "highball" and men took pride in their ability to produce. In their zeal, they pushed themselves to their limits and sometimes beyond. Their fame spread throughout the country until, like many heroes of history, they became victims of that fame. Each new day found these warriors locked in a duel with their personal reputations of the day before. In a dangerous occupation that demanded ability, many were accorded the highest acclaim possible. Their contemporaries would, respectfully, call them "highballers."

Change is a hungry wolf that lurks at the perimeter of all occupations and industries. Ever vigilant, it inspires movement and strengthens those it stalks. Or it devours.

Loggers improvised until improvisations became innovations that became systems. It must have seemed that they continuously had to learn new skills. And learn them they did.

Eventually some imaginative and daring logger slung a couple of hundred feet of light rope over his shoulder, climbed a tree, cut off the top, passed the end of the rope down to someone on the ground and pulled up a light block and secured it to the tree. Then progessively larger blocks and lines were hauled up until a bull block hung near the top of the truncated tree, through which the large steel cable mainline was passed from the steam engine to the timber waiting for skidding. They had a spar tree. The B.C. logging industry had produced a new hero, the high rigger. People across the country and around the world thrilled to photographs of these men performing their daring tasks 150 feet or more above the ground. Teenaged boys closed school books to seek employment and adventure in the coastal rainforest.

In just a few decades the high rigger would be gone from the forest, replaced by diesel powered mobile spars, driven to skidding sites, and the fully-rigged steel spar raised under its own power.

It would be 1950 before chainsaws would replace handsaws. Today a single faller, using one of the modern lightweight chainsaws, can fall more trees in a day than could six men using old hand-pulled crosscut saws.

Railways served the forest industry well as long as there were comparatively flat, virgin valley bottoms to cut. But eventually all the easily reached areas were exhausted. Demand for timber and profits pushed the loggers farther up the mountainsides. Railways couldn't negotiate the switchbacks and steep grades of the higher elevations. Trucks could.

Railways were abandoned, the tracks pulled up, and the roadbeds were widened to accommodate massive screaming diesel trucks with fourteen-foot bunks. Three hundred gallons of water carried in a tank behind the cabs cooled the brakes when loads in excess of a hundred tons pushed hard against the engine retarders on the hair-raising trips down the mountains. And schoolboys dreamed of trucks.

From the corporate point of view, the coming of the trucks would initiate an unforeseen change. The network of roads required for the trucks would open the forest to the public.

For the first time, timber operations were exposed to public scrutiny. People who selected a lake on a map on Wednesday evening arrived at their destination Saturday morning to find a scene of utter desolation with the trees clearcut to the water's edge and the shoreline choked with debris. Rivers and streams ran brown with topsoil and lake bottoms silted over. On steep hillsides where all the trees had been cut, great patches of soil

had sloughed down and trees would never grow there again. Every logging road was travelled, every destination pursued by people in their hunger for wilderness. The explorations revealed that, wherever the roads went, destruction followed close on the heels of the road builders. And parents sat with their children around campfires in clearcuts and dreamed of trees. And the loggers, now maligned, went about their hard and dangerous work as corporations dictated, while governments turned a blind eye.

When citizens began to demand an end to clearcut logging, corporations mounted public relations campaigns to justify their methods. Union officials thunder at length about environmental safeguards costing jobs, in an industry that loses thousands of jobs annually to environmentally destructive automation.

Great changes are coming to the coastal rainforest. Those changes, if they are to be beneficial, will demand heroism from many. When government vision supersedes individual careers and pension qualifications, governments need only to point the way. The loggers, those inventive and irrepressible heroes of British Columbia history, will make that change, if they are in the bush instead of the history books.

H.R. MacMILLAN

Does H.R. MacMillan belong in this anthology? The younger editors were dubious. Could the principles which inspired the Clayoquot spirit be compromised by too zealous a striving for a "balanced" viewpoint? The older editors thought about the fifties and early sixties, when the odour of pulp mills and wood chips smelled like prosperity, and the dictatorship of Big Business still seemed benevolent. Rewriting our past is not a useful step towards understanding our present or influencing our future. But are some things best forgotten? After much questioning of ourselves and each other, we decided to remember. This is how it was . . .

Everyone admired the men who made things happen, and for the first half of British Columbia's twentieth century, H.R. MacMillan, J.H. Bloedel, W.J. VanDusen, and Walter Koerner were the lumber kings. With daring and imagination, they turned natural resources into economic prosperity. Self-made men, they became patriots and philanthropists, dedicating many of their hard-earned millions to the enhancement of the arts and sciences. Vancouverites named some of their most prestigious public buildings for them: the MacMillan Planetarium, the Bloedel Conservatory, the VanDusen Gardens, the Koerner Library.

In Empire of Wood: the MacMillan Bloedel Story *(Douglas & McIntyre, 1982), Donald MacKay traces both the evolution of the company from timber broker to multinational, multi-faceted industrial empire as well as the personal story of MacMillan.*

The H.R. MacMillan Export Company started business in 1919, and by the 1920s, patterns for the industry were being set. Twenty-five percent of the province's work force was in the lumber industry. During the First World War, MacMillan had travelled overseas and made contacts that served him well for years to come. The MacMillan Export Company pursued foreign markets, usually dealing with a single important wholesaler in each country. In 1923, when an earthquake and tidal wave ravaged Japan and large amounts of timber were required for reconstruction, federal civil servants bypassed the usual channels and communicated orders and contracts to MacMillan directly.

In 1922, MacMillan moved into manufacturing by purchasing a tiny sawmill from the Blue Bird Lumber Company near Qualicum Beach on Vancouver Island. The mill closed within two years, but the step in this direction had been taken.

MacMillan's training methods and work ethic attracted ambitious young graduates from the University of British Columbia. Eager to learn the ropes from a master, they joined the company at junior clerical levels and worked their way up the corporate ladder on the strength of their merit and performance.

When other companies and industries failed to serve his needs, MacMillan expanded his company to fill the gap. In 1924, a lack of shipping facilities drove the MacMillan Export Company to found the Canadian Transport Company. The decreasing supply of white pine from eastern Canada and the need to guarantee a log supply led to the purchase of smaller logging companies and camps on Vancouver Island. In 1935, a withdrawal of lumber suppliers necessitated MacMillan's move into major sawmill operation and land acquisition. The merchandising company grew into a corporate parent firm involved in all aspects of the lumber trade.

MacMillan worried about his international contracts. Japan's invasion of China had halted the Asian business. Perhaps the company was too dependent on the British market? Such difficulties, however, were postponed by the Second World War.

After the war the industry took a new direction: pulp and paper. In 1949, after twenty-nine years as president, H.R. MacMillan became chairman of the board, but kept tight control of many operations, including construction of the Harmac sulphate pulp plant near Nanaimo. B.M. Hoffmeister was president, VanDusen vice-chairman, and Ralph Shaw vice-president in charge of marketing. When citizens attended a meeting to complain about the smell of the pulp mills, MacMillan is reported to have stomped to the mike and said, "When you stop smelling that smell, you stop having jobs."

In 1950 MacMillan began negotiating for a merger with Bloedel, Stewart and Welch, which owned or controlled over 300,000 acres and operated five logging camps on Vancouver Island. On April 10, 1951 the Vancouver Sun estimated that the proposed merger would mean "the creation of a single integrated forest operating unit worth in excess of $100 million."

The merger did not proceed without problems. On August 6, a Sun editorial worried about thirty percent of the coastal forestry industry coming under one manager. Even their criticism of MacMillan was a sort of tribute: "As an able man, as a great Canadian, and great British Columbian, H.R. MacMillan deserves a better fate than to be known as a great monopolist." MacMillan replied that the degree of efficiency demanded in supplying a commodity interested for world trade could be provided only by a big corporation.

A worse threat came from the Canadian Income Tax Division, which set its sights on $16 million in undistributed income held by Blodel, Stewart, and Welch. MacMillan, his lawyers, and the Tax Division sparred for three months until MacMillan announced he wanted the merger enough to pay the price— $2.3 million, to be paid by the merged company.

As his last act before retiring at the age of eighty-seven, J.H. Bloedel signed the documents of amalgamation. MacMillian & Bloedel Limited was officially born on October 1, 1951, although legal details were not completed until the end of the month.

MacBlo became a giant. Operations were integrated, from logging, through milling, to marketing and shipping. Over the next few years mills expanded, and machinery and methods were modernized. Loggers who learned the business on the job began to suspect they were losing promotions to MacMillan's bright young university graduates. Early profits were sometimes disappointing, and MacMillan began to warn of the dangers of selling seventy-three percent of the province's lumber production outside Canada, forcing Canadian sawmills to compete in a foreign market.

MacBlo worked with the government to establish four Tree Farm License areas. A Tree Farm licensee managed Crown Land on terms acceptable to the British Columbia Forest Service, providing for replanting, fire prevention, and harvesting on a sustained yield basis. "Stumpage," the price paid by the company for the government timber, was fixed annually. At first the licenses were granted in perpetuity; after 1957, they were renewable every twenty years. To MacMillan, the licenses looked like a relinquishing of business freedom, but he overcame his misgivings when no reduction in annual cut occurred as a result of the new policy.

In 1956 MacMillan, now seventy-four, retired as chairman of the board, but retained command as chairman of the finance and policy committee. He remained a public figure, a Grand Old Man and Public Benefactor, until his death twenty years later.

Following his death, his mansion was demolished and heritage-minded home-handymen could pick up pieces of the panelling and stained glass. University librarians were invited to rummage through his books. His company became a bigger player, and a bigger pawn, in the titans' game of industrial mergers, takeovers, and corporate empire building.

Fifteen years after MacMillan's death, Craig Piprell observed in Monday Magazine: "H.R. MacMillan was a pretty big fish in his day. But [he] would probably be appalled at what has become of the firm he founded."

—Phyllis Reeve

MIKE, MAC, AND ME

If Mike bought Mac with money from Me
I might not mind if Mike was kind,
But Mike told Mac that things were fine
So Mac makes money with money of mine

If I could choose just how to use
My tax I would not buy an axe
Nor would I wed my fate with Mac's
as Mike has done, these are the facts

It's simple, anyone can see
The trouble with Mike, Mac, and Me
The problem at its simplest be
The conflict is of interest

Gee, I wonder if Me, Mac, and Mike
Will ever learn to think alike
and leave the money in the trees
For all to share, Mike, Mac, and Me

SHORE PINES

Mostly the conifer is a responsible
Citizen in his great task
Of upholding the North West
As far as it can go,
Giving way only to implacable
Force in tundra, mountain or ocean;
But here at the edge a few do
Become wild boys
Putting on a fantastic mask,
Waving limbs in long slow motion,
As in abandon they twist and bend
To the uncompromising
Choreography of the wind.

IN THE PLACE BETWEEN

My family knows a hunger
and the boss
he gives me money, a few denarii only
He lives away
in a house of slate
and does not know my name

At night sometimes
I leave the tent
and go outside into the dark, beneath the stars

and the cedars, they sing

they sing of Sahara
of swift shifting sands

In the morning, we work
our axes biting
flashes in the sun

My family knows a hunger
and the boss
he gives me money, a few centavos only
He lives away
in a house of brick
and does not know my name

At night sometimes
I leave the hut
and go outside into the dark, beneath the stars

and the canopy sings

it sings of strange cattle
of high choking dust

In the morning, we work
our chainsaws screaming
hidden in the smoke

My family knows a hunger
and the boss
he gives me money, a few dollars only
He lives away
in a house of stone
and does not know my name

At night sometimes
I leave the shack
and go outside into the dark, beneath the stars

and the old firs, they sing

they sing of stripped mountains
of clot running mud

In the morning, we work
our grapplers reaching
clenched tight in the rain

My family knows a hunger.

TOO MUCH WILDERNESS

The Wilderness is too much for me.

My children thought of Wilderness as our three weekend acres. Just beyond the clearing of house, raspberry bushes, and pear tree with hummingbirds' nest, the brambles were unconquerable. If we strayed from the path en route to the sea, we risked sinking into layers of organic mysteries. And every year a single trillium returned to the same niche at the base of the same tree, bidden by no human will.

For years my Wilderness was Mount Assiniboine, of all the peaks on our trips through the Rockies, the one I could see but never attain. It shone austere and inviting, terrible and reassuring. I wanted it, and it was too much for me.

Or, Wilderness was a tangled trail in the tropics, where a missed step could mean a lethal sting. My father had been lost here, and found himself. Following via log bridges and vine trapezes, I could not tell my guides, whose hereditary land it was, that it was too much for me.

Often now Wilderness is the sea, beloved and indifferent, in league with wind and tides to threaten my existence. I have it, and it is too much for me.

Wilderness this year has been the forested heartland of this island community. After thirty years, it is too much for the loggers, and we can have it. But we are afraid of the responsibility. The darkness is too much for us.

How much more comfortable to clear the trees and let in the light, to tame the old growth forest into tidy twenty-acre hobby farms. We control the land, and nothing is too much for us.

Is Wilderness wasteland? wasted land? unpeopled and therefore empty? Is it the emptiness which is too much?

Or is it the fullness? Is Wilderness too full to tame? Wilderness teems and envelops. It is not emptiness, or nothingness, but Everythingness.

What if we enter it now?

From SETTLING CLAYOQUOT:
AN AURAL HISTORY

Ted and Dorothy Abraham

MRS. ABRAHAM: Ted told me he was from Canada [c.1920] and he said he had 160 acres on an island. Of course you know when you're young—I would have gone to the end of the world with him. And I did. We used to talk about our little home in the West.

I can still remember the day we got there. We first had to put on clothes suitable for going through the bush. Then we went along a narrow, narrow trail with trees all around us—oh, it was frightening! Half the time you were under water. There were no fields, no grass, no people, no anything! And then we got to Ted's beach and I thought, "What desolation!" There was a great rock out there and the sea was surging up against it. I didn't know what to do and then Ted said, "Isn't it beautiful, darling?" I didn't know whether to lie or not. I am not a very timid sort of person, but this was a loneliness unknown and unheard of. There was nothing there, just the long beach and the wild sea. My heart sank and I had quite an argument with myself. But you cannot pretend with your husband, can you? So, then and there, I told him I could not endure such loneliness. I am afraid he was very disappointed. However, we decided right away to build on the other side of the island, next door to my in-laws.

I suppose I was still a bit lonely. I remember how much I missed tennis. It seemed I should never play again. Though, I must say, we had great fun. We went hunting and shooting and bathing. And we loved the Indians when we got to know them. But, oh, I was frightened of them at first. Terrified. . . .

Fred Tibbs

MR. ABRAHAM: We were on Vargas Island [four miles from Tofino] so we didn't know [Fred] Tibbs that well. He used to swim from his island to Tofino. He was a good swimmer. But he drowned.

MRS. ABRAHAM: He was found in the kelp. . . . I can remember plain as punch, "Tibbs is drowned." We never really invited him to things. Perhaps we should have.

ALMA SLOMAN: He [Fred Tibbs] must have come about 1910 or '11. People wanted to get a road here, so they wanted more settlers, and sent these brochures to England advertising the West Coast. Most of the Englishmen went to Vargas, but Tibbs was at Long Beach. . . .

BILL SHARP: . . . Then he sold that property. Everybody thought he was crazy but I guess he got $5,000 for it, which was a lot of money in those days. So he was just passing his time on that island. I used to see him working all the time. I'd row over and we'd talk about, oh gosh, clearing land. That's about all you did in those days is talk about what you're going to clear and how you're going to do it and how you're going to take this stump out or that other thing. Then I'd row back.

Ian McLeod

It was after my uncle left that the liquor started to come in. The sealers and people like that used to have their own supply and they supplied it to the Indians. Then we got the beer parlour on Clayoquot. It was a bad place for a beer parlour. Any place you have to go by boat to the beer parlour, it's not good.

But it [Clayoquot] was sure a great place to go for sports. On the 24th of May, that was the place for your competition. I was good at the running broad jump. When I was seventeen I could make twenty-one feet, but Isaac Charlie, one of the Indians, he could make over twenty-four feet, twenty-five maybe. According to Major Nicholson and the judges in those days, he broke the world record, but it was unofficial.

You had some of the toughest competition in the world. There would be twelve or fourteen hundred people from Tofino, Ucluelet, the reduction plants, the sawmills, the hatcheries, the mines, Hot Springs Cove, Ahousat, Nootka. There would be dozens and dozens of fishboats. The first day you had feats of strength, running and jumping, and then on the second day it would be water sports, boat races, the greased pole. The big event was the tug-of-war, with the biggest men in the area for anchormen. Arnie Lista, he was the anchorman for a while. He could lift a 400-pound anchor up to his waist. People would stand back and sing for each side, Indian songs, Norwegian viking songs. I heard my dad singing a Gaelic song one time. He was the anchorman and he was singing a Gaelic song to the Norwegians.

My dad first came out here to visit my uncle in 1912. I guess these mountains reminded him of the Highlands, so he stayed. He brought my mother back after the war. He told her it was tropical and beautiful here with fruit trees. Mind you, he was partially right, because the weather was much better then. Now you get more wind in the summer and the blossoms don't stay on the tree. We don't get fruit now, but in the early days they grew pears and cherries and lots of apples. It's the tilt of the earth. The Japanese current used to come right into the inlet. Now it's 200 miles out.

John L. Gibson

Meanwhile, Dad had become associated with Bower and Winch, or Winch and Bower, very substantial people. In 1912, Winch ordered six Rolls

Royces and gave one to each of his family. But anyway Bower and Winch, Winch and Bower—they were later connected to the Spencer family—they were like dentists and lawyers today who have a vicarious interest in mines and wilderness, that sort of thing. They employed Dad as a partner in this exploration work, so when there was a big gold rush on the Bridge River in 1896, Dad went in on Winch and Bower's behalf. Then the gold rush started in the Yukon and Dad headed up there.

Shortly after that, the government of the day threw open the Crown lands for timber staking, so Dad went over to the west coast of Vancouver Island. The entrepreneurs of the day were staking the west coast in mile-square timber lots and then going down and selling them to lumber companies and investors in the United States, because they were the people with money.

In those days you could pretty well take timber wherever you wanted. There was so much of everything that, if there was anything you could sell, they let you take it. Better to have you doing that than going on relief in 1916. The provincial government has always been very good.

As a timber cruiser, my dad followed some very basic principles. He used to say that you should always stay where people can get in touch with you; if there's business going and they have to hitch a dog team to reach you, you won't get the business. So he got on the steamer line, got on the telegraph line. Then he went and got the best harbour on the west coast, little Matilda Creek. It had good water and it had the Ahousat Indian village for a labour market, and that meant customers too, for a store or any enterprise that you have.

In 1918, Dad was taking out aircraft spruce for the Imperial Munitions Board when the war suddenly ended. But the Munitions Board was very good about it. They made a settlement with him which gave him all the timber—which was valueless; I mean, what the hell do you do with it in the middle of nowhere—and probably a bit of money. Evidently he had enough to buy an old sawmill. Then we put in a shingle machine. You see, it just sort of evolved.

Sam Craig
Sam Craig is a prospector, and at the end of our interview I asked to tag along if he was going on any short trips. "Well," he said, "there's a claim we could stake just up the inlet. It's quite a climb but it will only take a day. We could go tomorrow." I asked him, "What if it rains?" "We go anyways," he said, "meet me at 7:30." I said, "How about 9?"

We met the next morning at 7:30. It was pouring. The ride up the inlet was slow as we warily felt our way along the channel, steering by the dark grey of the shoreline glimpsed through layers of rain. We turned up a narrow arm, followed it several miles, then anchored.

There was, however, a setback. Since Sam had last been there, the bottom third of the mountain had been clearcut. There were no trees standing and no trail markers. In the distance we heard the buzz of a chainsaw, the toot, and the rolling crash of timber.

Sam stood a few moments figuring a course, and then we started up through the slash—the tangle of stumps, logs, bucked limbs, branches, and debris left after the falling. In slash there is no horizontal. You climb, jump, duck under, and pull yourself through it, using tree trunks as bridges. If a log is pitched on too steep an angle, you go up it on all fours. "There's no shame in that," Sam said.

A few hundred feet up we came to a new gravel logging road. When the gravel stopped, we continued on in the mud of the road bed. Then more slash. When we at last reached standing timber there was a red ribbon hanging from a branch. "Good," said Sam, "that's the trail."

The trail was steep and distinguished from the surrounding woods only by the occasional ribbon. It led to an abandoned cabin. Gold had been mined here. Fifty years ago [1930s] the men carried the equipment on their backs, rigging block and tackle in the trees to bring up the great steel balls that now lay rusting on the floor of the cabin. Sam's gamble was that the price of gold would rise enough to render this unworkable site valuable.

We ate lunch and then staked the claim. To do this, a tree of the proper girth is felled at the proper height. Then the stump is squared and a metal registration card tacked on. This is all done just so. Then you go back down.

The downhill walk is the hard one, the one that left so many miners lame with arthritis. Gear that weighed 100 pounds on the way up, weighed double or triple that on the way down so that each step jolted, and strained the cartilage in their knees. After enough years, the knees just wore out.

We were carrying little more than lunch and an axe, but still the going was slow. Then Sam slipped. He grabbed at a branch to catch himself, but it broke, the end stabbing deep into the palm of his hand. He balled up some Kleenex and squeezed on it as we continued down. We cut three more stakes and blazed the trail with the axe. Then back through the mud, down the road, and over, under and through the slash. Sam would disappear in the maze of limbs and branches and then reappear farther down. The muscles in my arms and legs trembled. Finally we were at the boat, finally back at Tofino.

Sam Craig is seventy years old.

SAMMY CRAIG

Sammy Craig related to me his struggle to try and save the Clayoquot Public Working Circle during our interview in Tofino on March 30, 1991.

In trying to stop B.C. Forest Products, Sammy was also trying to protect his own right to acquire timber. Like many others, he felt the small contractor had to speak up against multinational corporations and government meddling.

In the British Columbia woods, many a sapling, such as Sammy, has been chopped down to make room for the bigger trees. But no matter how noble and dignified these timber giants appear, some of them are rotten to the core.

TOM AND JOE LEARN ABOUT LOGGING

The following year [1917] Dad took an order for telephone poles from Jim Horel who was responsible for all the phone lines on Salt Spring Island. We were shown how to select and fall cedar trees that would produce twenty-five- or thirty-foot poles with at least a five-inch top. By working long hours three or four poles were produced in a day.

We had a six-foot falling saw and a sharp axe. Tom did the trimming with the axe while I peeled with a drawknife. About every third day we harnessed that horrible horse, Dan Patch, and skidded the poles to a rollway built on the high side of our road. Tom would handle the cable and chains while I did the driving.

By the end of the summer we had managed to get over fifty poles ready on the landing. We later helped Dad roll them onto our light wagon and deliver them along the roads. To drop a pole at the markers, Jim Horel had put along the new lines, we just chained one end to a stump or tree and drove off.

This was our first experience at logging. The delivered price for a pole was $1.50.

World War One ended in the fall of the next year. Dad had arranged for Tom and me to do the logging for Captain Justice's small lumber mill, which was capable of producing some 2,000 board feet of lumber per day. Being so young, we were kept hustling to get enough logs cut to keep the mill supplied. We fell the trees together. When we had enough on the ground, Tom would cut them into specified lengths, using a six-foot bucking saw. Justice sharpened our saws each evening and eventually taught us the art. It was my job to drive their team and haul the logs to the mill. This was a great learning experience for both of us.

The pay was twenty-five cents an hour. To keep track of our earnings, we devised an unusual system. We each chose a big stump near our road. On the way home each evening we put a small rock on the stump for every dollar we had earned that day. For eight hours, two stones went on each stump. If something happened that allowed only six hours of work, we would put one rock in the tight little pile and place another a few inches away until the full dollar was earned.

We were paid in cash twice a month. On paydays we placed the money on the stump and put the required number of rocks on each bill. A one-dollar bill got one rock, a five-dollar bill would get five rocks. If bills and rocks didn't balance, we would go back and let Captain Justice know about it. Finding we were short one month-end, we walked back the half mile to tell our boss. He asked us how we kept track of our wages and, when we explained our system, he was so impressed that he made up the difference without going to check our count.

We worked there for two summers. Clive was the eldest of the Justice family and taught Tom the basics of cutting logs into lumber. I learned about the woods.

In the summer of 1920, we were kept busy cutting cedar poles for export and skidding them out to the public road. In mid-December it turned very cold. The ground froze and we had six inches of snow. Dad now owned two horses, a big Clydesdale and Dan Patch. With this lopsided team, working from daylight till dark, some 200 poles were skidded from the top of the hill to the landing at Ganges. If we met any traffic on the way down, passing was a problem. One of us always walked well ahead of the team to advise cars or buggies to pull off the road and let us by.

We bored a hole through the top of each pole before it was put into the water. A cable was then threaded through some fifty poles to produce a raft. These rafts were chained together and towed to Montague Harbour. Here they were loaded on a ship and exported to Japan. Montague, at that time, was the only exporting port in the Gulf Islands. There was one lone building in the harbour, a combined house and store operated by the Grey family.

Dad, Tom, and I camped on the beach to help load our poles. This was Easter holidays of 1921. I remember Tom working as a boom man, in his bare feet for the full two weeks, putting the poles into slings to be hoisted aboard. Dad was on deck as tallyman. I stayed in camp, washed dishes and hunted crows.

THELMA GODKIN, LOGGER

It was difficult for Thelma to find the right size clothes and a pair of logging boots to fit. There just weren't any size four boots around. They searched the whole district. Finally, Ladysmith Trading found a pair of leather work boots in their basement that were small enough. Johnny the Jazz, an excellent shoemaker, put on heavier hard leather soles and drove some logging caulks into them. He gave her a mixture of seal oil and bear grease to put on the boots every weekend, and showed her how to rub it in. Those boots didn't smell too good but they kept the water out and lasted three years. When it began getting colder in the fall, Thelma bought herself a grey wool, double-backed cruiser's jacket to wear when it wasn't raining. This was much warmer than the stiff tin coats.

"I felt like the tin man in *The Wizard of Oz*. That tin coat was most uncomfortable, but very necessary when it was pouring rain," she remembered.

Thelma started as a whistle punk on the cold deck machine. She can still remember the signals:

	HIGH LEAD WHISTLES
Ahead mainline	THREE SHORT
	(Prior to 1950 - one short.)
Ahead on straw-line	THREE SHORT—pause—ONE SHORT
Back on the haulback	TWO SHORT—pause—TWO SHORT
Slack haulback	TWO SHORT—pause—A SERIES OF SHORTS
Slack mainline	SERIES OF SHORTS
Slow	ONE LONG whistle precedes any signal
Stop all lines	ONE SHORT
Tighten lines	THREE SHORT—pause—TWO SHORT
When butt rigging is at tree to send out strawline	THREE SHORT—ONE LONG
When butt rigging is at tree	TWO SHORT—followed by a SERIES OF LONGS indicates the number of chokers required to be sent out

Grant promoted Thelma from the home tree to punk whistles at the landing a month later. She was now accustomed to wearing caulk boots, and walked just like any other logger. Grant hired Dolly Mae, a young girl from Duncan, to take over on the cold deck.

"A Chinese crew, ten of them, did all the falling and bucking. There were no power saws in those days. It was all done by hand, using saws the guys called 'Swede fiddles.' One of the older Chinese was kept busy just filing saws and sharpening axes. Spring boards were used to fall most of the bigger trees. The Chinese fallers seemed to have about five different straw hats. When one wore out, they just put a new one on over the old one. I can still picture that in my mind," Thelma laughed. "They lived in one small bunkhouse and always walked in line, one behind the other. Each one had an oil bottle hanging out of his back pocket and a sack with sledge and wedges hung over one shoulder, with their axe and crosscut saw over the other. It was the way they worked in those days."

Thelma started in 1940 and worked in the woods all through the war. Most logging crews were a mixture of old men and teenagers—either too old or not old enough to go overseas. In 1942 they finished dumping logs at the Ladysmith lagoon and moved to Mount Hall.

"That's where the forest fire burned us out," Thelma remembers. "Everything was tinder dry, and it was scary. I had never before seen a crown fire, and didn't realize that it could travel so fast. It just roared through the tree tops, flashing from one tree to the next. It burnt all our machines and most of the bridges. We eventually had to run out the other end to save our lives. All I could do was pack water from a creek by the bucketful. It was so hot and smoky we could barely breathe."

REQUIEM FOR TALUNKWUN ISLAND

Talunkwun Island, named after the Haida word for phosphorus, lies in the South Moresby group of the Queen Charlotte Islands. In recent years clearcut logging on the steep slopes of this island has caused massive erosion and landslides, and has made reforestation impossible.

I

You need not think they will make such a continual noise of singing in Skedans Creek as they used to in your previous existence.
　　—Haida mourning song

The sad ghost of a
dead art I come
down out of the mountains.
I am weak with hunger
and my hands, oh like the
cedar trees, are stumps.

The animal inside me
sniffs the breeze.
It is all lonely darkness
breathing in and out like the
sea. Over the slick rocks at the
lip of the falls I fell
back through my father's words
and into the womb of my mother.

I almost feel whole again
remembering how it was.
I could move among the trees,
embrace heaven and rock when
gods dwelt in all places
and everything was singing.

I was raven, eagle—
I flew up up up into the top
of the salmonberry bushes.
The sky was a wilder place
in those days, wider and cleaner.
I recall you could travel

just singing and flying,
with the sea all phosphorus
lighting the way below.

Now I sit and stare at
the ocean. Sometimes for days I sit
and watch. Who hears the songs
when the voices are silent?
Who remembers the great sound we used
to make, on the shores of an island
we thought would last forever.

II

What do they think they will attain by their ships
that death has not already given them?
　　　　　　　—William Carlos Williams

The submerged rocks sleeping
like whales did not stop them,
nor the winds that beached
our canoes and sent
the kelp gulls crying inland.
We thought their sails were clouds
and how could we have known better.
The sky was overcast and black;
my old grandmother picked cloudberries
and hid them under her hat.

The ships had come to trade—
what wealth we had was little then,
and nothing now.
My mother had to go begging
that winter. A young girl she grew
quieter and older.

If my hands were good I would
carve her something—the moon
gripped in a raven's beak—
but where would I find wood enough,
or the right spirit.

I lit a fire instead and stood in the
coals. A ship sailed out
and darkness tossed the sleepers
from its hold.

I felt tears on my young face
like rain down a mountain rock.
Something was lost; I could feel it
as I followed a deer trail to the
seacoast.

It was a day's journey
but it took me all my life.
At the end I found a highway
and people living in houses.
The trees were cut down and the
land had been sold for a pittance.
The old names were gone and the
ravens, for once, were silent.

I took the eyes of my owl
and stitched them into my head.
I took the wishbone of a foetus
and pressed it into my breast.
I sailed up into the clouds
and blackened the sky with earth.
The sky would mourn, too, the way
death does, in the roots.

III

But they could die for years, for decades,
so tall their silence, and tell you nothing.
                    —Howard Nemerov

They were sacred.
Their silence was something we
lived by, not the noise of machinery
stripping the thickets.

The trees were our spirits;

they have gone into nothingness.
They have become mortal, like us;
we diminished them and they have become
human.

Eternal life is unlivable
yet men rut like fat bucks in the
bush and women go on sighing.
It's a sad thing to be lonely in the
body, but to have no body at all—
that's the loneliest.

If I had the penis bone of a bear
I would point it at that woman.
Now there are no trees left to
shelter us, and the grass where we
could have lain is withered
and unyielding.

I wish there could be forests upon
the earth again, a place for our
children to gather. I wish the trees
would return during our own lifetime,
take hold and grow that we might
live again under their silence.

Now men talk of the wood they must
carry, they speak of the weight in
tired voices. I remember a time
when the whole world was singing,
and a love that kept us bound
by things we could not know.

IV

The wind blows where it will, and you hear the sound of it, but you do not know whence it comes or whither it goes; so it is with every one who is born of the Spirit.
        —John 3:8

They took my hands
and threw them into the ocean.

I saw them scuttle towards Skidegate
like white crabs with supernatural power.

It is sometimes necessary to sit
and say nothing,
to watch what takes shape,
and changes, out of that silence.
It is sometimes a necessary violence.

They left my skull, I suppose
it told them nothing. My eyes had seen
the rivers full of fish but now the eyes
were older and, like the rivers, empty.
The salmon have gone elsewhere to find
their origins. Like the ghosts of my
people, they have no country.

In my chest there is something that
hurts. It once was a heart
but now it's a hole and their
fingers are eager to probe it.
I cannot tell them how life is when the
soul has left it; the body does not die
but how can they know that.
They do not remember why they were born
They only hope to find mercy.

SPIRIT RISING

They tell me there's no connection—
But I hear them talk about the rape of the land
and I feel like I've been violated

All around the world women are rising,
women are singing, and women are holding hands.

They tell me there's no connection—
But a "virgin" forest says something to me

I saw a man stand in awe in the ancient temperate rainforest
"He's a big one."
I heard the roar of the chainsaw
and
   I
     heard
       her
         scream
"She's coming down fast."
When did that spruce become a woman?

I feel her anger and hear my own.

They tell me there's no connection—
But I hear them talk of manufacturing in Mexico
"No environmental laws, cheap labour and blow jobs are five bucks."

All around the world women's voices are calling,
women are screaming and women are fighting back.

I saw a powerful waterfall surrounded by ancient forest
become a trickle of water at the side of the road.
I drank the water and tasted salt on my lips.

They say there's no connection—
Yet I've heard of a woman raped because she fought for clean water
the river polluted by pulp from her forests
destined for "feminine protection"
money in their pockets

All around the world women are nurturing, women are caring
and women are sharing their wisdom.

When they follow me home at night I feel fear and anger—
When I follow the truck on the logging road
follow the smoke rising up into the sky, follow the soil
as it washes away
I feel the same fear and anger.

We hear her call.
Growing inside her is the spirit rising.

AN ENVIRONMENTALIST IN PROGRESS
Notes from a Clayoquot Blockade

At the centre of the swirling controversy on Clayoquot Sound is a very small minority of people trying to steer forestry policy in the direction that many of us know it should be headed. However, many supporters, as though held back by centrifugal forces, sit back on the periphery, look into the centre, and hope the "activists" can effect change on their own. Some of us may even give money to support the cause and feel like real environmentalists but we manage to talk ourselves out of really getting involved. At best, we are peripheral environmentalists.

This category probably best describes me. Oh sure, I've written a letter to the Premier, gone to a couple of rallies and given a few bucks to help out. But the idea of going to a Clayoquot blockade—I mean, I own a home in Victoria's prestigious Oak Bay (with wingback chairs inside), I'm nearly forty, hold two degrees, and the thought of collecting welfare is as remote from my reality as the thought of Adam Zimmerman bounding around in a Greenpeace zodiac shaking his fist at a Norwegian whaling ship. Surely blockading is for the so-called "radical fringe."

But there is something about this Clayoquot issue.

It's just before midnight on November 9 [1993] and I'm sitting on a bus outside the Clayoquot Resource Centre in Victoria waiting to spend the night driving to Clayoquot Sound to be part of a blockade that will protest MacMillan Bloedel logging in the sound. I've managed to talk my wife and three friends (who are also baby-boomer home-owners) into joining me.

Just as we depart, the co-ordinator tells us he just received word that a message went out to 700 loggers asking them to be part of a blockade against us. (Previously loggers blockaded a bus of Victoria businessmen from going to the Kennedy Lake bridge blockade site.) This supports rumours we heard earlier that the logging community is really annoyed because of the previous day's blockading by Greenpeace International.

I look around the bus at the mix of protesters. There are the young "radical fringe" types, many of whom we are told spent time at the Clayoquot Peace Camp this summer and have previously been arrested. There are the former '60s flower children (now flower adults?) but there are lots of "mainstream" types too. I find that the older lady across from me is a professional gardener; there is an engineer here too (how unexpected), and a businessman who tells me he went to the Peace Camp this summer, ended up staying for five weeks, and continues to work on a full-time, volunteer basis to save Clayoquot Sound. There is a fellow from the United Kingdom who tells us he is going to get arrested.

The atmosphere is quite light and chatty until we enter Port Alberni. It's now 3 a.m. and the logging town is eerily deserted. This is the first potential site that loggers could attempt a blockade. A sense of unease permeates the bus. We continue through the streets with no sign of protesters. We pass a late-night gas station and are given unfriendly gestures by two employees. We near the area where loggers prevented the businessmen's bus from passing several weeks ago. We pass by and see no one. It looks like we have made it over the first hurtle.

As we near the Clayoquot border, it is decided that the bus will stop at Kennedy Beach. We are early and this will be an opportunity to find out procedural details at the blockade site about thirty miles from here, and have a little spiritual connection. A windy, bumpy side road takes us to the parking area. As we disembark we are greeted by a star-blanketed sky. A short walk brings us to Kennedy Beach, silvery light reflecting off the gently lapping waves. We form a circle and the veteran "peacekeepers" fill us in on what should unfold at the blockade site. Following this, we have a brief "love-in," as one of my friends described it. One can see how love is inspired by this place. There is a sense of great solitude and peace here. I have spent many clear mountain nights looking up at brilliant, starry skies, but on this clear, crisp night, there seems to be a special lustre and closeness to the heavens.

Back onto the main road, we set off for the planned blockade site, the Kennedy Lake bridge—where over 700 people have already been arrested this year. As we approach the turn-off to the bridge, the bus becomes quiet. We can see vehicle lights on the road filtered through a light mist. I feel unnerved now as I watch people mill about in the shadows.

We soon determine these people are our allies, mostly local people from Tofino, it turns out. They tell us there is a logger blockade further up the side road at the bridge. Soon another bus arrives, full of protesters who have travelled from different parts of Canada to join us. On board are fishermen from Newfoundland, an older couple from Ontario. I see a sign from Prince Edward Island, and another group identified as Albertans. Somebody does a count and says there are now 287 people here and judging by those I can see, many are my age and older.

Soon the media arrive. Their camcorder lights spray through the mist. More vehicles arrive. The scene is getting quite surreal, something out of *Close Encounters*. Next, vehicles from MacBlo show up. The lead truck has floodlights mounted on the cab which imbue the proceedings with the sense of a movie set. Then the RCMP arrive. One of the policemen has a camcorder and he shines light on us. Then a MacBlo employee with a bodyguard in tow also blinds us with the light from his camcorder. We feel like aliens.

It's at about this point we hear: "Why don't you get a job, you bunch of fucking welfare bums."

We've been told to expect verbal abuse and to not retaliate. Nobody does. We are read the anticipated court injunction and told to move to the side of the road. All but eighteen people respond to this request. These eighteen people are to be arrested.

The scene is intensely solemn. I look at the arrestees as they are read their rights. Acute emotion strains their faces. All the pain they feel over the decision to log here has finally welled up and is wholly manifested in their expressions. A thirteen-year-old arrestee sobs quietly. Others are on the verge of tears. One of the east coast fishermen is arrested. The English fellow from our bus is also taken away.

They are very courageous people. Unlike many of those previously arrested, they are aware of the stiff sentences that have been handed down to those before them, including both jail terms and fines. Yet, they still choose to be arrested themselves.

As they are removed one by one, there is clapping and shouting of support from the protesters, which incites more derogatory comments from the loggers. Several protesters engage them and tension rises for the first time. The exchanges are lively but both sides keep their cool.

I listen to the comments from the loggers: "We open the roads up so you can hunt and fish up here"; "There are enough trees here for ninety years"; "The cut in Clayoquot has been decreased significantly." If these remarks fairly reflect the views of loggers, I realize how great the chasm of understanding is between the loggers and environmentalists.

As the sun begins to spread natural light on the scene and the MacBlo trucks move past the spot protesters stood not long before, we wander back to our bus. We all agree it has been a great experience, but that more peripheral environmentalists need to be at these blockades. We feel ourselves drawn a little closer to the centre of the issue. We are fighting that centrifugal force and being here at the blockade has helped us win this round.

THREE HAIKU

under pale mist
the woman wrapped in homespun
passes for Mary

old growth forest
firmly rooted in our hands
after centuries

protesting children
carried away by police
suddenly tearful

IT'S HOWDY DOODY TIME

I spend much of my life on the sidelines. That's not an easy admission to make. It suggests dullness and conventionality. Such an admission, I'm sure, will taint the otherwise dynamic, outgoing and wildly creative (did I mention sexy?) impression I normally leave people with when my children and I appear at the grocery store or the post office. Oh, I quietly entertain radical sentiments from the privacy of my journals or with a small group of people who spoke up first, but when it comes to going public, I am consumed by a matrilineal compulsion to be nice so people will like me. "Do Not Offend Or Make Waves Of Any Sort" is the first commandment of niceness. When it comes to my daily life, those radical sentiments, known as passionate beliefs, are suspended in a heavy emulsion of routine and predictability.

Last week I bodily flung myself out of routine and predictability and onto the road blockade at Clayoquot Sound. The trip came together in less than twenty-four hours. It wasn't easy with two small children (their dad was away at logging-related work) but it was entirely possible. That's one thing I learned about at the Peace Camp and on the blockade: *possibilities*. There are all kinds of them. B.Y.O.Possibilities, the more the merrier.

I went because I am infused with awe and respect for the ancient forests (oh oh, sounds like a passionate belief). With so few Vancouver Island watersheds left intact, I believe it is time to preserve a small share to be as nature made it. Clayoquot Sound is priceless. I knew I had to act. Now, I'm "going public" to share my impressions of what took place.

The Trip. Drive, winding road; road of labour, road of leisure. Take for granted no field of vision left unscarred. And this is only the view from the highway. It's just the way it is. Get there.

The Black Hole. Huge expanse of hills and mountain-sides all stripped, ravaged, burned. There thrives the Peace Camp: growing, flourishing, strong.

People. Many. Young, old, men, women, rich, poor. Together in an environment of co-operation, an environment of openness, an environment of trust and growth on this land replanted once, twice, three times, but the trees refuse to grow.

Busi-ness. Workshops, kitchen hustle, chop wood, carry water, tend fire. Visitors, residents, dinner for 100, then meet as the Pacific fog climbs up from the ocean and rests here for the night. It erases everything but our Fire Circle. Organize, strategize, inform for the pre-dawn.

Night. Children sleep, adults wake. No holiday. Something big ahead. Nervous anticipation. 3:45 a.m. comes early. Wake cheerful to tuneful accordion renditions of "Roll out the Barrel" and "It's Howdy Doody Time."

Embark. Long luminous ribbon of headlights floats down highway, logging road. A steady stream probing the dark with purpose.

Wait. Move about in wonder—of the black surrounds, of the imminent future. Hover near the bonfires. Allies waiting to show solidarity.

Act. Runner calls out. Assemble. Few words spoken. Lights bear down. No longer in the dark. Alone and in the midst of others. Standing. Trusting. Staring, clear-eyed at possibilities. Standing for our dearest vision of life. Power. Power from inside out and all around me. Acting now, fearlessly.

Witness. Injunction read, boundary reached. Will I stay? Not this time. Barricade parts. Flank roadsides. Turn, look back through the light-pierced fog and dark. Eight stand their ground peacefully. Faces lit, faces victorious, faces noble and brave. Particles of mist touch my face. Suspended animation.

Celebrate. Cheering, singing, voices clear or emotion-filled. Dawn.

I stood on the beach one day and watched a man and woman as they admired the view of the coast mountains across the water. "Beautiful," they said. "Fantastic." He pulled a package of film from his camera bag, discarded the box and canister at his feet and, after loading the film, snapped half a dozen pictures.

It's not just a nice picture of something over there. It's the air we breathe, the water we drink, the earth beneath our feet. Didn't they know they were standing on the view—the view to the future? Maybe this sounds flaky to you but, what the heck, I am a flake, a speck, a mere particle of sand on the beach of life—or, maybe that should be the oyster of life. Oh-oh, I feel a passionate belief coming on.

HOW TO DRAW A TREE

Trees as you know have twigs. They have a thousand things. The light on one part of one leaf. The insect crawling that has lost a wing. The bark so cavernous and full of deep ravines.

Tree with the energy of breath and bark someone cut letters on. Its roots have pulled themselves out of the earth; its roots have grown around a stone. The stone is white. The tree is brown and green. It is composed of oxygen and light, carbon and darkness. Night. Coming from nothingness, from nut or seed. It carries what it does not own, your mother's bones, the songs of birds, their love and grief, their homes. The arguments and tenderness of living things. The wind. Rain. Snow. Death in its leaves. Sap in the spring. Worms at its heart, roots in the ground where you can't go.

ARTIST'S STATEMENT

European explorers who were among the first to view this coastline had an astounding reaction (and I use these words out of context): "desolate, wantonly forlorn, dreary and inhospitable, gloomy and dismal, mournful, peculiarly uninviting, dull monotony, awful in its solitude, an astonishing and awful combination of objects."

One hundred and fifty years later, we are all, Europeans and Asians alike, still newcomers, immigrants, displaced persons whose seeing and sensing has accumulated at most within a few generations. We are regarded as plunderers and rightly so, but *changes are taking place* in a consciousness towards this land. Perhaps a sensitivity is developing as this landscape pervades our collective beings. If you stay anywhere long enough, someone once said, you will know the spirit that rises up and into you from the land. (Yet how do we measure "long enough"?)

Within this haphazard mosaic of peoples, like so many others, I go to the land seeking sources, sources towards a cultural identity. It seems to be still at a raw beginning. For me, six generations have passed and there is no other place called home, no other land where distant family lives. I can read about and look at the art history of Europe, and I can do the same with the art on this coast. My own "fit" seems in neither place. I've walked with envy in fourteenth-century villages in Europe imagining the inhabitants as exempt from this ever present search for place. No wonder this displacement is continuously present in dreams.

In those dreams or that place of partial sleep and partial wake, there exist unfolding and unrolling images of dwelling places, dens, interiors that are also exteriors, shelters and places of refuge amidst a profusion of unexplainable sequences, an irrational configuration of objects that encompass protectively within intricate panoramas. And there is a curious absence of verbs that could possibly explain or give reason for all this imagery.

Here in a huge new metropolis (perhaps the largest clearcut in all of British Columbia), I gather up the discarded materials from our perpetual need to renew—from thrift shops, second-hand stores, back alley dumpsters, anywhere that stuff has been abandoned. Just about anything has potential for art making, and the reason to gather borders on obsession. I leave the city frequently to walk narrow trails in tall forests, feasting on the magnificent intricacies of abundant natural growth. There are expanses of beaches where the bleached-out drift logs become another form of pathway. Again, the intricacies as recurring seasons pile more abandoned segments of harvested wood on top and between existing logs.

I attempt to speak of this land visually in the strongest possible voice because it speaks to me and allows me to enter it.

—*Written in conjunction with the sculptural installation titled* Desolate Combination of Objects with Long Assemblage *(length: 29'4", height: 13'; found wood objects, rope, sisel, papier maché, laser prints, slide projection, etc.) at the Pitt Gallery in Vancouver in March 1994.*

WRITERS FOR CLAYOQUOT

I was asked yesterday: "If you speak out, aren't you worried about showing contempt of court?" I replied that I am far more worried about courts that show contempt for justice.

I'm not a lawyer, like some of you, though in my time I've played a lot of judges' roles and dramatized a lot of famous trials. I've worked closely on these with great legal minds—from Bora Laskin and Roland Michener to Frank Scott (who was also a great poet)—far too closely not to have respect for the law, and deep sympathy with judges who have to play Solomon in tough cases. But in this tough case, I believe with all my heart that the court is miscarrying justice. There has got to be a better way, in our society, of handling civil dissent—and let me repeat the word "civil"—than jailing hundreds of patriotic citizens who may very well turn out to be more socially responsible than those intent on seeing them put away. What do I mean by "contempt for justice"? Today an attempt is being made to mislead the public by claiming that an injunction is a piece of legislation passed by a democratic government. It is not. An injunction is a judicial order, the responsibility for which lies with the judge who issues it. The notion that anyone who disobeys an injunction is somehow seditious—that is, out to destroy the whole democratic state—is a piece of unworthy intellectual dishonesty. So is the argument that courts don't make the laws, they only apply them. That's a half-truth. Courts are given considerable leeway, and make laws by setting precedent. The excuse that "I don't make the rules, I only carry them out," was the one used by Adolf Eichmann to send Jews to the gas chamber. It is an alibi for moral failure. I'm not saying to our jurists that we writers can give you lessons in law-making; I'm saying you should listen to writers on the subject of myth-making. That's our business. There must be a better way of handling dissent—a better way in the interests of the legal system—than making heroes out of dissenters. In years to come, the conscientious objectors of Clayoquot—young and old, regardless of individual motive—will be seen as martyrs to a great cause, and will be honoured for it by their children, and yours. Remember Louis Riel. You may choose to ignore our advice, but I want to add that our voices are not to be sneered at as those of mere fiction-mongers without clout in the real world. The arts in this country employ more people than the fisheries, more than agriculture, and three times as many people as the forest industry. You might not know this from some party platforms in the present election—or lack of them—but we intend our voices to be heard. And here they come.

—*Presented at the Writers for Clayoquot rally in Victoria, October 11, 1993.*

THE INNER FIRE
Organizing the Great Clayoquot Writers'
Reading and Literary Auction

July 21/93 Long Beach
Well, we made it up. All five of us piled into the rental LeMans, caught the ferry at Horseshoe Bay, had a walk through Cathedral Grove, a coffee in Alberni and are now settled in the Pacific Sands Hotel. I am so angered by what our government chose to do about the Clayoquot. The entire drive up I thought I'd be asked to put a sock in it as I fumed along the highway pointing out another clearcut patch on a mountainside. I make this trek at least twice a year to recapture my sense of self. The power of the waves and the stability and sacredness of the trees, the presence of spirit in the air soothes whatever ails me. My marriage is teetering and Stephen and I both know it.

August 20/93 Vancouver
Bill Deverell and I have just finished a day of Writers' Union meetings. Over dinner at the Japanese Deli our conversation moved from political activity through the union to an idea Bill and Brian Brett have been kicking around. First Brian and Patrick Lane wanted to get arrested at the blockade, then decided instead to do an event to publicize the destruction of the Clayoquot. Pat dropped out of the picture (he may do something in Victoria) so Brian asked Bill if he'd like to work on a reading to raise funds for and profile of the Clayoquot. From Bill's eagerness in the preamble, I was already listing on a napkin names of writers who'd be sympathetic.

October 27/93 Vancouver
Yesterday we sent out our first press release about the Benefit November 7 and today an article in the *Vancouver Sun*! Writers, artists joining fight to halt logging. At 9 a.m. today, MacMillan Bloedel rang Brian asking to have a display. Brian told them, if so, they must donate something to the auction.

October 28/93 Vancouver
I am informed late today MacBlo is donating a helicopter ride for two over the "pristine Clayoquot," so I guess they'll have a booth. I am confused. Brian is drafting an official letter of acceptance. Who's calling the shots here? Am I abdicating my role in some way, not taking responsibility? Borders of my mind are blurring, and nausea stirring.

A benefit for
Clayoquot Sound

**1:00 pm, Sunday
November 7, 1993
Commodore
Ballroom
870 Granville St.
Vancouver**

*Doors open at noon
for auction preview*

Tickets: $12.50
at any Ticketmaster
Outlet (280-4444)
or at the door

\huwaji / *Grizzly:* BILL REID

The Great Clayoquot
S O U N D
Writers' Reading
& Literary Auction

🔊 Master of Ceremonies: PIERRE BERTON

🔊 Hosts: WILLIAM DEVERELL & SUSAN MUSGRAVE (first set)
MYRNA KOSTASH & JOHN GRAY (second set)

🔊 Readers & Speakers: JOY KOGAWA, AL PURDY, AUDREY
THOMAS, STAN PERSKY, LILLIAN ALLEN, LEE MARACLE,
PETER C. NEWMAN, PATRICK LANE, LORNA CROZIER,
HERB HAMMOND, BRIAN BRETT, MARILYN BOWERING,
WILLIAM GIBSON, *and special surprise guests!*

🔊 Auctioneers: PIERRE BERTON & ALMA LEE

🔊 Auction items donated by: BETH APPELDOORN & SUSAN
SANDLER, MARGARET ATWOOD, ROBERT BATEMAN, BRIAN
BRETT, ROBERT BRINGHURST, ROBERT DAVIDSON, WILLIAM
DEVERELL, WALTER DEXTER, DOUGLAS & MCINTYRE LTD,
TIMOTHY FINDLEY, GRAEME GIBSON, ROBERT HARLOW,
PATRICK & ROSEMARIE KEOUGH, PATRICK LANE, CHARLES
LILLARD, FARLEY MOWAT, SUSAN MUSGRAVE, TONI ONLEY,
P.K. PAGE, GEORGE PAYERLE, PRESS GANG PUBLISHERS,
BILL REID, LINDA ROGERS, JOE ROSENBLATT, JANE RULE,
JACK SHADBOLT, ROBIN SKELTON, JACK WISE, GEORGE
WOODCOCK, *and many others!*

October 29/93 Salt Spring Island/Vancouver/Pender Island
I awake feeling queasy about not being part of the decision or process; Bill
and Brian are all for it. I feel degraded, alone, bad, confused politically and
personally. It's been twenty-nine days since Stephen left, no one to bounce
ideas off. Arguing all the way around me whether to say yes or no to
MacBlo—Brian has agreed verbally but not in writing. We should keep
this quiet, he says, to use in our final press release next week. Then Jacinta
French, Coordinator of Vancouver Temperate Rainforest Coalition (VTRAC)
called. She's heard a rumour that MacBlo is attending, she wants confir-
mation. I'm put in a precarious position of not wanting to lie, but I don't
feel allied with the decision and want to denounce it. Mix this with feeling
run-over by Brian, the lack of consultation with me and Bill, and now Al
Clapp, Artistic Director is quitting because of MacBlo's presence. I'm ready
to fling in the towel. So I decide to play the cards close to my chest with
Jacinta and to confront Brian with the secrecy. How far does it stretch?
To the organizing groups as well? Jacinta made it clear that if MacBlo
attends, VTRAC will have to reconsider its help, and perhaps boycott the
event. The Western Canada Wilderness Committee and Friends of
Clayoquot Sound might do the same, she warned. I'm on the outside of
a very important decision, one I am in collusion with by my silence. I
have to speak up.

November 1/93 Vancouver
I had the worst sleep in months last night. With adjusting to sleeping alone
after ten years, the political pot boiling in my head, and the fact I'm
implicated in a decision in which I didn't have a voice, the stress is maxing
out. I awoke at 7 a.m. and phoned Gary Cristall to see if I could strategize
with him. We drafted a *pro* and *con* list:

pros	cons
+perception of balance	–lose Al Clapp
+make money on heli ride	–possibility of violence
	–positive PR for MacBlo
	–energy/attitude of event will change
	–possible boycott by environmentalists
	–able to denounce MB for trying to buy us off

I need concrete ideas, words to articulate the frustration of not agreeing
with the right for anyone to have a display at this event. I am dumbstruck
and Gary urges me into speech. I realize this isn't a debate; this is a partisan
event. It's like inviting a rapist to a healing party. This is not the exercise

in freedom of speech Brian and Bill believe it to be. If MacBlo really wanted to do something they should just stop logging. On the phone, I go down my pro and con list point by point with Brian, who calls me a chicken-shit. Each of us knows we will not convince the other, yet we go round in circles trying. MacBlo is accomplishing what it set out to do: divide and conquer. It doesn't know how deep, the saying goes. I won't let them have the pleasure of my quitting. But I don't have to like it that they'll be there. Finally I am on my hands and knees, phone in hand, tears streaming down my face, and I see my reflection in the window. I will not humiliate myself further. To have MacBlo wagging its tail amongst people who have been arrested, who have literally changed their lives for a cause, to face their oppressors in a time of celebration, solidarity, and strength, is wrong. I steady my voice: "Brian, let's stop arguing and agree to disagree. I'll call Bill and tell him in a vote I am outnumbered. I will not quit the committee but I'm only continuing because I believe in the end result. I will not back down nor away." The jackhammer has been silenced. With Bill it wasn't so heated. He has a more subtle manner, he only called me spineless. The last call of the day was Al Clapp, who compared my staying on the committee and having MacBlo attend to working with the Nazis during the Second World War. Two men and a woman engage in a political struggle to fight an injustice we see, get drawn into our own politics, and almost destroy one another. This is democracy?

The fax rings from Salt Spring Island.

Angela:
The phone lines are dead tonight. Magic must be afoot. Or disaster. Who knows? Was it a storm in a soup tureen? Will we pay tomorrow? Does it matter? . . .

I wish you had agreed, but I'm glad you stood your ground. The same for Clapp. Myself—I guess I would always rather fight—I've been doing that for some years—no matter the holes it gets me into, and so I feel good about where we are.

I want to thank you because you've stood your ground, and have been pushed hard, many times. Regrets are almost a luxury, one that we pay for later—or take out on credit—yet despite the things I have done in my life, I haven't many. Still, as you may have guessed from our conversations, I yearn for the reaches we didn't accomplish, and will not accomplish.

I'm signing off for the night. I just wanted to thank you now before the shit or success comes down. It's been a wild run—and I do love and worship the wild runs—

"There is nothing stable in the world; uproar's your only music." (Keats—yes, I know, another Dead White Male)
Brian

A phenomenal success. To see 700 people attend a literary reading and auction, to raise over $23,000 in one afternoon, is I'm sure absolutely unsurpassed. I raced over from my Union Racial Minority Writers' Committee meeting to witness five camera crews and as many tape recorders stuffing sponge-covered microphones in Bill Deverell's and Pierre Berton's faces. I was the proverbial bumblebee with my gold-sequinned vest and black boots flying from back to front of stage. Acquiescing Al gave walk-on cues and directed traffic. Reader after reader did their bit beautifully—and then the auction. That was the only time I slowed down to watch Alma Lee and Pierre Berton in action. I felt disengaged. Perhaps that's the nature of these beasts: all the work occurs before and by the time it's happening, it's happened.

Apparently mid-show, a woman approached MacBlo's booth asking in-depth questions which were answered openly. The woman then asked if she could take some brochures to give to family and friends, which delighted MacBlo. When the woman piled three-quarters of the pamphlets from the entire table into her arms and started to walk away, MacBlo twigged that this woman was absconding with all its material. Their undercover security grabbed the woman but she struggled and managed to get away. Other than that, no SHARE or environmentalist groups protested outside the Commodore, no fights, no blood. Civility. And we were fair.

November 22/93 Salt Spring Island/Vancouver
I am hungover from a night of argument, tension, too much scotch, and being a fifth wheel. The wind-up gathering at Brian and Sharon's with Bill and Tekla started out with a good critical post-mortem of the event but wound down, as the alcohol did, to a morbid evening. Today I'm hungover with depression over the state of poetry and its place in our society. Haven't felt this beleaguered or downtrodden since my marriage ended. Even then, my personal worth and identity weren't up for questioning. Brian has a way of speaking about poetry in Canada which makes the proverbial razor blade inch out of the drawer towards me. Questioning my life, my choice, being a poet on a dead-end street. On this ferry I am lulled into depression. These are friends? Today, only the stupor of hopelessness, helplessness, and doubt cloud my eyes.

November 22/93 Vancouver Public Library
As I was preparing for my reading tonight, I had to ground myself in an identity further than that of simply writer. There was also me as political person, me as community organizer, me as loyal and good friend, environment

lover. The part of my identity associated with writing is low, debased, squashed. I need to anchor myself on the shores of other parts. I'm sailing in a storm of poet identity on my way to a reading. Last night Brian kept saying what's the use of publishing anyway—no one buys the stuff, never mind reads it. I'm exhausted from trying to convince him, and I guess ultimately myself, that that is not true.

At first glance I could only see unknown faces: library types, students, a few street people wanting shelter from the rain. Just as I'm beginning to read, in walk Jacinta, Terry, Craig, and Michele, four friends I made through working with VTRAC on the Benefit. After the reading all of them gave me huge hugs and invited me for coffee. Terry and Craig wanted me to know that the Clayoquot Reading was the first literary event they'd ever attended and they were so inspired, they decided to come to mine tonight. They had thought it a bit conspicuous that Bill and Brian read on November 7 and I hadn't, but were pleased to see I was reading just two weeks later. Not only were this minister, banker, community environmentalist, and government employee moved to attend more readings, but they all decided to tap into their own literary juices on a trip to the Carmanah. They'd never seen dedicated, high-profile artists put their art towards a political cause before. Their spirits had been lifted during that afternoon to such a degree that a new-found energy, faith, hope, and commitment appeared. I just about wept. The words were more than Polysporin to the burn patches of my soul.

I finally see a point. They saw it too, only earlier. We create art to create art. Because we have to. Perhaps it has meaning for some, perhaps by virtue of its existence it has meaning. Without political motivation and intention, art can still have political ramifications. It can empower people to act in new ways with newly tapped sources of energy, vigour, and commitment. These four people were at my reading because three writers acted politically and invited others in the artistic world to speak publicly.

December 5/93 Crystal Cove, Long Beach
I return with friends, for a few days of reflection and writing. The wind again whips up emotions and carries them off to far-away shores. I let go and let the world in. The rawness of anger and aloneness is gone and I feel blessed to have weathered through it. These two men, Bill and Brian, whom I respect very much on the one hand, remain complete enigmas on the other. Walking through the fire with someone will either kill you or make you stronger. Now, back to some poetry.

CLAYOQUOT IS IN OUR BACKYARD

Trying, as always, to find the good
   I think, "Perhaps"
as my heart tears with the ripping bark
"this could mean seeing more clearly . . . "
   new vistas?
ah, seeing a way clear . . .
More light, by any chance?

   I think not—
look away in anguish as she falls—
a clear view now of distant neighbours' dormers,
   TV antennae.
   empty sky.
Vision stopped at the gaping orange mouth
Fuzzy city street illumination of
   telephone wire and electric air.

   Thinking does not bring her back
godly and embracing pine, she who watched over
the children of these woods, then pastures,
dirt, then black-paved streets for generations;
home to uncountable cycles of creatures,
   to sun and shade,
to my first peaceful gaze of morning,
   and the heady boughs of Christmas

   These my son and I gather now in July
crying as the bulldozer spins above us, and thinking,
   "How will we keep your branches
   ever green?"

FOREST INDUSTRY USING SHARE
TO DUPE ITS WORKERS

"Save a job . . . kill a hippie!" snarls a large spray-painted graffito on the highway west of Port Alberni. Urging loggers to protect their jobs by killing environmentalists is an extreme but typical example of how the forest industry is responding to the crisis at Clayoquot Sound.

The industry strategy is two-fold: on the one hand, a slick public relations campaign aimed at picturing the companies and workers as "reasonable" and "willing to compromise," and on the other, a covert campaign of threats, intimidation, and character assassination aimed at anyone who does not support clearcutting three-quarters of the Clayoquot rainforest.

This ill-considered campaign produced the ugly scene near Port Alberni when two busloads of ultra-respectable business leaders were recklessly hijacked on a public highway. Previous to that, an environmentalist had a finger broken by an out-of-control zealot who was subsequently charged with assault. Two hundred litres of human excrement were dumped outside the Western Canada Wilderness Committee's information booth. Enraged pro-loggers drive past the Clayoquot Peace Camp blaring truck horns and screaming obscenities.

One might conclude from these unhappy events that all loggers are booze-addled bruisers looking for a punch-up. But the truth is far more complex. Afraid of losing the only work they know, caught in a historical vortex they do not understand, the more gullible among them are easy prey for professional manipulators.

This is the short-term genius of the SHARE groups. Funded by industry and staffed by disciples of American guru Ron Arnold and his odious Centre for the Defence of Free Enterprise, SHARE groups are fake grassroots organizations whose express purpose is to manipulate workers into doing the companies' dirty work.

We know that forest and mill workers have been laid off by the thousands in recent years, victims of an increasingly mechanized industry. But has there been even one peep from the SHARE groups in defence of working people's livelihoods? I don't think so. The SHARE movement exists to protect capital, not workers. By deliberately pitting workers against environmentalists, it has eliminated uncomfortable scenes like the one in 1988 when 300 angry forest workers protested outside Fletcher Challenge headquarters, demanding sensitive logging that protects jobs.

While seeking to liquidate the ancient forests of Clayoquot Sound, MacMillan Bloedel is removing thousands of acres of land from its managed forests on the east coast of Vancouver Island and the Gulf Islands in order to flip them for land development windfall profits. With deeper soils, flatter terrain, and more sunshine than the west coast, these are prime growing sites perfectly adapted to a tree selection management system that would employ far more people per log cut.

Do we hear any SHARE group outrage over this loss of "working forest" land?

As a person who grew up in a blue-collar home, I'm saddened to see working people manipulated in this way. Doubly unfortunate for them, the campaign into which they have been seduced is clearly destined to failure. Every act of intimidation and bullying works against them, and against the New Democratic Party, which has squandered so much political capital in the Clayoquot debacle, it should perhaps declare bankruptcy and be done with it.

By comparison, the campaign to save the Clayoquot rainforest is a classic example of non-violent civil disobedience. It is characterized by an extraordinary discipline. Participants maintain a friendly, open, and respectful attitude towards loggers, police, and company officials.

What is happening at Clayoquot is both remarkable and hopeful. I have no doubt that it is history in the making. Here at last is a realistic opportunity to halt the butchery that has for too long devastated our public forests and put far too many forest workers out of work.

The Clayoquot campaign is not against logging or loggers. Rather, it is a principled refusal to accept the wholesale destruction of the Clayoquot rainforest which will result from present government policies. I urge all who have hung back, all who have procrastinated, all who have been afraid, to go now to Clayoquot Sound and stand on the road for a better tomorrow for all of us.

—*First published in the* Victoria Times-Colonist *during the Clayoquot blockade.*

SOLIDARITY

One morning, during the weeks when everyone in our collective felt most overwhelmed by the tasks necesssary to compile Witness To Wilderness, *I awoke with "Solidarity" in my head. I remembered sitting on a grassy slope at a huge rally with my then-teenage daughter. I remembered my feelings of devastation and outrage at the TV image of Jack Munro, then a leader of the International Woodworkers of America (IWA), and Bill Bennett, then premier of B.C., standing on Bennett's porch with their arms around each other, laughing and joking with the TV crew. I couldn't remember the issues that sparked the Solidarity movement, nor the year, but I knew it was during a period of rapid technological change and concomitant job loss in the forest industry, about which the IWA, in retrospect, was relatively silent. I thought that if I had forgotten the issues, others might have too, and that anything to do with the IWA is relevant to Clayoquot Sound. With thanks to Bryan D. Palmer in* The Canadian Encyclopedia *(Hurtig, 1988) and to Jean Barman's* The West Beyond the West *(University of Toronto, 1991), here are the facts:*

There was a recession in B.C. in the early 1980s and people were worried about economic reliance on resource-based industries. Bill Bennett's Social Credit government was re-elected in May 1983. Two months later, Bennett introduced a "restraint budget" and twenty-six prospective bills that fell loosely into three categories: abolishing watchdog-type bodies; undermining trade union practices and collective bargaining; and cutting social services. In response, the B.C. Federation of Labour, under Art Kube, allied with community and advocacy groups and organized a massive protest movement, Solidarity, which joined together those concerned about the proposed cutbacks (minority groups) and the long-term implications of the increasing shift toward non-manual labour (public sector and resource workers). Although it looked and felt like a grassroots movement, Solidarity was funded and controlled by the trade unions.

Momentum built; there was talk of a general strike. By October, most of the restraint bills had become law. The Socreds used closure and all-night legislative sessions to stifle debate; Dave Barrett, leader of the NDP opposition, was ejected from the Assembly. The B.C. Government Employee's Union (BCGEU) contract was due to expire on October 31, resulting in numerous job losses. When the BCGEU went on strike on November 1, Solidarity organized escalating strikes which threatened to put 200,000 workers on the street. When teachers walked out two weeks later, the B.C. Federation of Labour leaders began to worry that outright confrontation might force Bennett to use repressive back-to-work legislation which would bring promised job action in the private sector; that is, Solidarity would have been out of their control.

Solidarity was stopped by the officials who had started it. They backed down from the movement's demand for broad repeal of the legislation and settled on a new contract for the BCGEU. On November 13, Jack Munro, vice-president of the IWA, flew to Kelowna and shook hands with Bennett.

Thus ended the largest protest in B.C. history. Some people continue to believe that a resource-based economy can support people during a recession in the style to which they have become accustomed during prosperity.

—Sandy Frances Duncan

THE BLACK HOLE
For the Protesters and Loggers of Clayoquot Sound

Birds don't live here, there is no safety
in the tiny tasselled hemlock, fireweed,
kinnikinnick.
The twisted blackened trunks
and stumps clothe each rise and hollow
on and on, until the eyes lose focus
and make the distance abstract,
black and white.

It is human to seek the familiar,
see torsos in the wreckage.
The mind provides personal horror,
unbidden.
It is human to see faces
in the mountains
as the shadows move on the ruined slopes,
the grey plinths of the dead still standing.

The mind names it, necropolis, wasteland,
crematorium.
There is no sound but the wind,
and easy to hear voices in it,
keening through the desolation,
a thin sound, one reed.

We thought we lived
in a botanical eternity,
that the simple wisdom of the plants
was the background to
our complicated stories.
We thought we had forever
against the green.

The mountie who arrested me
was a woman much younger than I.
She said, "I am doing
what I have to do,
just like you."

As the jail bus crosses the bridge
the lake is red and silver
in the dawn.
We wait in the loop
by the forest wall, where the great trees
rise from the grey bush,
for the logging trucks to come,
who have the right of way.

It is human to be afraid
of an unknown future,
to look after one's own.
We thought we had forever
against the green.

THE WILL TO COMMUNITY

The world is full of signs—signs that direct us, that tell us which fork in the road to follow. Trees are a sign. In *Itsuka*, the narrator says that "trees are the sign of an active mercy in the world. Year after year they continue to give us the breath of life." But one character argues that mercy is wasted on people who are unaware of doing wrong. "Therefore justice before mercy," she says. "Therefore name the crimes."

The business of naming crimes is a dangerous one, as you who have stood before the courts know only too well. The naming of crimes too easily deteriorates into the demonizing of people. Those of us who have been involved in political endeavours know how passionately we can believe that what we stand for is right, and what the other side stands for is wrong and demonic.

Clayoquot Sound, for me, symbolizes a special challenge. It's a challenge to the will to community, a challenge to refuse to engage in the demonizing of people, a challenge to transform enemies into friends, to do as the trees do, and to breathe mercy and oxygen into the choking economic and philosophical complexities at Clayoquot Sound. Specifically, we are challenged to forge links in a human chain between the strong and the weak, the hungry and the well-fed, between loggers responsible to their families, environmentalists responsible to earth's ecosystems, government leaders responsible to economic realities, corporate giants responsible to shareholders and courts responsible to the upholding of laws. Weaving in and out among these and other entities are the communicators, the chain-makers—the media, the artists, the prophets, the people of prayer, and each one of us whose responsibility is to help forge the links wherever we can.

What fuels successful human endeavour is a strong sense of correctness, a belief and a trust that right is being done. The moral imperative declares that it is right to stand together with the weak and disadvantaged. In the crisis at Clayoquot Sound, I believe we must form strong empathetic links with those who are struggling to provide adequate food, shelter, and clothing for their children. The solutions to their problems are to be sought in solidarity.

I claim little understanding of the ways of commerce and industry, but I have heard it said that, with great effort and with a healthy will to community, locally-based, locally-owned value-added industries can thrive. In the book, *For The Common Good: Redirecting the Economy Towards Community, the Environment and a Sustainable Future,* Herman E. Daly and John B. Cobb Jr. offer solutions. They point to community nurturing enterprises as practical and achievable if the practise of economics is made into a moral discipline, one that never loses sight of people or of ecological health.

Some people argue that local industries are unsupportable pipe-dreams, retrograde, romantic notions that have little place in today's competitive world of big business and mega economics. Paradoxically, it's big business that has brought us vast computer and communications networks. By connecting millions of people to one another, they have paved the way for a huge base of information and power sharing. So now, because we are linked around the world, we are ensured that local regional activity need no longer be insular. Rather than being retrogressive, could it be that local industries, riding down the electronic roadways, will show the way to a sustainable future?

I hope with all my heart that it is not too late. We hear that certain irreversible and catastrophic trends are already upon us, that species upon species are gone forever, and that some of the best correctives and possibilities are also gone forever. But I know it's not too late to learn from the trees and to act with mercy towards each other. It's not too late to develop the will to community. We can organize meetings like this one, we can think and listen, read and learn, we can petition and lobby, we can be part of immense computer networks, and every single one of us, the very least among us, can still make a difference.

—*Presented at the rally to save Clayoquot Sound, Orpheum Theatre, Vancouver, November 7, 1993.*

From THE LAY OF THE LAND

It was in August that I decided I had to go to Clayoquot Sound if I was going to have anything intelligent to say on the subject. It was the end of September before I actually went. In the meantime, I followed the controversy closely. I didn't feel that I had a great deal to contribute to the discussion by offering anything pretending to be an expert opinion or even a fair evaluation of one. I had to defer to a host of experts on sustainable forestry methods, clearcutting versus selective logging, the value of the logging industry to the economy, or the amount of oxygen produced by a given tree. If one expert said one thing and another said something else, I was in no position to dispute either of their professional opinions. The nature of the controversy itself interested me even more than the substance of either side's argument.

By the time I actually left for the west coast of Vancouver Island, a curious pattern had become apparent. There were some thoughtful and provocative pieces written by people who held the opinion that the protesters were basically criminals who were threatening the very fabric of democracy by their wanton defiance of the law. There were similarly impressive pieces contributed by those who felt that the civil disobedience being exercised at Clayoquot was similar to that practised by Mahatma Gandhi and Martin Luther King. The odd thing was that, by and large, the writers defending the actions of the protesters had actually been to the scene of the controversy, while pro-logging ones had not.

Was it that the views of the pro-logging advocates were objective, reasoned opinions offered by people unsullied by raw emotion? Certainly their arguments often condemned "tree-huggers" for their appeals to emotion rather than to the hard facts. But why was it that whenever somebody came back from the Clayoquot, he or she seemed to have become passionate about protecting those trees from those chainsaws?

Although the summer had been relatively rainy, September was magnificent. By the last weekend in the month it seemed as though summer would last forever; sunny, warm, and drier than the west coast has any right to be. It was Saturday, just before noon, when I saw on the left-hand side of the road a banner over the entrance to an old lumber road. This was the Peace Camp. It was located in the remains of an old clearcut affectionately known as the "Black Hole." Tangled creepers and thorny bushes were everywhere. Here and there you could see small cedars just starting to establish themselves while the entire landscape was punctuated by occasional grey, almost metallic spires; these were the skeletons of trees left behind after the slash had been burned. As a result of the hot dry weather, everything was covered in a layer of fine dust. Looming over the camp was the face of a mountain, also shorn down to stubble, looking as elegant as the skull of a Marine recruit. These hundreds of acres of devastated forest sitting next to the magnificent Pacific Rim National Park served as a constant reminder of the desecration that the campers were protesting.

The gate to the camp was a ramshackle three-sided structure with a bulletin board, literature provided by the Friends of Clayoquot Sound, a couple of camp chairs, and on the ground, a small perpetual fire to keep coffee hot. Past the gate, one walked down a narrow, dusty one-time logging road for a hundred yards or so, passing a variety of vehicles parked precariously at the side. While there was a wide range of vehicle taste (new BMWs to ancient VW microbuses) and bumper sticker sentiment (*Faculty Parking, U.B.C.* to *Give Peace a Chance*), they all shared a uniform layer of dust. At the end of the road was the camp itself.

The centre of activity at the Peace Camp was the circle, a dome-like framework about forty feet across made of cedar poles lashed together and holding up a canopy. In the centre was a circular fireplace. Around this, the daily circle meetings were held, as well as most of the socializing among the visitors and the residents of the camp. About two hundred feet away was the co-operatively run kitchen, set up to serve hundreds of people. There were tables for chopping vegetables and several beat-up gas stoves hooked up to large propane cylinders. Behind the cook tents there was a path going up the devastated mountainside where the more permanent residents had pitched their tents amid rocks and brambles.

An air of quiet friendliness permeates the camp. One hears snatches of quiet conversation among those who haven't taken this opportunity between blockades to visit Meares Island. People smile and nod at you, and occasionally someone offers to show newcomers around or answer questions. Someone is always ready to sit down with a cup of coffee and talk about the protesters' philosophy of passive resistance. Back at the gate, where at least one "greeter" is always on duty, cars pass by honking their horns. Sometimes the drivers or passengers hold up a two-fingered peace sign; more often, however, only one finger can be seen. Frequently an obscenity is shouted. During the night, it is not uncommon for anti-protesters to drive by or even enter the camp waving guns. Occasionally a truck load of human excrement or fish guts was dumped at the gate. No charges are ever pressed or laid.

Once or twice an hour a car or R.V. pulls off the road and the occupants hesitantly approach the gate. The overwhelming majority of people asking questions are appalled at the ravages they have seen. In one afternoon it is not uncommon to hear from visitors from a half dozen different countries, all expressing outrage at what they have seen as they drove by the forest.

Petitions are willingly signed and postcards to MacBlo and the provincial government are taken along, to be sent back from foreign countries. One Finnish woman, a schoolteacher, tells me that stepping into a clearcut from an old-growth stand had actually made her physically ill. There is sympathetic agreement all around. One simply cannot grasp the full extent of the obscenity without first-hand acquaintance with it.

Late Sunday afternoon, the camp fills up with people. By dinner (a ratatouille made by a team of volunteers, along with fresh baked bread donated by a Tofino bakery on the condition of anonymity), there are at least two hundred people preparing for the circle. Some of the drop-in visitors from the weekend have opted to stay for Monday morning's blockade. As coffee is drunk, a strategy session is held. For those new to the protest, the morning's schedule is laid out. At 4 a.m. the camp will be awakened by a group of musicians (today, a guitar, violin, and oboe) strolling among the tents. Volunteer drivers will be parked along the road with their hazard lights flashing until their cars are full. Volunteers will prepare food baskets for the arrestees. Coffee and bread and peanut butter, jam, and marmalade will be laid out so everyone going to the blockade can fill up. All drivers are to follow the lead truck which will carry the Friends of Clayoquot banner. The convoy will depart at around 5 a.m. and turn onto the logging road at 5:15. By 5:30 the convoy would arrive at the Kennedy Lake bridge. Vehicles are to pull off to the clearing to ensure that the road is clear. The second truck will have all the makings for tea and coffee. By the time the last car is parked, a fire will be going and water heating. A brief outline of the actual blockade and arrests follows, and then those who have volunteered to be arrested are each asked if they're sure and if they understand the implications of a criminal record, and are told how they can change their minds at any time. The twelve volunteers then go to a separate strategy session that includes a discussion of the philosophy of non-violence, as well as some practical information sharing. They are each assigned a "buddy," someone who will be their direct link to the outside world while they are under arrest. They are told what to expect in terms of arrest, incarceration, mug shots, fingerprinting. They are briefed as to how long they can expect to be held in custody before they are asked to sign the peace bond. They are told the maximum penalties the court could inflict.

Before dawn, the protesters would be starting a day that would change their lives; for the loggers, it would be business as usual.

CALLING ALL THE WORLD

Calling all the world,
at eight o'clock today,
we were so far away,
and falling.

Riding through the stars,
the universe is ours,
locked in a metal world,
and falling.

Calling all the world,
to tell you where we've gone,
we're on our way beyond
your imagining.

Calling all the world,
we've gone so far away,
much further than we'd planned,
we're travelling.

Calling all the world,
calling far from home,
we're out here all alone
and falling.

Sailing on a sea,
invisible but free,
in cold, in dark,
in beauty.

Calling all the world,
at eight o'clock today,
we were so far away,
and falling.

Calling. Calling.
S.O.S. The Whole World.

A DAY IN THE LIFE . . .

The sound of an accordion playing "Roll Out the Barrel" jangles my brain. It is 3:45 a.m. and this is the wake-up call. My eyes slowly open and I reluctantly push aside my comforter. Time to rise once more for my daily gate duty at the Clayoquot Peace Camp. The blockaders will soon be trudging down the path toward the road, ready to pile into available trucks, vans, and cars, and head for the Kennedy Lake bridge.

My role is different. I was arrested in 1992 and my two-year probation states that I cannot attend any "illegal" demonstration or be closer than 200 metres to any active logging road in British Columbia. I must stay back in camp while the others do their daily "civic duty," our term for civil disobedience.

Those of us who remain behind look after the security of the camp and pull closer to the fire in the sudden silence, waiting for the dawn. We talk of many things—our lives back home, happenings in the camp. It is enriching, though sometimes I would rather not hear the conversation and choose to walk further down the road to listen for nighthawks or owls.

The two-hour shift soon ends and it is time to trek towards the kitchen, my boots crunching on the stony road. Perhaps there are leftover dishes to wash from the previous evening. The huge pot of water for the porridge must be put on to boil. The preferred job is washing dishes in the morning, as it warms the hands in the cold misty air.

Soon the blockaders return—seventeen arrested today—and the line-up for the morning meal forms. "I have never felt closer to tears than when that giant logging truck went through," a young man says, his voice softly trembling. This is his first day. "It doesn't get any easier after two weeks," someone else says, pulling her favourite flowered plate from the stack on the table.

And so the day begins. We sit on the benches in the tent-like fire circle, its plastic covering flapping in the morning breeze, devour our breakfast of porridge and fruit, and wait until the morning circle starts. Today I will be the facilitator, but first I must do an interview with a young man from Edmonton, who is putting together a video about Clayoquot Sound. He is curious why a grandmother would stay in these bleak surroundings for so long—I am beginning my eleventh week—and I reply "I love the people here, that is why I stay."

By now some of the arrestees are returning, and a cheer rings out. I raise my hand in the air, others follow suit, and there is silence to focus the circle. Some people do not care to join in, preferring to go back to bed. Blockading is tiring for many, both physically and emotionally. But there is camp business to be done: dishes, meal preparation, digging of latrines, and gate duty. And there are non-violence or peacekeeper workshops to be planned for the afternoon. These workshops are my main job. Sometimes I find it hard to stay awake and I long for a morning nap.

And so the day goes on. Dinner at six is followed by the evening circle and strategy planning for tomorrow's blockade. The process sometimes lasts for several hours as 200 people, many of them beginners, struggle with the consensus process.

Every time new people join the group there is a cry for more rebellious actions. "Can't we do something to slow down the trucks so that we can stop them from logging a few more minutes?" "I have a great idea—let's build a huge barricade on the road!" "Maybe we could jump out from behind the bushes and surprise the police."

Patiently someone explains that this type of strategy will not further the campaign. Making the blockade accessible to people from all walks of life has made it successful. It is usually decided that blockaders will sing songs until the police arrive, and have a single heartbeat drum as each person makes a short statement while being led away by the police.

Sometimes there are other issues to talk about and the meeting goes late. Some of the headier ones are gender issues, nude bathing at the lake nearby, cigarette smoking, and drumming. (It is hard living with people ranging in ages from babies to people in their seventies.) We try to solve each problem as it comes up, but the turnover is quick in the camp and some coming only for a few days immediately wish to change things to suit themselves. It is difficult to "leave your ego at the gate." We know all things are connected and each issue must be examined; therefore great patience is required. We have so many things to learn and so many to unlearn.

We join hands to sing one song before heading off to bed. We consider ourselves lucky if we are finished by 9:30. I once more crawl into my van and quickly fall asleep. Another day is over.

CONTROVERSY

He talks about forests all the time.
In the morning I pick pine needles
out of my breakfast cereal,
listen to the crash of harvest licences.
At lunch, my friend's latest bon mot is
buried under an avalanche
of falling firs.
Our bed is a vast clearcut,
our pillows full of sawdust.
When I inadvertently start a story
about a bear on a logging road,
it is swept away in the undertow
of watershed destruction.

My favourite words, salmon, cedar, snow
are kept hidden and locked.

I have to defend myself against a crime
I am not committing. I am a stand-in
for everyone who buys a morning newspaper.
I want to scream like a seagull,
"Get off my back," fly out
to the far kelp beds.

Every old cedar that falls, the damp earth,
the crushed salal, speak to me, too.
I keep trying to say that.

I keep trying to say, All I need is
a piece of paper small enough
to write this down.

From TERRACE LANDSCAPES

2

Terrace landscapes—landscapes of heart and mind—not just trees & clouds & straight streets looking south—a long mile—when dark all the "Terraceness" goes out of it, there's just a dark space, a sense of trees & houses & a mile away, low down, lights of a street, gas station & neon of a hotel, as if that were the only street in the universe, all around flat land, or rising land, then mountains. Fog settling over, riding the flat of the airport hill—in the morning rising, restlessly writhing upwards, from the river, & following the river, a river of fog or mist atop a real river under.

The parking lot outside Safeway is the centre, at night a few cars still parked at the north edge, close to Lakelse, maybe the glow of a cigarette visible, moving.

The imagination of the town fights with the imagination of the land. The imagination of the land is creative, its forms come out of the land, appear out of the hills, the creeks between low hills, stride into the centre. Not Indian, or animal—bear—nothing so specific. Maybe they are geometric, Platonic—they are forms into which people and animals can fit their dreams.

The imagination of the town is imposed, a ledger. The streets are the lines, they line us up. Driving we imagine we are walking, the tree-lined streets (of Manawaka), on our way to the stores, the bank or the credit union, the library, the doctor. A dream of a town out of a primary reader.

City sophistication an added element. When you eat at Don D, exotic foods served by neat boys and friendly women, you can lose yourself in the world it creates—imagine Terrace a community in harmony with other communities in a pacified world—the places cornmeal & papayas come from.

More disconcerting, the last vestiges of the local—the Co-op cafeteria— the oldest old men on canes in the sunlight. And that reality isn't there either, disappears when you look back to the Indians, back to the land. You realize you look back at nothing. Again, there is nothing. It is all made up. Except the forms.

15

The MacEachern decision. The faces of Natives, seen, or looked at, anew. In the mall & the one or two in my classes who come shyly in—when asked to read from Shakespeare they have soft, almost inaudible voices, but they don't trip over words, or race over them, like some of the white boys. I think of jet planes bombing Iraq, tens of thousands of boys dead, like those Hamlet imagines will die in Fortinbras's attack on a "straw" of earth *which is not tomb enough and continent/to hide the slain.* Today napalm reported, the jellied gasoline shot from helicopter gunships, but in the *Sun* the letters say we should approve or disapprove according to whether it's pro-American or anti-American. Language slipping sidewise, to evade the point, any way, not to answer, respond, but to speak again, shift ground. They are to blame, MacEachern says, for not having grasped the opportunity, always there, to become part of the mainstream.

And where is the mainstream, is it the stream of "goods" that flows from the mall to the house & garage to the dump? And how to grasp it?

Valleys. Looking from the air at the snowdrifted mountaintops no one, no goat even, has set foot on, in niches the glaciers, in the valleys the crooked lines, like pen & ink, of streams, the grey curves of highway. Then encapsulated, riding, at a comfortable speed, home.

Look up close. Trees in a Margaret Avison poem
ragged on/the windward sides—
prepared
for onslaught when the obliterating
blasts sweep in again.

Let the tree stop the words, let it stand in front of the "decision," immovable, at least not movable by language, bendable by wind, but returning to its growing space. Bodies, living, of the Indians, moving—of the beings we name glibly as trees, or fish, no matter how precise you get, as forester or biologist, do you know the species, the subspecies, the individual? No way to let this language, this "decision," into the landscape, to let it come between people and the land—the land, another glib abstraction?

16

Insisting, in my mind, on a subject. For "sense" to be made. Sense, meaning. But not knowing, not caring really, if there could be meaning in the fields, meaning on the roads, the geese in the fields, pools of melted snow, sodden earth.

For the geese who come some way we call "home" or "north," we feel complimented, start to smile on their return, as in fall we feel fallen, found wanting & waiting for the emptiness that is our reward. The description of anything is a scheme, & I'm tired of schemes, tired of needing to know.

Need to know means playing a part, having the facts to hand, or the general lie of the land. Poetry dies, willingly. Its last, left, nothing is now but everything unnamed & surviving. Lasting. Like the black necks, white-ringed (memory swoons), brown-feathered, the blue, the white, the wet, the calm, the oval, the ovary, the delta. Escaping. And all flowing away, the incline, the trickle on that slight gradient of the cool seeping from under the grey, cold, evaporating, upward, the skillful pools, the turning. Bugs. Birds. Sodium. Let live. Shadow on glassy, of the tall, bending, & then the geese flying over & the sound, undescribed. No feeling. No one to feel. The slight sound of coughing.

There is such a wanting in all things whether one or many, to be free, & whether part of a separate, & whether entangling or loose. Untouched. Unknown.

Such a need not to be touched, not to be known. Up the road that follows the river, up the slope, the tree aquiver, the star that booms in the dark, way far away, around & back again, & back, away.

From TURNING THE TIDE

Voices echo in the hills, singing and calling in the early morning darkness. The sound is haunting and beautiful as I lie in my tent. Closer by, two people are walking up the gravel road, strumming a guitar and singing Bob Marley's "Redemption Song." It's 3:30 a.m. Time to wake up. It's Monday, August 9. This morning 300 people will be arrested for blocking a logging road into the old-growth forest. . . .

I came to Clayoquot Sound to support the blockade, to learn and write about the process of the blockade, the Peace Camp, and the roles women are taking. I arrived . . . on a Saturday, with a busload of others. "Welcome to the Black Hole," says the driver. . . .

We are warmly greeted at the gate. The woman leading us in says, "We ask you to read the Code of Non-Violence and agree to it before you enter the camp." Non-violence workshops are offered daily and all blockaders are expected to take one.

We trudge down the old logging road, past the communal fire circle and the kitchen, dubbed "Clearcut Café." Following the gravel road uphill, past a line of tents on both sides, I'm amazed at the number of people—it's like a small village.

The trail divides at the top of one hill. I take the west road and set up my tent between a small tree and a charred log. To protect the regenerating land, we must camp on the road. It's very rocky and I'm glad I've brought sleeping pads. Some people have been here for weeks. Taut expedition tents sit next to faded and tattered ones, perhaps pressed into one last use for the cause. . . .

On my first night, I meet Tzeporah Berman, an organizer with Friends of Clayoquot Sound. She agrees to an interview when she has some free time; as it turns out, that's not till my last day.

We talked about the prominence of women on the blockade. "The women are the ones who are making decisions here, doing the organizing, mostly." . . . Almost all the non-violence trainers are women. "There's been a lot of problems at the camp, but at the same time, it's a wonderful place to be. I feel like we've created a safe space for women and for people of all backgrounds to come here and protest." She qualifies this though. "I think, that to say there isn't sexism, or that this is a totally safe space, is to be completely naive, because our own socialization is incredibly pervasive, and we have homophobia and sexism and racism in us." . . .

Berman comments that some men have promoted "unsafe and machismo actions" such as "jumping in front of the trucks right as they go by" and "building a big thing in the road," and these are usually the same men "who want to drum twenty-four hours a day. What we've seen is people needing to enlarge their egos through that. And all of these people, in my experience, have been men."

"The feminist focus of this camp means we try to work that out in as open a way as possible within the camp. We've had women's caucuses. At one, a woman said she had been sexually harassed on the way up to camp by someone who was in camp. We supported her and talked to her and tried to decide what to do." They contacted male allies and named the perpetrator, calling on the men to deal with it. "That wouldn't have happened if there weren't so many strong women here willing to support, and if the organization hadn't been feminist-based." . . .

I found one of the most powerful aspects of the camp is that many of the people involved are committed to fundamental changes in society, beyond the blockade. The struggle against the malaise of cynicism and powerlessness that sees the current economic and social system as inevitable and which mocks our deep feelings and dreams is revitalized by this commitment and energy. Clayoquot Sound is just one struggle among many to "turn the tide."

THE PEACE CAMP, CHRISTMAS 1993

There wasn't much left of the Peace Camp. After the trial and execution most people picked up their garbage and drifted off. We went back to the fishing boat. It gave us something to do, and a little money in the bank wouldn't hurt. Only there wouldn't be much to bank if the fish didn't start to bite. Every year of fishing was the worst yet, and this year was the very worst.

We kept pretty close to land. We liked to keep the trees in sight, after all we'd been through. They came right down almost to the beach, and looked as if they went back inland forever. They didn't, though; there were bald spots on the mountain. Looking back to shore, I tried not to think about them. Then I saw J.C. on the beach. He had the camp stove set up and was waving.

We'd been trying to figure out what was happening to J.C. Since he'd been dead, he kept coming and going unexpectedly, never staying very long, and this made us waffle about getting on with our lives. He'd been hinting that these flying visits would stop soon. We still didn't know what to do.

Peter got excited when he saw J.C. He'd always been excitable, but was much more hyper since he'd perjured himself at the trial. Odd though, he'd also become totally non-violent—ever since J.C. wouldn't let him cut off the policeman's ear.

The activist streak seemed to run right through his extended family. His mother-in-law, for instance, after she was cured of the fever, joined the Raging Grannies and sat down in front of the temple to block the money-changers. Then she joined up with that Samaritan woman J.C. met at the well, and they marched back and forth on the road to Samaria so people had to stop stoning each other.

She'd been at the Peace Camp when the High Priest came. He thought we might be the first thrust of anti-imperial resistance, and he'd better be seen with us, just in case. He wore a purple checked shirt and brought a couple of cameramen to record his moment of solidarity with J.C. But J.C. wasn't there; he'd gone to Tofino for a picnic with the Women's Institute. So the High Priest sang a couple of songs with the Grannies, but their tunes weren't contemporary enough for him. And he had his picture taken, arm-in-arm with someone from the Tribal Council, standing meaningfully in front of a very large tree.

After the High Priest left, J.C. came back. He'd been listening to loggers' wives, and then to four Nuu-chah-nulth women with their own story to tell. He was looking tired. He wanted to save humans as well as trees, and that was hard work. Maybe the hardest part was convincing the rest of us.

So when Peter saw J.C. on the shore, he got very excited, and more so after J.C. signalled us to move the nets. We did and the fish came until they broke the rope. We never figured out how J.C. did that. Peter had been working stark naked, for the convenience, but I guess he thought that was not quite seemly, now that he knew who J.C. was. So he pulled on his shorts, jumped overboard, and swam to shore. The rest of us took the dinghy, dragging the heavy nets to safety. We didn't mind much. We already suspected we were going to need Peter's way of charging ahead and getting things done. We were right too; it wasn't many months before he'd led us in and out of jail a few times, introduced us to a few angels, and started the catholic church.

J.C. had the food ready—the usual loaves and fishes, but he sure knew how to cook them. We all talked a lot, and some of what was said came out wrong in later reports. J.C. asked questions which made us all squirm a bit, but he looked satisfied, or at least resigned, with the answers. He said again that he'd be out-of-sight soon, but it wouldn't matter, he promised. He would make one more appearance, to that Paul fellow who kept stoning the wrong people and sticking spikes into trees. He'd send him in his boat to keep an eye on Leviathan and talk to the Greeks about their unknown god. Also, J.C. was convinced that Paul was the person to spearhead the letter-writing campaign.

But what about the rest of us? J.C. fed the leftover loaves and fishes to three eager seagulls and a couple of crows, and sat comfortably on a piece of driftwood that looked like a dragon with eagle's wings.

"OK," he said, "here's what you have to do."

THE SPLITTING OF THUNDER
A Profile of Joe and Carl Martin

"Many moons ago, there was a widow in this village. She had a son and as the son grew older, some strange things began happening in the village. People were dying. People didn't know how the people were dying. They were puzzled by it. So they got the councils together and appointed some people to watch over the village every night.

"One night someone had seen this young man come out of his house and he went back in just before daybreak. Sure enough, in the morning someone else was dead in one of the houses. So they figured out it was this fellow that was doing the killing. And they planned to capture him. But the fellow knew already and he escaped into the forest. It took a long time for them to catch him, but when they did, they brought him back to the village and the council sentenced him to death. They got a big pile of logs and they tied him up to it. They lit it up; and the fellow was dying and he was laughing and laughing very hard and he told the people: 'I'm going to suck your blood. I'm going to suck your blood forever.' And as all the ashes blew up they all turned into mosquitoes. That's where the first mosquitoes came from."

Mosquitoes serve as a powerful metaphor for the many "mosquitoes" sucking the life and spirit out of the Clayoquot Sound First Nations. But although the Nuu-chah-nulth people have been drained by decades of violence—overt and subtle—they have also maintained the strength to face adversity and overcome oppression. The Martin family, in particular Joe and Carl, personifies that invincible spirit. Well-known to journalists reporting from Clayoquot Sound, government officials and industry representatives, these two brothers of the Tla-o-qui-aht First Nations have become increasingly vocal about the destruction of their land and the disrespect shown to their people.

Storytelling, they say, is only one aspect of their culture that has been eroded. The disappearance of their language, land, and resources are other casualties in a two-century-long war that puts money over people and White people over Natives. However, while storytelling may be endangered, Joe and Carl are still telling stories of the distant past and creating mythology from the present.

Our elders used to tell stories like this one, says Joe Martin of his mosquito story. "My dad sometimes talks about the stories they used to tell. I never hear them anymore.

"Before we had electricity, people would be in bed just after dark, probably telling stories. Now we have microwaves, TVs, washers, dryers, everything to save us time. But we never have time for each other."

While the largely White town of Tofino rapidly becomes an international tourist resort, Natives keep to their reserves. The influx of commercialism, in all its forms (tourism, forestry, fisheries), has always occurred at the expense of local Native peoples. Naturally, some Natives aspire to the material wealth and consumerism around this once-quiet peninsula: new cars, high-tech equipment, expensive sneakers for their kids, and that invasive North American poison—junk food.

"If you stand on the dock on the weekend," says Carl, "you'll see lots of people running off to the city. They're caught in the system. Everybody's so dependent. The government keeps throwing money at them."

According to Joe, the loss of culture has a lot to do with the proliferation of television. "All our stories have to do with nature and respect for nature. It's not very often you sit down and listen to someone talk about our connection to nature through these stories," he says. Satellite dishes have become a treasured status symbol on most reserves in Clayoquot Sound. In Opitsaht, a reserve of about 200 people on Meares Island just across the water from Tofino, where Joe and Carl grew up, two totem poles stand flanked by satellites. It's a strange contradiction and a symbol of a deeply-imbedded dichotomy. Do you or can you go back to the traditional ways as Carl would like? Or do you adapt to and adopt the White man's games?

Either path is paved with pain. Decades of residential schools, Christian indoctrination, the Indian Act (which is still law in Canada) have all created wounds so deep that, upon close inspection, they reveal the bones underneath. "Just about every family in our village has had a suicide," says Carl. "Everybody's hurting. We lost two nephews to suicide recently. In that same month, there were four other attempts.

"I think about the traditional ways," he says. "How our people were close-knit tribes and worked together. If a house was needed, people would get together to help. Now you can't get anyone to lift a finger. That's not a community.

"We're all numbers," says Carl, touching his arm as though it was imprinted right there on his brown skin. "I'm 240. Then if you work for the White system, you need other numbers. It's kind of like how the jail system works. They have us right on our backs."

When Joe was at school, nuns would come over the trail in four-by-fours from the residential school at nearby Kakawis to teach the children of Opitsaht. The teachers were "nasty," says Joe. "They'd wallop the hell out of you with rulers. They had no right to do that. That has a lasting effect; it's created serious social problems."

"The abuse the boys and girls took from them is incredible," says Carl. "We can't bury that stuff. . . . How many people have died here due to

alcohol? The numbers are so high. It's all like a madhouse to me. I could blow up talking about how people are blinded by it. Our villages were burnt, our canoes trashed, things taken to museums like we were a dying race.

"I don't think it's right the way my people are treated and what's happening here," says Carl. "I want out of the system. I want to bring things back.

"A university student once asked me if I would go back to the old ways. And I said, 'If you go back.' Because we still have a chance here. But we're not given that chance. We're told where to live, where to fish. If we were to leave the land alone, let the trees grow, leave the salmon stocks. . . . "

As he is talking, there's a loud blast in the distance. "Did you hear that?" I ask. "What are they blasting?"

"The earth of course," says Carl.

Joe's daughter, Gisele, says that although a lot has been lost, the power is still there: "I remember an elder saying at a cleansing ceremony for the new moon that the power of our culture is stronger than the white government because of our connection to the land."

Gisele is only sixteen, but last winter she went to Europe with Joe where she met European Parliamentarians and stood with her father at the United Nations in Geneva as he made a presentation to the conference on the International Tropical Timber Agreement. "We showed them that we exist," says Gisele. "That we're not just people in Walt Disney pictures and books.

"They were expecting us to walk in with buckskins and feathers," she says. "And here I was with a tie-dyed shirt and a black sweatshirt inside-out. My dad was wearing a tie he'd gotten recently as a joke that had Bugs Bunny on it.

"Do you ever notice," she says, "that Native people are constantly laughing at White people and White people never know it. It's always very subtle."

But when Joe or Carl talk about what's happening to their land, neither is laughing. "We are in the middle of a struggle to defend our land and culture from forest policies which are not only not sustainable, but which we believe are actually contrary to the Canadian Constitution," Joe told the United Nations. He talked about the B.C. government's April 1993 decision to open Clayoquot Sound to even more clearcutting and how the decision was made without any First Nations input. "As hard as we have tried, we have never been able to secure a final agreement or treaty from either the federal or provincial governments recognizing our land and resource rights, and giving us the right to make such critical decisions ourselves."

That may change, however, with the implementation of the new Interim Land-Use Agreement signed by B.C. Premier Mike Harcourt and Nuu-chah-nulth chiefs in Ahousat in March 1994. On paper at least, the agreement will serve as a "bridging mechanism" until the resolution of land claims. So as not to destroy the land before First Nations get any part of it, the agreement sets up a joint management board which gives Native people a veto over all land-use decisions in Clayoquot Sound.

Carl doesn't like the agreement, doesn't trust the government's motives. "It doesn't mean anything to me. It's all the same. Nothing has changed. It's work as usual, roads as usual. They're talking about negotiations and they can't even tell me what they're negotiating."

Carl and Gisele said they tried unsuccessfully to get copies of the agreement before it was signed. "The elected chiefs haven't talked to people in the cities," says Carl, referring to those members of his family who live away. "I have no idea what's going on. They're not saying anything to the people."

"Sometimes I read the agreement and I think, no I don't like it," says

Joe. "But then you go back and think about all the time that our people have been attempting to have something like this with the government. And there's a chance. A chance for us to work together."

The agreement is complex, written in legalese. No one is really sure what it means for the wilderness of Clayoquot Sound. Concerns have been raised by the environmental movement that, given the power, Natives will log it all. "People always point at us like we're another Hitler," says Carl. "Like we're going to chop down all the trees and take all the fish."

"Our people have been using the forest for thousands of years," says Joe. "But I don't think our councils would act the same way as multinationals. . . . I don't think people know us that well. In Canada, if you look at it, everyone has been at arm's length all this time. Only now are we beginning to come together."

That coming together has its roots in what Gisele calls "a struggle for keeping the wilderness wild." And the Martin family has played a large role in the controversy. In 1984, when Natives joined forces with environmentalists to stop logging on Meares Island (land claimed jointly by the Tla-o-qui-ahts and Ahousahts), Joe, Carl, their father Robert, a hereditary chief, and Robert's partner Ruth, built a cabin on Meares "to welcome people to the tribal park." They spent three months at that cabin where Joe helped build his first dugout canoe. Today, Joe and Carl are some of the few Natives in Clayoquot Sound who possess the knowledge to carve canoes.

During the Meares Island blockades, Joe, one of the main instigators, was summoned to court in Vancouver. "They tried to throw me off the island," he says. "But when they found out I was a Tla-o-qui-aht, they dropped it like a hot potato."

Joe's recognition of environmental destruction began about fifteen years ago when the Save Our Salmon Committee came to the site where he was logging. He was working as a chokerman for Millstream Timber at Kootowis River, just behind where the Tofino landfill site is now. "I was hiding from the film crew," says Joe. "I didn't want to be seen doing this work."

Part of his job was dragging logs through the streams, streams that Joe says were full of debris. "I remember looking at the mountains on a clear day where I'd been working. I knew what it was doing to the fish. You don't have to be a rocket scientist to realize what has happened.

"I grew up fishing with my dad in Browning Pass. We used to fish there up until mid-November. There were thousands of coho salmon in the area. Now it's been logged over and the salmon are gone."

Robert Martin still fishes. One beautiful Sunday in Opitsaht, he is cleaning his boat, the Sea Raven, in preparation for the summer salmon season. Wearing hip waders and a sad smile, he mourns the loss of a resource that once sustained his people. The salmon season has dropped from seven months to two, he says. Now he also has to fish for ling cod because of the declining price and stocks of salmon.

"I don't think there's really been overfishing in many of these areas," says Joe. "I think it's mostly from destruction of the salmon habitat."

When Joe and Carl were growing up, they used to help their father with his trap lines. At that time, only one or two people had power boats; everyone else travelled by canoe. The two brothers lived in a house looking out at Tofino. They would lie in bed and see only three lights coming across the water. "I remember one day it was snowing," says Joe. "My grandfather was fishing just off Opitsaht and we saw him catch a big fish. We were yelling from the house. . . . The winter spring salmon are really small now. The largest we caught last year was six pounds. We used to catch thirty pounders."

"We're going forward too fast," says Carl, "knowing how things were when we were kids. The language has been broken. That's a big part of it . . . regaining our values. We have to regain the values we were told we didn't have." Carl has been collecting information from Native elders for years. He prods his father, Robert, for knowledge Carl says he is quickly forgetting.

Carl has put together a dictionary of the Indian names for local birds and animals, and he has an amazing collection of artifacts, most of which were found when a waterline was put in at Opitsaht. Among the harpoons, fish hooks, and war clubs, a mass grave was discovered. The smallpox epidemics, says Carl, killed a lot of people around here. His grandmother escaped the sickness by taking her sisters up to the Clayoquot River valley.

"I look at these things," Carl says, pointing at the artifacts carefully displayed on his living room table. "I think about them all the time. This is us. People have tried to bury the ways we've tried to survive. But my family is doing a lot to keep things somewhat alive."

A recording of his grandfather singing Tla-o-qui-aht songs is playing on a small tape deck in the kitchen. "I know where our roots are," he says. "I've dug for them. I talk to my brothers, sisters, and children all the time about who we are, about the traditional ways. I want them to realize we were a much happier people. That we have the option not to be controlled."

I ask Carl how much land Natives lay claim to in Clayoquot Sound and he looks disappointed, surprised that I do not yet know the answer. "How can we lay claim to something we already own?" he asks simply. "We never gave it away."

They never gave the thunderbird away either. It is still part of the stories, the myths.

On a trip back to Tofino from Hot Springs Cove, Carl's son asked his father where thunderbirds came from. "As we were approaching Catface mountain," says Carl, "my son pointed at Lone Cone. 'They live up there in the sky,' I said. 'You can't see them but you can hear them in the wintertime.'"

Then one afternoon, while his son was playing outside, thunder rocked the sky. "My son came in the house, shaking. 'The thundering bird is here,' he said."

From **A STRAIT ARROW EDITORIAL**

Racism is the biggest obstacle to a just land claims settlement in British Columbia. The general public and even the Native people have to be educated as to what a land claims settlement will mean. For sure the attitude of colonialists *giving* Native people something through land claims is totally off base; the reverse is true—that is, Native people are giving up something so guests can live in harmony in our country. . . .

A land claims settlement will allow guests to live in B.C. *legally*; as it is, non-Indians are breaking their own laws by living in B.C. without a treaty settlement.

TREE HISTORY

For six years the wind has shaken this tree. Has pulled the leaves their windy dresses off the snakeskin down. Scissors have fallen from the branches. Fingers lean and painful. Snipping and poking at our broken sides our failures. The days and years have sped by. Rings of wood round and numbered. Unfolding sand and pearls, gardens and walls, barbed wire, a typewriter held back held back. And the mornings and midnights reach around and under me. Time pushing me slowly gently along its river route waterway, no turning back, no stopping or getting off, through thunder rolling and the wounds of love and war. At the end a Gem a wisdomstone or a full-blown Tree. The fingers tear under the skin's layers. The serpent curls up the spinetrunk. When Time passes like this there are roots to unknot or bury deeper. Rivers to catch. Tears to flow. Birds strain in their string nests. The wind the wind gets inside of me. Wild flowers push up from the base basement. Between the human edges. Broken glass. The Mirror you once held. Children and Wishes tumble out of the trunk like birds or bright ribbons into the sky. No law of gravity here. The wind sweeping them as many coloured as light as waves or shells. As strong as the sun. Bright and different packages. Dreams gulling. Stories of Time running ahead out of the veins. Time with boats and brave ones.

LETTERS ON CLAYOQUOT SOUND
IN THE EYE OF HISTORY

Introductory Note

The intent of these two letters, from my wife and me to Premier Michael Harcourt, will be quite evident. They call upon the justice of history, which will produce the answers Mr. Harcourt did not condescend to give, since—as is his practise—he ignored our letters. Here I should note another related fragment of history. Twenty years ago when Dave Barrett was leader of a NDP government, I wrote to him regarding certain practises of the Liquor Control Board that I had found were defrauding honest drinkers. Barrett not only replied; he took action and ended the abuse. Now I compare his responsiveness with his successor's silence. Presumably there are hundreds of other British Columbians whose protests have likewise gone ignored or unanswered, and long before the books of history get around to condemning, Harcourt and his associates will feel the effect of their arrogance in the ballot box.

20th August, 1993

Mr. Michael Harcourt,
Premier of British Columbia,
The Legislative Buildings,
Victoria, B.C.

Dear Mr. Harcourt

When my husband and I had an audience with the Dalai Lama in Vancouver a few weeks ago, I told him about the magnificent decision you and your government had reached regarding Tatshenshini and its million square miles of protection as a natural park.

The Dalai Lama was delighted; he threw up his arms and said: "What? No more hunting? No killing? No trees to be cut?" I felt proud to be a British Columbian.

Please have the courage to do the same for Clayoquot Sound. Thousands would admire your strength.

Politics is ephemeral, but nature is a heritage to be cherished and preserved.

Yours sincerely,
Ingeborg Woodcock

Mr. Michael Harcourt,
Premier of British Columbia,
Parliament Buildings,
Victoria, B.C.

Dear Mr. Harcourt,

I know you must have received many hundreds of letters about Clayoquot
Sound from people representing a great variety of viewpoints. But I find
myself impelled to add to that list because I am a historian—in fact the
author of *The History of British Columbia* which you may have read—and I
feel there are a number of ways in which you should consider the
perspective of events at Clayoquot Sound before you allow the situation
to reach what a historian can see only as a tragic extremity.

The first way in which all those who may be interested in the history
of British Columbia must be concerned is the obvious one, the destruction
of natural monuments in a region where the evidence of our distant past
is so scanty and fragile. Let us look objectively at what is happening. A
small crew of men go into the forest with their machinery and earn a
couple of thousand dollars or so, and a tree that ranks as a natural wonder,
that has survived since its seed germinated perhaps in the time of King
Alfred, is destroyed, never to be replaced.

Surely the arguments in favour of this kind of logging are thin indeed.
Even the matter of jobs, so industriously flogged by the union leaders,
becomes irrelevant when one sees MacMillan Bloedel's own figures. In a
two-page advertisement in a recent issue of *Maclean's* they talked of *100
direct jobs* and 300 indirect ones as being involved with Clayoquot Sound.
The other day I heard it reported on the radio that, after the arrest of a
group of idealistic protesters, a mere sixty loggers were into the timber.

I put it to you, Mr. Premier, that this is a pitiful justification in the eye
of history for wantonly destroying what by good fortune has survived for
twelve centuries. I put it to you that you would be better occupied in
finding means of multiplying jobs by developing secondary wood industries
on the spot rather than exporting our timber to be processed abroad. Surely,
quite apart from your legislative powers, the government could use its
position as a major shareholder in MacMillan Bloedel to achieve a change
in the company's policies. If that deal is to be seen as anything more than
the kind of government-capitalist scam with which we are too familiar in
this province's past, your social-democratic ideals would seem to suggest
the appropriateness of this kind of interference in the capitalists' "freedom"
which harms our other freedoms.

There are many other historical aspects of the situation that I could raise. But let me be content with one of them. In the long run of history, morality is usually better remembered than legality. Gandhi has become a world hero; the British officials who imprisoned him according to the law are considered petty tyrants. A generation or so ago, British Columbia governments and judges sent hundreds of Doukhobors to prison for long periods for their protest actions and tore hundreds of Doukhobor children from their homes to be forcibly retained in the small concentration camp at New Denver. Do you—any more than I—remember those past events with less than shame for our province which could not accommodate the beliefs of a minority? Do you wish to add more shame to our history by imprisoning hundreds of highly moral men and women who are willing to sacrifice their freedom for our most precious heritage, the great old trees that symbolize our history and should be allowed to die with as much dignity as you or I?

Yours sincerely,
George Woodcock

CAMP WILDERNESS

I met Matt in 1954 when I was nine years old. I was at a summer camp for girls in Algonquin Park and he was employed there as a guide. He was rarely to be seen around the camp itself, but when a canoe trip was about to depart from the big dock down at the waterfront, Matt would appear, rounding the point in the stern of a twelve-foot, green-canvas Peterborough. A slight and scraggy, middle-ageless sort of man, I remember watching him in wonder; he didn't seem to move at all and yet the narrow, tipsy little boat, full to the gunnels with gear, was being propelled through the water as if a small outboard motor were attached. I'd never seen anyone paddle like that, creating his own wake. When alone, he moved like a dancer, skimming the canoe over the surface like a hawk riding a thermal, and once I saw him spin 360 degrees with a single stroke.

Matt's trips were definitely the ones to get on, and his canoe the one to dibs. Not just because you could count on getting to the campsite early, but because you could also count on seeing amazing things no one else did along the way. Spectacular things like a bull moose lolling half submerged in the boggy recess of an inlet, or beaver kits racing through a grassy stretch of the Madawaska River. With Matt, though, you had to know how to keep silent so you could hear; so you could tell, sitting in the bow, paddling on the opposite side of the canoe, when he saw something and where he was pointing.

Camp life was something different, though; something straight out of Ernest Thompson Seton's "The Birch-Bark Roll of the Woodcraft Indians," in fact. We learned archery and canoeing, sang songs around the campfire about blue lakes and rocky shores and ate in a dining hall ringed with reproductions of Group of Seven paintings with titles like "Solemn Land" and "September Gale." Paradise was a northern forest and wilderness, we were told, was all around us. Well, certainly up by Lake Opeongo in the farther reaches of the Park where motorboats and tourist camping hadn't yet dumped enough garbage into the lakes to attract leeches. Real wilderness took a while to get to and revealed itself as something wild, unpolluted and unoccupied—as the Group's pictures were witness—Nature, as it were, *au naturel*, free of human contrivance. As I think of it now, the Wilderness venerated in camp lore was entirely imaginary. The narrative was always set in the past or some other time altogether implying, without being explicit about it, that human beings exist outside nature and are antithetical to her by definition. There were exceptions, of course; people who "learned" to move through the natural world (the Bush, the Wild, the North) without disrupting it. But that Wilderness couldn't reckon with someone like Matt whose people had been living in the place for several millennia and knew the land intimately. It also couldn't reckon with the recent history of European settlers whose nineteenth century logging activities had left the Park a shadow of its original, pre-contact self. Hardly pristine Wilderness, it was created *after* the giant white pine (Ontario's old-growth) were levelled; squared by broad-axe in the woods (shavings left to feed forest fires) and sent off in British ships to serve the Empire and the bank accounts of Ottawa valley entrepreneurs. The Algonquin Park I knew as a child was a theme park, and Matt was the only clue.

Does this mean, then, that Wilderness is a matter of subjective experience? That it is, and can only be, a question of ignorance, given that what's unknown and empty to me may be teeming with history to you, that my wilderness could be your grandmother's trap line? Intuitively, I feel there's still currency in the idea—so long as it is taken for idea or cultural construct, not geo-physical fact. Idea, ideal, desire, wish. Much, after all, has altered in mainstream Canada's view of nature and Aboriginal culture in the past thirty years. Histories which were hidden are being told now, and slowly recognition is building that our generation's responsibility is to establish a different set of values which neither sentimentalize nor immortalize Wilderness but seek a balance, draw a circle and draw all living things inside.

The dilemma for people like me—White European Canadians with tenuous connections to the Old Country—is how to place ourselves in relation to the landscape. By now our North American experience stretches over decades and generations, and the physical and spiritual character of the place has had an effect. How could it not? But the mythologies my culture passed on have lost their power and been discredited, and we have to begin somewhere else. We have to find the place where past and present, native and newcomer, nature and culture can meet.

Some years after I grew out of camp and saw Matt for the last time I discovered Marshall McLuhan's writings on culture. I remember reading his theory about technology being an extension of the human body—the car an extension of the foot and so on—and thinking of Matt. Matt settled in his canoe, slipping through the sparkling waves of a windswept lake, riding the current on wings.

ELEPHANTS

The cracked cedar bunkhouse
hangs behind me like a grey pueblo
in the sundown where I sit to carve an elephant
from a hunk of brown soap
for the Indian boy
who lives in the village
a mile back in the bush.

The alcoholic truck-driver
and the cat-skinner sit beside me
with their eyes closed—
all of us waiting out the last hour
until we go back on the grade—

and I try to forget the forever
clank clank clank
across the grade
pounding stones and earth to powder
for hours in mosquito-darkness
of the endless cold mountain night.

The elephant takes form—
my knife caresses smooth soap
scaling off curls of brown
which the boy saves to take home
to his mother in the village.

Finished, I hand the carving to him
and he looks at the image of the great
beast for a long time
then sets it on dry cedar
and looks up at me: What's an elephant?
he asks me
so I tell him of the elephants
and their jungles—the story
of the elephant graveyard
which no one has ever found
and how the silent
animals of the rain-forest

go away to die somewhere
in the limber-lost of distances
and he smiles at me
tells me of his father's
graveyard where his people have been
buried for years. So far back
no one remembers when it started
and I ask him where the graveyard is
and he tells me it is gone
now where no-one will ever find it,
buried under the grade of the new
highway.

THE SPIDER AND DANIEL ORTEGA

Back in 1987 I spent some months in the central highlands of Mexico, in Michoacán. One evening I sat by myself at the table of my casita, making notes. It was nearly dark. Supper leftovers, papers, and pamphlets were spread in front of me. On the short wave, an in-depth account in Spanish from Nicaragua: the Voice of America describing Daniel Ortega's latest peace proposal to the Contras, free elections and so on.

I felt a chill. The news report was hopeful, the evening cool, but I noticed my shiver had another source. Ten feet above my head, on the ceiling in the shadow of my lamp, was an immense spider. Not a tarantula, which have hairy legs, black backs, reddish bellies. This character was brown, two balls of body-mass, a solid figure-8 with legs. The back half was a globule the size of a golf ball. The front looked like a horse-chestnut, the kind we tied a string through when we were kids and smashed against each other's; conkers they were called.

Right then the araña was motionless. With legs clamped wide, a giant. I think it was a diriamba, indigenous to the highlands. He, she, waited. She—yes it was a she—had her place on the ceiling. Mine was down below.

Mine since a few weeks before. I'd gone to Mexico for a little peace. There was a novel I had to finish. Through increasing static, La Voz de América was explaining how Ortega was ready to settle with the Contras; the only condition, the U.S. stop sending armaments to those guys—did I really hear him say that? Estos muchachos? I'd been travelling for a few days and news had been happening without me.

I tried to imagine what the spider wanted. Was she watching me? Planning a chomp at my shoulder? But then she'd have pounced while I wasn't looking—if I'd seen her earlier I would've sat somewhere else.

A prickly feeling like a squadron of ants crept down my neck, across my shoulders, along both arms. I sat without moving. I'd had a couple of beers. I found myself asking, But which of us is the uninvited guest?

Time to be brave. I rubbed my arms free of itch, went to the refrigerator, poured another beer, sat down again in the same place and wrote what became the previous six paragraphs. I'd decided, since my friend Arañy up there was keeping the peace, I could trust her. The short-wave crackled. I put words down on paper, thinking clearly, concentrating—

Out of nowhere, I mean I wasn't looking for four or five minutes, two feet from my hand a great struggle exploded. I pushed off fast, landed a couple of meters away, behind me my chair crashed down. On the table, one huge spider, one monster cockroach.

A roach's roach, this one—three inches easy, broad as a fullback with thighs to match, long quivering antennae, stubby wings to give it hoist, manoeuvering power as if trained by dragonflies. In size, an even match-up.

The roach must have reconnoitred the tabletop from the crack along the wall, then advanced in search of my leftovers. When did the spider spot the target? The target, crossing the terrain in secret, infiltrating in the shadow of my papers—

The spider, silent, had dropped from the ceiling; no strategic web for her. She battled the insurgent, close in, strike to the flank—

Slow mighty thrusts from the roach.

The spider, with movement barely perceptible, half-turned. She pressed her chin to the intruder's abdomen. The needle penetrated. A slow final sway of struggle. Paralysis.

The roach lay on its back. The spider grasped it by the gills, lumbered to the edge of the table, dropped with her prey by a line she spun as she went. Static had replaced La Voz de América. The spider ambled out the open door.

In the electric light, a thin glistening thread.

CLAYOQUOT CRACKDOWN
Mass Clearcuts, Mass Trials

Janet McIntyre didn't plan to get arrested. The forty-two-year-old youth worker journeyed to Clayoquot Sound last August "out of curiosity." She wanted to see the ancient trees and the people who pledged to protect them. But when she watched police wrench a handicapped child from its mother's arms to break up a logging road blockade, she knew she had to act. "I was sobbing my brains out," Janet recalls. "The kid was screaming at a pitch that could break windows. Helicopters were swirling overhead. All these cameras were clicking. It was like being in a holocaust or something. And I decided if these women are willing to have this happen to them, then I can too." So Janet sat down.

Janet was one of more than 800 people arrested in Vancouver Island's Clayoquot Sound rainforest last summer and fall. All were charged with criminal contempt of court for allegedly violating a B.C. Supreme Court injunction that forbids obstructing MacMillan Bloedel on a logging road. The ongoing mass trials and jail sentences constitute the largest criminal prosecution of peaceful dissent in the history of this country.

But the portrait grows darker still. The provincial government's Crown counsels are prosecuting the opponents of a multinational logging company whose largest shareholder is the B.C. government. And RCMP admitted in court they gave MacMillan Bloedel Polaroid photos of all arrestees, including their names, addresses, and dates of birth, in exchange for the company's videotape of the daily blockade. Legal experts monitoring the Clayoquot crackdown believe the real defendants on trial are Canada's democratic values and the Charter of Rights.

"Picketing and mass demonstrations, even illegal demonstrations, have an important place in our democratic traditions," says Keith Jobson, a retired law professor from the University of Victoria. "Many Canadians believe the right to peaceful demonstration to be an essential supplement to the parliamentary process, particularly in times when the electoral process appears to be unresponsive to local needs and concerns. Far from the highway to anarchy, demonstrations are seen by many Canadians as a legitimate and treasured common law right and constitutional freedom."

B.C. Supreme Court Justice John Bouck disagreed. "Without the rule of law democracy will collapse," Bouck said last October in sentencing the first forty-four Clayoquot defendants to jail terms ranging from forty-five to sixty days plus fines of $1,000 to $3,000 apiece. "The strongest mob will rule over the weak. Anarchy will prevail," he concluded. That same day in an adjacent courtroom, a man who forced a five-year-old boy to perform oral sex was given a four-month sentence to be served at home on electronic monitoring. Bouck's people had to do their time behind bars.

Newspaper editorials slammed the Clayoquot sentences as unduly harsh. Environmentalists took to the streets asking why none of MacMillan Bloedel's officials has ever been jailed for any of the company's twenty-three environmental convictions. Victoria's federal Liberal candidate (now revenue minister) David Anderson condemned the provincial government for initiating a "vindictive process" and urged that the Clayoquot convicts be pardoned. From Amsterdam, Greenpeace International branded Canada an "international environmental outlaw." And in Clayoquot Sound the arrests continued.

But even more disturbing than the sentences themselves were the conditions under which the defendants were tried. Bouck refused all requests for individual trials, jury trials, and adjournments to allow defendants to find lawyers. As a result, many of the defendants represented themselves with scant understanding of the law throughout their six-week trial.

"The worst mother-raper and father-stabber will get an adjournment to get counsel," said Adrian Chaster, past-president of the B.C. Trial Lawyers Association. But Justice Bouck had no time for such comparisons. In a courtroom announcement that sent journalists scurrying for the Charter, Bouck said the Clayoquot defendants didn't need lawyers because the legal issues in the case were not complex, and because the defendants could read and write and express themselves. Crown counsel Brian Rendell went a step further and told the court the defendants were lucky to be here instead of in some country where protesters standing on the road are shot or disappear.

Columnists and editorial writers were flabbergasted at the daily redefinition of justice emerging from the Victoria law courts. Lawyer Jim Millar unsuccessfully sought a judicial stay of proceedings in the "Kafkaesque" trials, arguing that their continuation "will undoubtedly leave the impression that the attorney general is joined at the hip with MacMillan Bloedel in a judicially sanctioned assault on peaceful dissent."

Indeed, Premier Mike Harcourt's NDP government has been unable to expunge the image of collusion throughout the Clayoquot affair. In February 1993, the provincial government became the largest shareholder in MacMillan Bloedel when Noranda Forest sold off its forty-nine percent stake in the company. In a multi-million-dollar stock buy that was subsequently investigated by both an independent inquiry and the B.C. Securities Commission, the B.C. government acquired 2.1 million shares, increasing its total ownership of MacMillan Bloedel to 3.3 percent.

Two weeks after the stock purchase (and behind closed doors) cabinet made its long-awaited decision on the fate of the Clayoquot rainforest: two-thirds could be logged. MacMillan Bloedel holds most of the cutting rights in Clayoquot Sound, one of the largest temperate rainforests left on Earth. Environmentalists argue that the entire Clayoquot should be preserved so the world will have one remaining blueprint of this ancient and complex ecosystem that is rapidly disappearing.

When the arrests began last July, the province's Crown counsels petitioned the courts to raise the charges from civil to criminal contempt, thereby exposing the arrestees to stiffer sentences and relieving MacMillan Bloedel of hundreds of thousands of dollars of prosecutorial expenses. Judges complied, and by January, half of the 800 arrestees had worked their way through the clogged courts, receiving convictions, fines, and jail sentences—most commonly twenty-one days. The mass trials are scheduled to continue into the summer, just in time to welcome the world to the Commonwealth Games in Victoria. In a desperate bid to distance themselves from the Clayoquot debacle, five government MLAs (including four cabinet ministers) from pro-environment ridings in Greater Victoria sent a collective letter to their constituents shortly after the first sentences were handed down. "It was the courts that commenced and conducted action against the Clayoquot protesters, not the government," the MLAs stated in their two-page letter. Two of the five (environment minister Moe Sihota and forests minister Andrew Petter) are lawyers, as is Premier Harcourt, who verbally defended the letter.

It took the Chief Justice of B.C. Supreme Court to set them straight—and on the front page of every major paper in the province. "The fact is that the proceedings for contempt launched in July were begun and have been conducted by counsel from the Ministry of the Attorney General," Chief Justice William Esson told a packed Victoria courtroom. "We are entitled to expect better from political leaders and lawyers."

One party that has maintained a surprisingly low profile throughout the trials is the B.C. Civil Liberties Association. When contacted for this essay, BCCLA executive director John Westwood said his organization has issued no statement and taken no position regarding alleged civil liberties violations connected to the mass trials or to the injunction itself.

"They seem to be very ably represented," Westwood said of the hundreds of defendants, many of whom are still representing themselves or relying on legal aid lawyers who refuse to meet with them individually. As for the document that started it all, Westwood said: "We didn't discover any problems with the injunction as it was stated, i.e., that it was too broad or anything like that." This comes as a surprise to lawyers and environmentalists.

The validity of MacMillan Bloedel's injunction, whose scope includes the entire public, has been challenged by Greenpeace and the Sierra Legal Defence Fund. The two groups are currently awaiting a ruling from the B.C. Court of Appeal. Courts in Ontario, Manitoba, Saskatchewan, England, Australia, and the United States have all declared this type of injunction invalid precisely because it is too broad. But it will likely take a Supreme Court of Canada ruling to grant British Columbians the same liberties enjoyed by citizens elsewhere.

Many lawyers believe the entire process of a private corporation writing its own law to restrict the general public, and then using that law to trigger criminal prosecution, violates civil liberties. "This is non-legislative law-making," says Victoria lawyer Robert Moore-Stewart, who is representing some of the Clayoquot defendants. "The corporations, through their lawyers, write those laws [i.e., the injunctions], and then go to court and get the judge to sign the corporation-specific law."

Beyond the troubling problems posed by the injunction—problems which the BCCLA is mysteriously oblivious to—most legal experts agree that the criminal contempt charge itself undermines civil liberties and basic principles of justice. The charge of criminal contempt of court is the last surviving criminal offence under common law. It is centuries old, pre-dating the democratic system in which legislatures and not lone judges write the rules for society to live by. Unlike offenses contained in the criminal code, the criminal contempt charge is vaguely defined, the punishment is potentially unlimited, and the defendant has no right to a jury trial. U.S. Supreme Court Justice Hugo Black described the criminal contempt charge as a "despotic power" and "a drastic and perverse mode of administering justice usurping our regular constitutional methods."

So why did the B.C. attorney general's people opt for this despotic power when they could have just as easily charged the protesters under various sections of the criminal code? "These matters should proceed as swiftly as possible," Crown counsel Rendell told Justice Bouck last July in his application to take over the Clayoquot prosecution from MacMillan Bloedel's private lawyers. Charging the protesters under the criminal code would have led to time-consuming jury trials.

"The criminal contempt charge is subject to so many criticisms that people had thought in this day and age neither the Crown nor the courts would be wanting to use it too much," says Jobson. In fact, when Jobson met with senior staff in the attorney general's office to discuss the matter last May, they showed him a copy of their new guidelines "for restraint in the use of criminal contempt charges." But the guidelines must have been converted to parliamentary scratch paper, because the criminal contempt charge shot out of the starting gate before the Clayoquot blockaders could finish their first round of "We Shall Overcome."

But not all the news is bad. "The mass trials have served to catalyse the movement," says Valerie Langer, a director of Friends of Clayoquot Sound, the fifteen-year-old group that organized last summer's protest. "They have made the public more aware of how few rights we have within our public forests. People who have never been involved in forestry issues are getting involved because they're mad—and specifically about the trials."

Some of those people are likely to turn up in Victoria this summer if Friends of Clayoquot Sound proceed with their plan to erect a summer-long protest camp on the legislature lawn. Others have already shown their support by contributing more than $36,000 to the Green Party Defenders Fund, an ingenious scheme whereby the Green Party of Canada uses political contributions to pay the fines of "forest defenders" while reaping a hefty tax credit for the contributors.

"You pay twenty-five dollars—Ottawa pays seventy-five," the Greens announced last fall when they unveiled the fund. (A contribution to a federal political party entitles the donor to a tax credit of seventy-five percent on the first $100 donated, and a lesser percentage thereafter.) Fund coordinator Michael Timney says it's appropriate for the party to use political contributions (earmarked "Defenders") to pay the Clayoquot fines. "These people have essentially been doing the work of the Green Party, since the defence of the forest is Green Party policy," Timney explains.

Rather than foreclosing on public dissent, the Clayoquot trials are clearly galvanizing many Canadians to actively resist unjust authority. Thoreau urged citizens to "Cast your whole vote, not a strip of paper merely, but your whole influence." While Canada's boldest are casting their whole vote in B.C.'s public forests and law courts, the provincial government would do well to remember that a time will also come for British Columbians to cast a strip of paper.

—*An abridged version of this article appeared in* This Magazine, *April-May 1994.*

MURALS

At Long Beach I sit in a plastic lawn
chair facing the ocean, binoculars
raised. I am looking

for a whale. I would like to tell my children
how its gigantic body leapt
out of the waves
graceful as a minnow.
How it slid, a shimmering blade

back into the foam. I do not know
that sitting at the edge
of the Pacific
I am more likely to see an elephant
tapdance on water.
There is much

I don't know—that the last
whales mutated, their flippers transforming
into wings. That they churned
and flapped their tails
until their thunderous dark
bodies rose into the air.
They flew

toward the cities,
up and down the coast
they swam into the sides of tall buildings:
hospitals, banks, insurance companies.
Spread themselves across
the blank canvasses

on every street corner.
A storm whips across the bay.
I have been sitting so long and
I am cold, please someone, tell me
to go home, tell me they are
happy up there

pressed like colossal blue butterflies
against cement walls.

—Read at the Writers for Clayoquot rally in Victoria, October 11, 1993.

FACE TO FACE WITH THE FACELESS ONES

July 26, 1993 Demonstration, Vancouver
"Are you sure there is a vigil happening in front of MacMillan Bloedel today at noon?"

"Yes, at 925 West Georgia."

"Thank goodness. I am in the right place after all." I hang up the pay phone.

After hours of travel by van, ferry, bus, and then foot, with a fourteen-month-old baby on my back, a six-year-old in hand, a diaper bag over one shoulder, and a deer skin drum over the other, it was a relief to know the trip was not in vain. It had been a bit of a panic though. The bus driver had instructed me that the MacMillan Bloedel offices were somewhere down that street—no luck. A bike courier had said, "Well, maybe it is in that building over there," and another had instructed me that, "Yes, possibly in this building, but I think they have offices over in that one too."

Dealing with the "faceless ones" is not easy. There are absolutely no signs inside or outside to indicate the presence of this multinational company. Gazing up the towers, I again clarified my purpose for coming. How can people make truly sane and sensible decisions about the planet when they spend their time in rooms ten stories off the ground, in rooms without natural light and fresh air? How can they decide the fate of trees, life systems, and communities by looking at maps, shuffling papers and watching stock market ups and downs?

With my drum, a small piece of yellow cedar sample from Canada's oldest recorded tree and a pile of stickers of the Planet Earth taken by nasa, I hoped to bring a remembrance of the forest to the rush of downtown Vancouver. I planned to sing the "Old Growth Tree Song" so generously shared by Whis.stem.men.knee (Walking Medicine Robe) with the Red Cedar circle. This song, sung by his ancestors, has a slow beat to remind us of the time it has taken for these trees to grow. The song has low, deep, trailing sounds. They bring us to the healing, green sacred spaces of the forest.

Just the week before, my three young children and I had lain in an ancient forest at dawn recording the flight of marbled murrelets as they flew like shadowy ghosts in and out of the yellow cedars of the Caren Range.* Just maybe the beat of the drum would spark a remembrance of the heartbeat of the Earth. Maybe the beat of the drum would root people long enough to feel in their bones and soul what really matters.

About forty of us gathered on the street corner that hot afternoon. All kinds of signs were set up or worn while petitions, pens, and pamphlets were readily available. As the office towers began draining at lunch hour, workers started their brisk-paced, chattery breaks. Most chose to ignore our presence.

My six-year-old daughter, Katerina, wanted to hand out Earth stickers. She offered them with enthusiasm and determination. At one point a businessman with a briefcase clenched in his hand cleared the path frantically with his free arm. Without breaking his forward fixed gaze, he breathlessly passed, repeating, "*No time, no time, no time.*"

As I continued to beat my drum it sang of time. It made me think how these ancient rainforests connect us to our past, a past even beyond totem poles and cedar canoes. It brought me to the dripping of water off clouds and needles into mossy pools, of light filtering through the canopy in patches, of fungi growing in dark, moist places, of composting needles and trees, of marbled murrelets feeding their young—of something timeless. The drumbeat made me think how these ancient forests connect us to the future, a future beyond my children's children's children. It brought me to the dripping of water, moss, of light, of dark places, of composting and life feeding their young—of something timeless. It brought me to the present. How blessed I was to be drumming in this moment, my daughter holding the planet Earth in her hands.

* *The Caren Range is located behind my home on the Sechelt Peninsula. Two weeks later, Friends of Caren discovered the first active marbled murrelet nest in Canada.*

THE RAVEN AND THE CROW

Clayoquot, this is the raven's world,
Green wind, washed sky,
Sea dancing,
And trees, magnificent.

In court, this is the crow's world now,
Lawyers, black-backed,
Pecking into our lives,
Sifting our passions into argument.

Whose voice, then, should we listen to?
If you seek wisdom
Do not ask the crow.

From STATEMENT TO SENTENCING

As my actions were in no way intended to bring disrepute on this court, I offer the court an apology if it has mistakenly interpreted my actions as disrespectful. In fact, I believed my actions to be entirely in support of the court. I sat on that road to protest the continued abuse of the law by MacMillan Bloedel, a company which has been convicted twenty-three times (with an additional fifty charges still pending) for repeatedly polluting waterways, destroying fish habitat through negligent logging practises, and failing to report chemical spills. Actions which have adversely affected other means of livelihood, posed human health threats, and destroyed one of the world's unique and rare environments.

Still, the decision to be arrested was a difficult one for me to make. I have no previous criminal record of any kind, m'Lord. It was not until the final minutes of the demonstration that I took my place on the road. At that point there were only a dozen or so protesters left on the road, and there was no question that the logging trucks would soon go through. "Why then?" you may ask. "Why go on when it was clear that the day's protest was over?"

I looked upon that road, m'Lord, where the last protesters stood. They stood silently, slightly huddled together as the clouds had rolled in and it was getting cool. They stood there with this long empty space in front of them where 250 people had already been dragged or led away to jail. They stood there knowing that the police would soon be coming for them. In the middle stood Merve Wilkinson and his wife.

Merve Wilkinson is well known to local foresters. He has a long history as a Vancouver Island logger and forester who has set a clear example of how selective logging can be sustainable and non-destructive. I asked myself, 'Why am I not standing on the road beside him?' We both knew that not only are there alternatives, but that the destruction has gone so far that we must demand those alternatives now. We both knew that people can and must live by values which honour their neighbours and the sanctity of all life on the earth.

My body, my spirit, demanded that I act. Some physical and concrete act, no matter how short lived, to oppose the continuing public deception and needless environmental devastation.

That I had to oppose an already existing law is regrettable, yet history is full of examples of immoral laws which were justified and enforced by self-serving political leaders at those times. Slavery, the Final Solution, and Apartheid are just a few which come to mind. To protest those laws would have been engaging in an illegal activity. Yet today, those who did protest are praised for their stand against distorted visions of a just society. History has vindicated those protesters, m'Lord, just as it will vindicate those of us fighting for an open and democratic process and the protection of Clayoquot Sound.

From CRYING LIKE A MOUNTAIN

Shocked. My mind could not accept what my ears had just heard the judge say. I was being sentenced to forty-five days in jail and a fine of $1,500 for peacefully blockading a logging road on public land.

I was in the first group of forty-four protesters to be prosecuted for our participation in the Clayoquot Sound blockades of the summer of 1993. Certainly I expected to face the due consequences of my actions, but to receive a sentence comparable to that of a violent crime dissolved any confidence I had left in the legal system. In fact the whole mass trial process where one man presided in an autocratic manner, where our individual rights were repeatedly denied, had already drastically lowered my opinion of the courts.

From A RENEWED RESPECT FOR THE COURT

The judge's first words to the Reverend Graeme Brownlee and those other defendants who appeared with him in person in the Victoria Court House on November 3 were, "I am going to find you guilty."

The atmosphere was quiet and respectful and any tension that may have been felt by the accused was not evident. One sensed that here were a judge, officers of the court, defendants, and their advocates, who had been together for several days and had come to respect each other's integrity. . . .

In his judgement, Mr. Justice Murphy referred to Graeme's eloquence. Graeme had said, in part, "My Lord, for me the issue is deeply religious, deeply theological. It is a question of the relationship of the Creator to the Creation. It is a matter of our responsibility to our Creator. It is a question of rendering to Caesar the things that are Caesar's and to God the things that are God's. I chose to block access to the Kennedy River bridge because I chose the latter."

—*From an article by Peter Lucas in* The Diocesan Post, *Victoria, December, 1993. Reverend Brownlee, from Kindersley Parish in Saskatchewan, was the first ordained person to be arrested at Clayoquot Sound.*

A RESOLUTION FROM THE 38TH SESSION OF THE [ANGLICAN] SYNOD OF THE DIOCESE OF BRITISH COLUMBIA (1939)

That the Synod of the Diocese of British Columbia deplores the wasteful methods of logging in vogue on Vancouver Island, and the Coast generally, and the consequent destruction of the valuable forest resource upon which so much employment depends, together with irreparable damage to the watersheds and spawning grounds; and further expresses the hope that early steps will be taken to enforce selective logging in order that a large measure of waste may be eliminated and immature timber saved from destruction.

The Synod would urge that re-afforestation and the protection of the forests against fire receive immediate attention, and pleads for a forest policy which will ensure a perpetual timber yield and ensure better prospects of continued employment for the people of British Columbia.

CLAYOQUOT TESTIMONY OF THE ISLANDERS
MARCH 10-11, 1994

They planted themselves like trees in the courtoom
Standing their ground, rooted in their experience,
Towering upward and outward
They spoke from their depths.

Listen. You have to listen.
This is the wilderness calling
This is the cry of the earth.

—*The Islanders were mostly from upper Vancouver Island, as well as Denman, Hornby, and Lasqueti Islands.*

MY LEARNED FRIEND

In hindsight, I suppose that I should have been at least a bit suspicious when Legal Aid assigned me a lawyer who introduced himself as Clayton Greenspan.

He was a rumpled-looking fellow of indeterminate age. He wore a baggy suit, and I don't believe I've ever seen a tie more splashed with soup stains than his. But the enormous leatherette valise he dragged around bulged with so many files and books I couldn't help but be impressed.

He gave me precise and unequivocal instructions: "You don't say anything. This is a difficult and complex case. Lots of precedents. Lots of technicalities. I'll do the talking. Understood?"

At the time this seemed like an eminently sensible strategy.

There were about fifty of us defendants in the case. That first morning at court, I couldn't help but notice that I appeared to be the only one of the entire group who was not either a Raging Granny or a kid wearing dreadlocks and at least one nose ring.

About thirty seconds before the judge is scheduled to enter, Clayton realizes he's misplaced his robes. He dashes out of the courtroom while the judge comes in the other door, and we all rise to the solemn invocation, "Order in court!"

You could tell right away that this judge is not a happy camper. He glowers down at us defendants as if each of us is Clifford Olson. As he sits down, I recognize, and instantly empathize with, the unmistakable wince of a chronic hemorrhoid sufferer.

Clayton finally reappears. He's swaddled in obviously-borrowed robes big enough to fit Shaquille O'Neal. Before we even get to enter our pleas, Clayton pops up to present a preliminary motion.

The judge looks down at him like he's a cockroach. Then the judge says, "Go ahead, make my day."

Totally unperturbed, Clayton introduces a motion for adjournment on the basis of what he calls "a collateral attack on the injunction."

By this time I'm beginning to feel a tremendous surge of admiration for Clayton's courage. Still, I'm not entirely convinced that this collateral attack is such a good idea. Neither is the judge. He brushes it off like it's dandruff. Then we adjourn for lunch.

We head over to the Cherry Bank. Clayton knocks back a couple of bourbons. Then he splashes a bowl of onion soup all over Shaquille's robes.

By now he's really wound up. He keeps telling us what a sympathetic judge we've got. How things are looking up. How he, Clayton, has developed several ingenious lines of defense.

I try to explain to Clayton that I'm into Gandhi, that I want to plead guilty and accept my punishment as an integral part of civil disobedience.

Clayton finishes with a Napoleon brandy.

Somehow he convinces me that the Crown can't possibly identify me from the polaroids and videotape. "They can't tell John Doe from Joe Schmoe," is how he puts it. Then he plunks down his brandy snifter and dashes back across Burdette.

After that, the whole thing became one long and hopelessly Byzantine litigious blur. I felt like I was channel surfing across endless episodes of *Perry Mason*, *L.A. Law,* and *Street Legal*.

I do remember this: Clayton fought like a tiger every step of the way. He fought on the question of identity, and lost. He challenged the validity of the injunction, and lost. In what seemed to me a brilliant tactical gambit, he introduced a defense of necessity. The judge sneered at him. Then Clayton mounted a mighty bulwark he called "the defense of justification." The judge almost bit his head off. For the first time, Clayton seemed to stumble just a bit, to be slightly unsure of his footing. "But my Lord," he spluttered, *"mens rea!"*

Finally, backed seemingly to the brink of legal oblivion, Clayton played a last, desperate card: The Charter. The judge's laughter rang through the courtroom, eerily reminiscent of Jack Nicholson.

After each defeat, we retreated to the embracing confines of the Cherry Bank. No matter how dismal, no matter how disheartening the day's proceedings might have been, no matter how thorough the thrashing we'd been administered, after several bourbons, Clayton took heart.

He became convinced that the juridical tide had turned. That the Crown was in disarray. That our complete vindication was at hand.

As the days dragged on, I found myself caring less and less about my own fate, and worrying more and more about poor Clayton's. There was no mistaking the evidence that here was a man tumbling into emotional crisis.

He took to calling me late at night, long after I'd gone to bed, to whisper conspiratorially into the phone that at last he'd found the smoking gun he'd been looking for.

He began calling the Cherry Bank waitresses "my learned friends."

Suddenly, unexpectedly, he seemed to me entirely vulnerable, desperately fragile. What did it matter in the overall scheme of things if I were sentenced to some absurd electronic monitoring, ordered to pay some Mickey Mouse fine—here was a brave and noble human being falling to pieces before my eyes.

I remember well the fateful day of judgment. The judge, mounted splendidly beneath a coat of arms bearing the motto, *Dieu et mon Droit,* solemnly pronounced all of us, as we'd known weeks ago he would, guilty of criminal contempt of court.

As the judgement was rendered, Clayton gasped audibly. I saw his shoulders sag. His body was wracked by a series of tiny, heart-rending little tremors. His face—I could see it only in profile—seemed galvanized in astonished disbelief.

Afterwards, I led him sobbing from the courtroom. We found sanctuary in the adjoining jury room. Clayton collapsed entirely into my arms, sobbing spasmodically.

"Thank you, Clayton," I said over and over, seeking to assuage his awful pain. "Thank you," I repeated, knowing that I held in my arms a man plunged pitilessly into a dark night of the soul, from which there might never be complete redemption. "Thank you for everything."

And through his tears, magnificent even in defeat, triumphant at the very doorstep of despair, Clayton sobbed, almost inaudibly: "Just wait! Just wait till sentencing. We'll win out then, I'm sure. But don't you say anything. Don't say a word! It's a very complex case. I'll look after it. I'll look after everything."

—Part of a satire performed for a group of lawyers in Victoria at a benefit for the Clayoquot Resource Centre.

BLEEDING HEARTS

Much has been made of the tremendous cost being incurred by this government as a result of our arrests. But our campaign too, is being bled—and the blood is money, time, and a diluted non-violence.

We are watering down our truth, our focus, and our ethical stance. And with all due respect to our learned friends, much of this must be attributed to the nature of our involvement with the legal process.

We said we would be open, yet won't admit our identity; we publicly broke the law and then try to pretend we didn't; we said we'd accept our fate but act surprised when the state strikes back; we chose the fight and then react like victims; we said we'd respect all beings, but insult judges, sneer at politicians, and deride SHARE "fanatics"; we are trying to pressure the state, but assume everyone needs their fines paid; we are urged to play the legal game, yet every one of us loses anyway.

It seems to me inconsistent with the principles of non-violence and civil disobedience to "try to get off" in any way other than appeals to the Defense of Necessity, the judgment at Nuremburg, or some personal higher law.

Perhaps we should not only admit our identity and actions, but insist that we were there if there is any doubt. Maybe jail wouldn't be such a bad thing. Maybe we should gracefully accept every escalation by our "opponents" with genuine understanding and good humour. Maybe we should free up some of our lawyers so they can apply themselves where they are perhaps needed more. Maybe we should get on with our resistance.

RÉSISTANCE EN THE COURTS

It's often safer to be in chains than to be free.
—Franz Kafka, The Trial

When we commit acts of civil disobedience, we dictate the terms—we choose the place, the time, the shape of the monkey-wrench we throw into the works. We choose the chants, the songs, the costumes. We decide where the bodies will be placed. For the duration of the action, we create our own human space in the body of destruction. Our voices are loud or silent by our own choosing. Our clothes are colourful, or waterproof, or chosen for comfort in action. We hold hands, clasp arms, embrace our comrades, those we love and even those we don't particularly like—the risk and the action unifies us.

Then we are hauled off to police stations and jail, and while what happens there is a little less under our control, we are still able to carry the spirit of the action with us. Often we are crammed together in tiny cells. We make jokes, sing political songs off-key, leave our marks of bravery on the walls with chalk among the marks of desperation left in blood by people not as fortunate as us to be able to choose to be arrested. When we leave the police station, we walk into the arms of our singing cheering companions.

Then we go to court, weeks, usually months later. Suddenly, the tables are turned. We are most definitely not on our turf.

The courtroom is clean, peopled with three-piece suits, careful haircuts, and subdued voices. The benches are arranged in rows, facing the judge, not in a circle to give everyone equal input. The list of behaviours not allowed—no talking, no singing, no reading, no gum chewing, no dancing, no hugging, no talking back—is longer than the list of ones that are.

The judge is every authority we've ever run up against in our lives—father, principal, priest, doctor. All the behaviours we've learned over the years for dealing with these figures of authority come into play when we are summoned before the judge. We cease being free people, and revert to being frightened, shameful children.

The courts are not a benign bystander in the process of repressing resistance. Our fear of standing naked before authority is used against us in so many ways. It ties us to expensive legal bills as we give away our right and ability to speak for ourselves. It makes us *feel* guilty, makes us want to prove that we *are* worthy of the master's approval. Songs die on our lips. We find ourselves wanting to grovel. Gone is our courage, our control, the power of action.

The challenge before us as resisters is to keep in mind the integral role the courts play in keeping people repressed and obedient, and to use that knowledge to extend our action from the streets to the courtroom. Our challenge as non-violent activists is to see the humanity behind these tools of oppression.

Discussions of the court experience, even performing courtroom role-plays during our civil resistance preparation, can be useful, as can sharing our experiences of and reactions to authority. We can wage a political trial, introducing testimony from those affected by the oppression our action has resisted. We can make "creative" pleas—instead of the usual guilty or not-guilty, we can plead, for example, for an end to injustice or environmental destruction. We can stand up for our own people, and remain seated for the judge.

At the heart of these actions, however, must lie our own sense of integrity. We did the action that brought us to the court, of our own choice, in our own name. When we appear before a judge, it is our own integrity as resisters and as human beings that will permit us to stand as tall as we are physically able, to look the judge in the eye, and to take whatever "punishment" is handed out with strength, courage, and dignity.

There is no dignity in co-operation with evil, the banal, or the blood-thirsty. When we refuse to play the game of accepting community service or electronic surveillance, when we show ourselves unafraid of the harshest penalties the courts can give us, then and only then will we be truly free.

I began this article with a quote from Franz Kafka, partly because his way of looking at the courts and authority should not be different from our own, but also because the notion of freedom being unsafe is accurate. A free person does not fit in. A free person is not accepted. A free person is ultimately shunned by the society still in bondage.

However, if we truly value all that enslavement has to offer, would we have been resisting in the first place?

CLAYOQUOT EDITORIAL

I want to say thank you to the convicted Clayoquot protesters. While many of us were busy changing the baby, paying the mortgage, or cutting the lawn, you cared enough to take a stand. You cared enough about our environment, our economic future, and true justice to take a stand.

You join the ranks of others who have stood for land, against the state. I wish I could tell you that your efforts will be recognised and your names remembered. Then, who could have known at the time that "criminals" of the past, like Chief Joseph, Geronimo, or Louis Riel, would be remembered and their actions recognised as heroic in the eyes of history.

Your actions may also be called heroic. To stand for what you believe in, what many of us believe in, at a personal sacrifice, is the act of a leader. You are leaders for the many of us who feel as you do, but for our own reasons, are not able to stand as tall as you. Politicians know that a letter of criticism is representative of many dozens of votes. So I ask you, if over 700 are willing to be arrested, how many do you truly represent?

In the end it is not the provincial government, the federal government, or MacMillan Bloedel who you are responsible to. We all answer to our conscience and the Creator. History will truly judge your actions. Perhaps one day even the descendants of those who now persecute you will acknowledge and benefit from your actions.

There are times when the state is not just in its application of justice. In these times it is on the shoulders of the people to do what is just, in the interest of our earth, our children, and our true system of democracy.

The provincial government of British Columbia has shamed us on the international stage with its partisan application of "justice." Who will not question the Province buying 2.1 million shares of MacMillan Bloedel stock just two months before announcing the "Clayoquot Compromise"?

We in B.C. will be judged justifiably harshly for its mass approach to court proceedings, like leading cattle to slaughter. Am I wrong, or is a right to a "fair" trial not one of our basic rights in this country?

The court had made a grave error in mistaking civil disobedience for criminal intent. Clearly a group of bureaucrats in blue suits and red ties has met in some musty Victoria office and decided to set an example for anyone who thinks they can interfere with the wishes of the Province.

Civil disobedience is the last peaceful position to be undertaken by citizens wishing to influence the decision-making process in a democracy. Contrary to Judge Bouck's reasons for sentencing, Mahatma Gandhi did not invent civil disobedience, he only popularized it.

Judge Bouck believes that civil disobedience is not needed in a democ-

racy when in fact a country with some level of democracy is the only place it can work. Countries with more oppressive regimes drive the people underground into stronger, more direct measures.

Peaceful civil disobedience is not a crime, but a responsibility of citizens in a democracy. History has proven time and time again the just cause of the Native peoples of North America in past confrontations with the American and Canadian governments. Who today would defend the Indian Residential Schools, or the oppressive Anti-Potlatch Law?

When the needs of the earth and the people are set aside for the short-term corporate profit, civil disobedience becomes a democratic responsibility.

It is understandable that the B.C. government desires to look out for the interests of MacMillan Bloedel; it is after all a major shareholder, and also has an interest in the short-term gains from the Clayoquot timber. Never mind that the future economic well-being and determination of this Province has been handed over to companies like MacMillan Bloedel through Tree Farm Licenses.

Basically this means that the forestry resource is controlled by multinational corporations, and not the people of B.C. Does anyone really believe they have our natural resources and our long-term well-being in mind?

We should be clear that the logging industry is desirable, necessary, and a viable part of the B.C. economy. What is being questioned are the motives and accountability of the Province and its corporate cousins. What is unfortunate is that business interests have promoted the perception that we must log our old-growth today to ensure employment; short-sighted and questionable logic.

Once there were eighty-nine pristine watersheds on Vancouver Island; after the Clayoquot is logged, we will have five. Will we be debating the last one some day soon? Will the "tree-huggers" be trying to protect the last old growth tree one day not far off?

I have trouble imagining that there will be jobs in the forest industry for my children when they grow up. As part of the Nuu-chah-nulth Nation, I fear they will never see one of the great wilderness areas, and that of their ancestral land, only a fraction will remain.

Over time the stance taken by the convicted Clayoquot protesters will come to be viewed as the correct one, benefiting all future generations of B.C. citizens. For myself and my children I thank them for their sacrifice.

THE TREE SPEAKS

Get off my back,
I've had it up to here
with the humans,
let me grow old in peace,
fall over and die gracefully;
though I sometimes think
a quick cut of the chainsaw
is better than death by fire,
always a possibility.
Suffering. We know about
suffering. Growth is suffering.
But you know that.
And don't give me your stupid
human hugs. Listen to me now,
talking out of character like
a member of the human race,
look what you've brought me to,
so low that I'm only a foolish
projection of some old woman poet.

I have to listen to the ants,
beetles, lichen, chipmunks, mosses,
moulds, using my bark—and don't strip
it off me for your baskets, either.
Do you hear the raven up there
in my top-most boughs, tricking
and treating? I like that, I like
the feel of all that.

No, I don't want your hugs, I'm
sorry, or the chainsaw gangs,
or tongues of flame. Don't want
this poisoned voice. That old
woman poet can have it back.
For obvious reasons,
I've got to save my breath.

Let me winter back into pure
tree-life, species specific,

blowin' in the wind,
uttering only rarely a bleak,
humanoid word
of thanks, of praise.

CUT

I lie on Tofino soil
inhaling light.

Trees exhale my body.

JUST VISITING

The Police arrested magic, and magic went with them.
—Buffy Sainte-Marie

The Nanaimo Correctional Institute is nestled in a second-growth fir forest on a slope overlooking Brannen Lake. With its flat, windowless buildings surrounded by a high, chain-link fence, it looked more like a suburban elementary school than a prison. I pressed the button at the main gate. "Good morning. I'm here to visit a prisoner."

No answer.

"I guess I'm a bit early. Is this the right place?" I stared at the metal box, wondering if it was connected to anyone. I felt vulnerable standing there, unable to see whomever might be silently observing me.

"Visitation doesn't begin until 10," the louvred metal box barked. "Wait at the gate on your left." There, a sign informed me that only previously declared items would be allowed in; all other items would be considered contraband. Did that mean they could seize my case? I went back to the louvred box.

"Can I bring in my tape recorder and camera?"

"No."

"How about a book for the prisoner?"

"Title?"

"*Light in August* by William Faulkner."

"You can always try," the voice said, nearly drowned out by sounds of rude laughter in the background.

I locked my camera and tape recorder in the car, then waited at the gate with Barbara. She had called me the night before, having heard I was going to interview a Clayoquot protester, and asked me for a lift to the prison to visit her brother. At first I felt a little apprehensive about associating with the kind of people who visit prisons, but I consented. On the drive out, I learned that she and her brother had emigrated from Poland, and that he was serving time for blocking logging trucks at Kennedy Lake bridge. She was a young, dark-haired woman with a stoic demeanour. I asked her how she felt about her brother getting arrested.

"At first I was angry with him," she said in slow, careful English. "But after I visited the protest camp, I knew he had done the right thing." Then she explained how, on a sudden impulse, she joined the blockade and got arrested herself. She was awaiting trial. "In Poland there are no wild forests left," she continued, "so I had never seen one until I came to Clayoquot." She brushed her long hair aside and looked into my eyes. "In Poland there is an eight hundred years old tree—" She faltered. "It is the only one left. They keep it guarded inside a fence. To us this is very important. Do you see?"

At 10 a.m., a guard with a massive belly cantilevered over his trouser belt sauntered up to the gate and let us in with the small cluster of other visitors. He led us into a room that looked like a school cafeteria, painted mould green and egg-yolk white. I waited until all the prisoners had entered and greeted their guests.

One slightly-built man stood alone, patiently looking about the room. I was surprised by how young he looked. I introduced myself. We shook hands and sat at one of the tables. Christopher Phillips had short hair and a three-day-old beard. He wore, as all the prisoners did, baggy, faded-green overalls with numerous tears and missing buttons. Our talk was occasionally interrupted by the squawking sounds of guards telling jokes to each other over their radios.

Chris was twenty-one years old. He grew up in Nova Scotia and had come to British Columbia last March. He joined the blockade and was arrested July 19. His trial began August 30 and lasted seven weeks. Chris answered all my questions with gentle confidence, and without embellishment. Whenever he paused, he quietly contemplated the others in the room. I took an instant liking to him. I estimated about half the prisoners in the room were Clayoquot protesters, and felt the strong bond that existed between them. Barbara and her brother, who talked excitedly at the next table, smiled at us when we looked at them.

Chris said the trial was the most difficult part to endure. He and a few others chose to bypass lawyers so they could voice their reasons for blocking the logging road. He said he thought this annoyed the judge, who he believed gave them harsher sentences than if they'd had lawyers. The defendants in that first mass trial received jail terms from forty-five to sixty days and fines from $1,000 to $3,000. He was one of twenty-two prisoners who refused bail and home electronic monitoring.

I asked him how he was managing in jail. "Not bad," he said. "A bit rough at first. There was a lot of tension with the other prisoners. They're different from us. We're polite to them. Some of them are to us. A lot of them are also political prisoners; they just don't know it yet. Now that they're getting to know us, they agree with what we're doing."

Before the Clayoquot protesters could get too friendly with the other prisoners, officials separated them. To alleviate overcrowding, they had to open up two new blocks down by the lake for the female protesters. Chris said that the cook now gave them what "passes for vegetarian food."

There was one incident, Chris said. All prisoners were required to work from 8 a.m. to 3:30 p.m., with frequent military-like inspections. One day they were told to hack some bushes, and someone in their group didn't approve of it. A guard was sent for, but by the time he got there, the incident was settled and everyone had agreed to go back to work. "But by then it was too late," said Chris, "because this particular guard really overreacted, and started shouting, 'Your name is Inmate! My name is Sir!' Then we all refused to submit to him. So four of us were sent to the digger [solitary confinement]. It was horrible. The cells were six by six feet. A bolted door with a panel to let in a little light. No furniture. Just a bucket. I could hear some prisoner screaming insanely."

They were let out a few hours later. After that, the overreacting guard calmed down, as though someone had talked with him. Chris thought some high official ordered the guards to back off to avoid trouble. "The politicians have passed the Clayoquot problem right down to the correctional system. Most of the guards admit this institution really doesn't correct anyone. In fact," Chris said in a low voice, "some guards are sympathetic to our cause, now that they know us."

I asked him who in particular, but he said he didn't want to get anyone in trouble. I assured him I wouldn't disclose any names; I just wanted to interview them discreetly. Chris looked around and said, "They may have this place bugged. Let me use your pencil." He wrote a name on my pad and quickly handed it to me.

Chris's conviction was to be appealed in March 1994, based on the grounds that the mass trial denied the defendants their right to be heard. It was to have been attended only by judges and lawyers. But Chris has already served his time and, by not admitting his guilt, he isn't legally restricted from taking part in future protests. But his main reason for refusing bail is that by contributing to the crowded prison conditions he might save another protester from being arrested. Still, he doesn't begrudge those who accept bail or agree to be electronically monitored at home. "Most people have families and jobs and aren't able to do what I can."

Chris thanked me for the book, and said he had lots of time to read it. He didn't need anything else, had no regrets, no doubts, except—"Sometimes I wonder if anyone knows we're in here."

Walking out the gate, I suddenly felt happy. I thought about all the people who say this generation is apathetic. It isn't so. Thank you, Chris. I'll tell them.

CATCH AND RELEASE

*You're not supposed to watch a tree fall. You have to turn your back to allow the
spirit to escape. Trees have spirits. Everything has a spirit.*
  —Mary Hayes, Clayoquot Band

A calm attends October's drowsy creek
suspended in the alder canopy
over the pooled, residual water.

In the bird noise, the sporadic rattling
down of a brittle leaf, you can stand long enough
for crayfish to emerge and proceed, experiencing

every inch of the streambed beneath—
their progress so deliberate and complete

to seem always destination. A shift
of weight to the other foot and there

we are too, self-aware not a second too long
for a view just wide of the minnow. What is it

causes that imperceptible
break in rhythm on the stair, the precautionary
countermanded half-step/almost stumble

in my mental gait?
Here is thinking gone under bewareness

that nonetheless confesses to intrusion
of its shadow, and a stick's probe

near the reflex. Speedy in retreat
those antennae for trout-rise, the protruding

snout of the turtle, dimple of rain,
exorcize the dry spell, swing back

to the snagged fir in the roped-off area, anticipate
the night of wind and rain it will crash

through our sleep, the morning of plash
and hustle beneath the bridge we wake

with relief in the next world, the only one
alive to itself and our longing.

Our understanding of wilderness needs to be engaged in profoundly personal ways if the necessary political activity is to have long-term significance. Part of my work in this poem is to make Mary Hayes' enigmatic statement comprehensible on my terms; to meditate upon it with a respect and scepticism that is appropriate to its oblique, even playful "meaning." It seems to me something of a koan. What does it mean to "turn your back on the falling tree"? This is in interesting contrast to the Workers' Compensation Board's advice in The Fallers' and Buckers' Handbook, *for example. But it is also in contrast to the conventional environmental wisdom which stresses committed, focussed, political attention to logging. Why, and to where, does the "spirit" escape?*

The Hayes quote is from a statement accompanying photographs of her in a show of photos of Native Chiefs and Elders touring B.C. in the summer of 1993.

From A COPERNICAN REVOLUTION

I believe that we, at the close of this millennium, are in the throes of another Copernican revolution.* There was much disruption during the previous one. Many people suffered and some died agonizingly for claiming the heliocentric view that the earth revolves around the sun rather than the geocentric view that everything revolves around the earth. Similarly, many of us are now suffering for claiming the biocentric view that humans are a part of nature rather than the ego or anthropocentric view that "man is the measure of all things."

However, there are two main differences between then and now. Now, burning at the stake is not necessary: our co-dependent legal system uses more subtle methods (severe fines and imprisonment) whose result, they hope, will be the same—silence of those who try to change the status quo. Secondly, the results of resisting the new view of reality in this Copernican revolution are not theoretical, as before, but practical. If we continue to think that we are the pinnacle of creation, with power over everything and the right to destroy nature at whim, the results will range from loss of bio-diversity, beauty, destroyed "resources," to collapse of civilizations and death of our species as well as of most others.

Our species is not the centre of the universe, nature is not ours to dominate and destroy because we need a dishwasher or another car. We are a part of nature. Realization of this will do much to stem the Cartesian loneliness and contemporary alienation that afflicts us as we hurry to buy and consume more things in order to relieve this spiritual wasteland—called modern society—that we live in.

As a physician, I liken what is happening in the forests today to what was happening in families twenty years ago—that is, the problem of abuse. Just as twenty years ago, those in power denied physical and sexual abuse in families to the extent of mentally incarcerating those who spoke out, now the physical and spiritual abuse of our forests and streams is officially denied to the extent of physically incarcerating the ones who bring this message.

* *For more on this, see the Epilogue in Richard Tarnas' excellent book* The Passion of the Western Mind *(Ballantine, 1991).*

A LITTLE SOMETHING IN THE MAIL
ABOUT ELECTION TIME

If Harry and Hilda Smith should wake up one day
with a great idea about changing the political map
of the world, Harry or Hilda (whoever rises first
to put it into effect) should be placed on a small island
in a large lake of cold water, but every ordinary
comfort available at hand.
Now, in order to deliver their idea to any other soul
beyond the immediate family, Harry or Hilda
must swim across to the nearest telephone
booth, there to find instead of any telephonic device—
pen, envelope and paper. The glue for the stamp
must be very clearly poisoned and kept
where there is no other source of moisture bar
the tongue's.

All this, of course, is an improvisation on the messenger myth.

If Harry or Hilda Smith can bring his or her self to give their idea
the last lick of conviction, the sender of the good news
dies.

If Harry or Hilda can persuade any other Hilda
or Harry to lick and mail it, the original Harry or Hilda will have
committed murder and suffer the full consequence of the law
for their persuasion.

This is how we must address all our good ideas.

From THE HOUSE THAT JACK BUILT

Set: The back porch of a house in a new subdivision just outside Toronto. The stage is empty except for two rockers and a screen for slide projections. Under JENNY's chair is a capacious, old-fashioned knitting bag and a book. Under JACK's chair, a catalogue, two bottles of beer, a pair of binoculars.

Characters: JACK: A young man from Kapuskasing. JENNY: A young woman from Kapuskasing, married to Jack.

Lights go down, the whirr of the slide projector is heard. A slide of a forest is projected, aerial view, acres of trees. Lights up.

JACK: We had it as good as it comes. We was like a couple of love birds. Back then—
JENNY: Every year we'd go to the CNE—
JACK: Seasons tickets to the Blue Jays, not one, two, one for me, one for her—good seats, cost a fortune, smuggle in a six-pack—
JENNY: The home exhibition, the horse show, the fall fair at Orangeville, and at Hallowe'en we'd go down to the front of our building and hand out candy to the kids, in costume—me as a witch and him as a ghoul, every year—
JACK: Slow down. That was when we lived on Queen.
JENNY: Downtown.
JACK: Right. Living downtown's no good. No good for your lungs. Bad air. You live in a couple of rooms downtown, what do you know about spring? . . . So I built her a house. I mean, what more can a man do for his wife? You meet a girl. It's too soon, high school, but what can you do when she's the right one. Chew on your fingernails? Jerk yourself off? No. You buy her a ring, right? You buy her a ring and then you marry her. You do it right. You work for her, and you just have to hope she doesn't get herself pregnant before you've got her a house. . . . I bought the land in the spring. There was turtles out there. One day I saw maybe thirty turtles on the other side of the swamp. Before it got drained. They took the turtles away. They didn't die or nothin'. They didn't kill 'em. I know that. They loaded them up and took them away. To the zoo maybe. Someplace.

[Slide view of forest from the ground, burgeoning summer growth.]

JENNY: This is it?

JACK: What's wrong with it?

JENNY: It's wet.

JACK: Of course it's friggin' wet, what do you expect?

JENNY: It's a swamp.

JACK: Where else are you gonna find a fifty-foot frontage?

JENNY: What's that noise?

JACK: It's frogs, that's all. Just friggin' frogs. And traffic.

JENNY: What about a basement?

JACK: You want a basement?

JENNY: It's too wet for a basement.

JACK: You want a basement, you'll get a basement. . . .

JENNY: All these trees.

JACK: Yes. They said this is the only red maple swamp in—I dunno—This is the only red maple swamp.

JENNY: All those trees!

JACK: You don't like trees?

JENNY: Reminds me of Kapuskasing.

JACK: We don't have red maples in Kap.

JENNY: They gonna cut them down?

JACK: Sure. Course they'll cut them down.

JENNY: I dunno.

JACK: *[Leans forward.]* Billy and me, see, we got the foundations in in six weeks. 1750 square feet.

[Slide changes to a single tree in winter.] . . .

JACK: We'd been moved in three months—three months and we didn't even—not once. And we used to do it every night. I mean, how are you supposed to start a family if you don't—well, you know! *[Pause.]* I bought a futon for the guest room so that if my mom or her mom and dad wanted to come down for Christmas—we never had the room for them on Queen. Someone told me a futon's the thing to buy. So I bought it.

JENNY: It smells like earth. Like layin' on old roots. I might as well be layin' in the yard.

JACK: *[Hopefully.]* You don't have to sleep on it.

JENNY: I don't mind. *[She rocks.]* It was the first time I ever slept on my own in my whole life. I bought a poster of Meryl Streep.

JACK: She bought this poster of Meryl Streep. I took it down and hung it in our room. If she wanted to sleep with Meryl Streep that was okay with me, but I didn't see why I should be left out of the action, right?

JENNY: *[Staring straight ahead.]* I love you.

JACK: I love you too.

[Slide changes to a placard reading "Save The Frogs."]

JACK: One thing about not having a sidewalk you don't have to shovel it in winter!
JENNY: You never shovelled it on Queen!
JACK: We had a ton of snow that year. *[They rock.]*
JENNY: They drained the swamp. Endangered species include two varieties of orchid under our driveway. Mud puppies right where the double sink is—they're dying out. They use them for research. A Canada Goose nest under the garage. Geese mate for life. Treefrogs, Fowler's toads, lungless salamanders. Bullfrogs. We eat their legs. A frog. Does not. Drink up. The pond. In which he lives.
JACK: She found the first placard when it melted. Yeah. She musta been rooting around out there on the street. When I was at work. Yeah. When the snow melted. It was somethin' to do with frogs.
JENNY: Save the frogs!
JACK: The frogs didn't come back that first spring.
JENNY: *[Yells, full voice.]* Save the frogs!
JACK: I guess they found someplace else or they got sucked down the sluicepipe or somethin'. The frogs didn't come back but the woman who started it did. She came knockin' on our door. What do they want? It's done. Number 23 Pine Crescent. A whole friggin' street. It's done. Thirty-two houses with double garages and porch lights—fire hydrants, water and sewage. It's done, right? If I didn't do it, someone else would. Right? *[Rocks.]*
JENNY: Save the swamps!
JACK: It gave her somethin' to do. Didn't bring no money in, but I didn't say nothin'. She was on the phone for hours to this one and that one. Then I'd come home and there'd be all these women in rubber boots in our kitchen. I didn't say nothin'. *[JENNY rocks.]* First she baked for them. Then she started organizin'. She organized walks. She organized petitions— we had pamphlets up to the ceiling in the living room. She got guest speakers in, wine and cheeses, she even got her name in the *Star*. Up to then she'd never organized a friggin' raffle and all of a sudden that's all there was. Organizin'. And I'd come home and there'd be all these women leavin' coffee rings on my oak finish.
JENNY: *[Dismissing him.]* Oh, Jack!
JACK: The papers are full of protests. Nobody reads them. Who cares? It's done. You gotta live with it. Don't you know that? It's done!

JENNY: Their ancestry can be traced back twenty-six million years.
JACK: It's too late.
JENNY: If you stand in the bush and run your finger along the teeth of a comb, a frog will answer. *[JACK belches.]* When they're displaced they always return back to the place where they lived. They keep returning back for ten years.
JACK: She moved back into our room. Me and her and Meryl Streep. Things improved. As long as we didn't hafta talk too much things were more like they used to be. I never asked her what she did with her day no more.
JENNY: *[Shrugs.]* I never go back to Queen. Even when I have to go downtown I walk other streets.
JACK: I mean, how many guys would wanna come home from the shop floor and talk about frogs, right?
JENNY: They often lose part of their tail to escape an enemy but a new one grows back.
JACK: Hey—what did the leper say to the prostitute? You can keep the tip! You can keep— *[JACK laughs, looks at JENNY expectantly. No response.]* You see? I mean, I'm the one who wouldn't go huntin', she's the one used to tell me I was chicken. She was never interested in nature. *[Suddenly, violently, to JENNY.]* You coulda stopped me! *[JENNY rocks with her eyes closed.]* I put in a clothesline and built the steps up to it to make it easy for her. I brought in topsoil. Got a vegetable garden dug in out the back. It was a bit wet. So what? I bought her a freezer so she could freeze 'em. And all the time she was out there with those women, goin' on about 'Environmental Corridors'! *[Shuts his eyes tight.]*

[Slide changes. A cross-section of a tree trunk, showing the rings.]

JACK: It was the next spring. The next spring that they came back. *[JENNY suddenly becomes alert.]* They were in the basement. Just a few of them at first. Cute little green ones.
JENNY: Oh look, Jack!
JACK: Then they moved into the kitchen.
JENNY: I told you they'd keep comin' back!
JACK: The living room. They sat down to meals with us. *[JENNY draws her feet up, scared.]* *[Opening his eyes and getting into it.]* She went up to Kap for a visit and when she came back I told her they were in all the cupboards, in the sink—when you sat on the toilet—
JENNY: Where? Where?
JACK: I told her they were in the bedroom. They were jumpin' and

crawlin' all over Meryl Streep's face. They were in the friggin' bed. *[Jumps to his feet.]* The whole friggin' house is overrun! The whole street! *[JENNY screams.]* Like a slimy green rug, heavin' under your feet—and when you walk on it you feel it squelch—you feel it under your feet, and then you're up to your knees in it and then it's up to your chin. They're on your shoulders, in your ears—they're takin' over! It's frogs! Your friggin' frogs! JENNY: Do somethi-i-i-ng! I hate them! Kill them! Kill them!

[JENNY and JACK shrink back to either side of the stage and stand, transfixed. Lights go out, leaving the slide. This also disappears, leaving the screen blank. Finally the screen is also dark. Lights come up to reveal JACK and JENNY back in their chairs. JENNY is very pregnant.]

JACK: I decided against a lawn. I put down gravel and cedar chips. The weeds got through so I kept a bunch of weedkiller in the garage. It's not hard to control them if you get the right stuff. *[Picks up the binoculars.]* You can't go on livin' in the past. You gotta look forward. Right? *[Hands binoculars to JENNY.]* You ever look at the sky Jenny? You ever look at the stars? Really look I mean. Really look.

PLANET EARTH

It has to be spread out, the skin of this planet,
has to be ironed, the sea in its whiteness;
and the hands keep on moving,
smoothing the holy surfaces.
> —Pablo Neruda, In Praise of Ironing

It has to be loved the way a laundress loves her linens,
the way she moves her hands caressing the fine muslins
knowing their warp and woof,
like a lover coaxing, or a mother praising.
It has to be loved as if it were embroidered
with flowers and birds and two joined hearts upon it.
It has to be stretched and stroked.
It has to be celebrated
O this great beloved world and all the creatures in it.
It has to be spread out, the skin of this planet.

The trees must be washed, and the grasses and mosses.
They have to be polished as if made of green brass.
The rivers and little streams with their hidden cresses
and pale-coloured pebbles
and their fool's gold
must be washed and starched or shined into brightness,
the sheets of lake water
smoothed with the hand
and the foam of the oceans pressed into neatness.
It has to be ironed, the sea in its whiteness.

and pleated and goffered, the flower-blue sea
the protean, wine-dark, grey, green sea
with its metres of satin and bolts of brocade.
And sky—such an O! overhead—night and day
must be burnished and rubbed
by hands that are loving
so the blue blazons forth
and the stars keep on shining
within and above
and the hands keep on moving.

It has to be made bright, the skin of this planet
till it shines in the sun like gold leaf.
Archangels then will attend to its metals
and polish the rods of its rain.
Seraphim will stop singing hosannas
to shower it with blessings and blisses and praises
and, newly in love,
we must draw it and paint it
our pencils and brushes and loving caresses
smoothing the holy surfaces.

NATURE

Sometimes I wonder about nature.
It has a sort of magic.
When I hear the word nature I think of life.
I think of cool, refreshing air and
of great forests.

But now I think of logging and
contaminated water.
Animals scurrying from forests.
Their homes now gone.
And no one is doing anything about it.
Save our forests!
Save our wildlife!

SAVE CLAYOQUOT SOUND!

BEWITCHED, BOTHERED, AND BEWILDERNESSED

At Clayoquot Sound, as of June 1993, almost 150 people so far have been arrested for standing up for sustainable forestry practises, and the preservation of the largest tract of temperate rainforest remaining on Vancouver Island.

The government feels trapped by the need to preserve forest workers' jobs, and to protect the communities dependent on forest sector jobs. In New Zealand, the forest industry generates five jobs for every thousand metres of timber, while here it only generates one. Meanwhile, B.C. companies insist on the need to cut into the few remaining wilderness areas. But consider:

- For each sawmill job, 4.5 jobs can be created in the value-added sector by remanufacturing.
- B.C. forest companies currently ship logs down to Washington and Oregon for remanufacturing in their own plants.
- Mill workers say that high quality logs are often wasted, and turned into chips.
- Under the Small Business Forest Enterprise Program, smaller value-added companies are able to bid for timber, but applications exceed licenses granted by four to one.
- In its report on Lumber Remanufacturing in B.C., the Select Committee stated that the biggest problem facing value-added companies is the supply of timber: they simply can't get enough.

The bottom line is that we are cutting old-growth forests in world heritage sites because of a failure to diversify our forest community economies and provide alternative jobs for forest workers.

> *The existing forest tenure system is preventing economic development by entrepreneurs when it blocks access to public timber.*
> —Ray Travers, R.P.F.

So what is to be done?

If New Zealand (and Sweden and Switzerland) can do it, why can't we? What kind of positive policy would it take to increase forest-sector jobs, end the sacrifice of Clayoquot Sound, and save similar yet-to-be-logged jewels?

The Lumber Remanufacturing Report contains fourteen detailed recommendations, and a further seven, written "in the event that these recommendations are not strong enough, or major licensees do not respond in a positive manner," which were deleted from the final report.

The recommendations are very simple. They start with setting a goal of doubling the number of remanufacturing jobs in B.C. by the year 2000, and again by 2010. They would establish an agency or association to work on behalf of the value-added sector in B.C., with regional committees charged with doing whatever it takes to increase value-added enterprise and remanufacturing.

They go on to suggest ways of increasing the timber available to value-added businesses through the existing licensing system, expanding the Woodlot Program, and setting up training and market development initiatives.

The recommendations deleted from the final report include enacting the recommendations of the Forest Resources Commission to reduce timber allocated to licensees to fifty percent of present levels, and buying a major license and using it to feed remanufacturing facilities around the province.

It would also be possible to add community clauses to tree farm licenses, just as they are in Cable TV licenses, obliging license holders to undertake community economic development activities in areas under their control, designed to diversify forest community economies, in conjunction with the Ministry of Economic Development and local groups.

And yet still, nothing happens. The province, along with the Ministry and the Minister, has been bewitched by the major forest companies—and now we are all bothered and bewildered—while our land is being bewildernessed. Meanwhile, at Clayoquot, the conflict continues.

THE ISLAND OF VANCOUVER

A trace of lines left in the sand
A pearly shell clasped in a hand
Wind blows the water and starts it twirling
From the sea a fog comes whirling
Golden sun gleams from east to west
Geese break form, then join the rest
Mountains strain to push back the sky
And the waves go rushing by
The island of the sun

Majestic trees tower high
And with their branches touch the sky
Around their crowns the ravens fly
The air so sweet, each leaf so green
A half-seen mist like in a dream
A gentle cocoon, calm and serene
Flowers scattered here and there
A lovely fragrance everywhere
The island of the rainforest

By the shore a road runs by
Where earth and water meet the sky
And the ships go sailing by
The island of the sea

Waves blown by breezes break and shiver
On the shore they dance and quiver
Through the sands that run forever
The Island of Vancouver

WHEN ROOTS GROW BACK INTO THE EARTH

I've always been skeptical about loving the whole planet Earth. For me, you can love it best when you love a particular place, and even then, you can't do it in a moment, but only as you know that place and are involved in it over a long period of time. So I dateline this essay very specifically: 1st. Concession, Locheil Township, Glengarry Country, Ontario. Spring 1994.

I've read that the women who used to live here went off by themselves when it was their bleeding time. In sacred menstrual huts, they sat on the ground, on beds of moss. They rested, meditated, and visited with each other while their blood seeped out of their bodies and into the living earth.

I think of this as I walk between the trees I helped to plant as a girl. Every spring, beginning when I was eight, we planted trees here, in the thin, hard soils of eastern Ontario, on a run-down little farm my parents had bought in the 1950s, in lieu of a summer cottage. Armed with shovels and buckets, we tramped the land where it slopes up from the river, digging hopeful seedlings into the inhospitable ground.

I worked the ground with my bare hands: scratching among gravel and stones, finding the edge of rocks and prying them out, then foraging around for handfuls of precious soil, sweet black humus with which to cover the roots of the ten-inch nursery trees. The idea was to re-forest the land, which probably should never have been cleared in the first place. The soil had become too poor for farming. "Barren," they called it in the soil-testing lab: leached and eroded from having been used too hard, then left open, and exposed to the elements. The 200-acre farm had been abandoned like so many others around here after the Second World War, when mechanization imposed its implacable choice: get bigger or get out.

The trees came through a government reforestation program. Red pine, white pine, and spruce, they arrived in bundles of twenty-five packed in peat moss in slapped-together wooden boxes made of spruce lathe. Once, the year we planted 13,000 and my mother carried a solution of soda and water in a screw-cap bottle to keep herself from throwing up, there were ten boxes, each five feet long and three feet deep. When the last tree had been taken out and planted, my brother and I made forts with the empty boxes, our hands too tough to catch the splinters.

It's my hands in the ground I remember the most: eight-year-old, nine-year-old, ten-year-old hands. And the ground perpetually cold, with frost still glinting amongst the stones. I'd bang away with my shovel, trying to find a way in for the trees, and hitting rock after rock under last year's withered weeds. The reverberations jarred my head, and I threw the shovel aside.

On one side of me, I sensed my older brother and sister moving steadily ahead. On the other side, my mother kept an eye on my little brother while working her own row of trees. She worked doggedly, stooping but never once getting down on her hands and knees—a girls' school product even there. My father was, as usual, way on ahead, never stopping, never even slowing down. But I knew he'd double back, then help me catch up. He had a shiny, round-mouthed shovel, which he sharpened regularly so it would cut fast and neat.

My hands are stiff with cold, and puffed up pink like sausages. I know this, but I don't really notice as I work in a universe reduced to impenetrable earth riddled with stones and rough-edged gravel. I've pulled or shovelled aside a scruffy brown patch of last year's twitch grass, along with the collapsed seedhead of a burdock plant. The burr barbs are lodged in the skin between my fingers. My fingers are caked in half-dried mud as I rake through the ground, seeking passage for the tree roots. The stones here are a mix of shale and granite, the tag end of the Precambrian Shield littered like bones beneath the surface. I find the edge of the stone I'm up against, and yank to pull it out. Nothing happens. I scratch for a fingerhold deeper underneath, feel the dirt drive farther beneath my nails, the nails separating a little from the skin. Still I push, past gravel and frost crystals hard as diamonds. I get a grip and brace myself, knees apart, on the thawing ground. I pull hard, shoulder and stomach muscles straining. My fingertips burn as they slip from under the unyielding stone. Tears run down my face. The rock's too big. I'll have to dig another hole. Warm salt water drops onto the backs of my hands, moistening where the dirt has dried. My head throbs as I dig again, kneel again, and struggle with the stones.

I plunge my hands into the bucket. Sweet release. The water's cold, yet seems warmer than the ground. And the wetness soothes my fingers. I pull out a tree. A seedling with its spritely main shoot, its tentative side branches, and its prodigious roots.

I hold the tree by the stem, my swollen fingers tingling. I tuck the root filaments carefully into the hole. I curl them around so they all fit in, and push the tips down into the fertile hole. I do this with every tree, an extra boost so they're sure to take root here, and survive. The root tendrils lie there like a hank of my own fly-away tangled hair, kept in place only by my twelve-year-old hand. Still holding, I pile the precious black soil in on top of them. Crumbs of still-fecund living earth for them to cling to, draw nourishment from.

Take, eat. This is my body. . . .

I scoop a handful of muddy water out of my pail, pour it off the tips of my fingers, and watch it seep into the ground, down among the root hairs.

I rake last bits of dirt into the hole, then plunk the patches of turf back on top, and press them in place with my hands. One tree planted. One out of thousands and thousands and thousands. And now they blanket the slope, a skein of green in infinite tones and variations, with the wind sighing through them, lightly or heavily, depending on the weather.

Now their trunks are thicker than my body. Their roots are gnarled fingers worrying the edges of the few still-protruding rocks. Whether it's new soil building up or the rocks themselves subsiding, I don't know. But now only the boulders are visible.

The biggest boulder we pulled out of the fields, a fisted hunk of pink-tinged granite, is now a sort of family monument. It's parked along the path between the hayfields in the lowlands close to the river and the higher ground where we planted the trees. My father hired a stone mason to write on the rock, beginning with the phrase: "They cared for this land." He listed all our names, and our birth dates. Then, at the head of the list, he put the name of Duncan "the Night" Macmillan. Some research I'd done in the archives established that he was the first to clear this land. And that's how my father counted things.

The man was nicknamed "the Night" because he was such a fine, hard-working Presbyterian that he worked at night if there was a moon to see by. He cared that much for his family: children of emigrant Scots seeking a better life in the New World. I can imagine him out there day and night, hectoring his workhorses as they strained to pull out the deep, resisting tree roots. I can imagine his relentless labour, and the faith that kept him at it. Until he'd broken the land to the plough and the discipline of crops.

It never occurred to me while planting those trees every spring that it was his diligence I was covering up for. Nor did I consider the compulsion to be productive as anything but admirable. He was hard-working. So were we, pushing ourselves from early morning 'til nearly dark those cool, sometimes cold and wet, spring weekends. I have no memory of what we did after we returned, exhausted, to the farmhouse and the stew Mum simmered at the back of the woodstove. We were weekend pioneers, with little time for contemplation.

When my father died, we buried his ashes at the memorial rock, and I visit it often when I'm walking these woods. The rock is overshadowed now by the trees. A thick branch of a spruce droops down and brushes the top. Lichen and moss creep microscopically across its surface, obscuring my father's chosen words.

I gaze at the bough of spruce, its deep dark green turning black in the shadows beyond. I see the buds where new growth will emerge, fragile as seedlings, in the spring. I see where old needles are sloughing themselves off, cascading across the rock and settling on the ground. I understand these trees, know them as minutely as I know the flesh of my son named after my father and now twelve years old himself.

It's strange I came to love these trees, after all I went through helping to plant, then tend them through their first years of life. Every spring we walked the still rock-strewn land where we'd dug in the seedlings, trying to find them under the collapsed remains of last year's overwhelming weeds. Spotting a toothbrush bristle of green, I'd pull the grasses apart and frisk the tiny branches free of entangling debris. It sometimes took days to find all the buried ones, and not all of them in time.

Then it was the snow itself which posed a threat. The red pines got it the worst, with their bushier boughs and thicker needles. The snow took them down, and by spring, they'd be bent right over, twisted sideways and unable to right themselves. It became our chore as children to scout out these cripples and set them straight, using broken branches from dead elm trees, or hawthorns and other scrub bushes that had infiltrated the long-abandoned fields. It wasn't hard work. In fact, I remember actually enjoying it. At some point too, I crossed over, and continued doing it on my own. For them. For us. I'd encountered the word "pantheism" by then, and I was a pantheist; though still a church-going one.

It was pleasant solitary work, and I used to alternately talk to the trees and sing to them: hymns in the early days, then Beatles' tunes about love, love, love.

There's been a little rain, and now the sun is coming out. I walk toward it, up the path through the woods, in the direction we moved with our buckets and shovels over thirty years ago. A mellow, honey-thick glow slants through the trees and onto the path, which is spongy with moss and fallen pine needles. The sun comes through the branches of an overhanging pine, and I stop to contemplate a water droplet hanging, like a diamond, at the tip of one of its needles. I duck in under the branches knowing it's drier there, and sit on a mound of moss-covered ground.

I think of my mother, busy as ever and still battling headaches. I think of my older brother, my younger brother, and my older sister: one's a lawyer, one's a doctor, one's a telecommunications manager. Then there's me, busily writing to meet the next deadline, to have another book in print. A drop of water descends from a branch above me, and lands on the back of my hand. It occurs to me that the whole bunch of us could be out there clearcutting at Clayoquot. It's that much in our blood, the diligence and hard-working spirit; what Nietzsche called the endless becoming, with no horizon but the perpetual invention of new objectives: the next tree to cut, the next one to plant, the next cause to write about.

The drop of water slides down my hand where I rest it against the ground. But I think it's not the will and the diligence themselves that are so bad. It's their monopoly within us: our hearts, minds, bodies, and souls all dedicated to the dynamo of doing, without respite. No time for rest and contemplation. No time for rooting and taking root. No time for remembrance and reciprocity.

I watch the drop of water, now warmed by my skin, roll steadily down my hand, and slip away into the earth. I feel the moss soft beneath me, feel its moisture seep into my jeans. Around me, shadows drift up like root hairs seeking passage. A breeze whiffles the upper branches, light as surf bubbles caressing a shore. I sit on the moss, enveloped by these trees I helped grow into this ground over so many years. They're in my blood now. I feel them.

When I take the time
to remember myself as part of them,
and remember them
as part of me.

—*The information about Native women's menstrual rites comes from Anne Cameron's* Daughters of Copper Woman *(Press Gang, 1981) and from Beth Richard's article, "Blood of the Moon," in* Herizons *(Vol. 7, No.4).*

TREE-PLANTING

I need a piece of paper
   to write this
To stay still, hang on to a pen
    that wants to two-step
        wants to stomp up & down the page

I'll rip out the middle page from
    my journal—the page where when I pull out one
    I magically get two

Because there is so much to say

Couldn't write
sat in my ATCO-trailer
   sameness/numbness/nothingness
and
had nothing to say

Needed a televison a diversion
   something to think for me
   something to cover me
     inability to think
something to hide the truths
with neat half-hour segments
with superficial glances at unreality

And in the ATCO-trailer logging camp
I had nothing to say

Although—if you listened
    if I listened
   my pores were emitting
    a high-pitched whine

    a shrill scream
       sweating out of my body

while I worked/walked/struggled

putting new trees in the ground
(to decorate the stumps
to cover the ground
to reassure)

But that was at first.
    Then I adjusted
        maladjusted
        disappeared

And the body I left wasn't
    content
    but fit better
        into the ATCO-trailer
            sameness
            numbness

Stay longer your world can be one of fourteen days on four off steak on Satur-
days and single beds in ATCO cells

I don't cry when I see a clearcut
I don't gasp scream shriek or
        feel shame

I call it a *cut block* discuss the *bid price* and *run a line*. Then I *fill*.
That is my shell my numbness my armour

I intellectualize   laugh (bitterly) at
the lies   hypocrisies/hypocrazies
read the treeboxes
spit out the slogans

HELPING MOTHER NATURE GROW BETTER FORESTS
FORESTS FOR THE FUTURE
TREES FOR TOMORROW

I'll plant them
    wander through the
        burned scarred rocky muddy dusty clearcut

at the end of a contract drive
away, escape, forget where it was
drink in the bar grimace at
the word lies. *Reforested Restocked Replanted*

Every piece was made the same
Full of stumps
full of attacks on truth
        on my soul
        on my body

And then I pay my bills
        start again
I can do it—so much around
    reinforces the numbness

Where How Why When
    did we become
            so wrong so lost
            so detached?

Can I gather enough energy
                    vision
                    truth

        to say *no   stop   what next?*

When do we ask?
When do we listen?
When do we talk?

TREES

trees
cathedrals
brooms ladders
landships lookouts
globes plumes and arrowheads
squirrel highrises highways trapezes
playgrounds flicker feeders bird airports
nest holders fruit danglers seed droppers
animal shelters haunting faces water savers
sap rivers sugar makers kite grabbers helicopter mothers
green dresses graceful dancers shade makers summer's leaf-heavy
rustle and flip fall's orange yellow green and red palettes smeared on hillsides
winter's pen and ink on wan sky Christmas evergreens of pine and spruce and fir
spring's pinkblossom sweetsmell chlorophyll giants weathervanes erosion stoppers
earth lungs air conditioners oxygen farms sky fillers rain makers
stormhorses wind sculpture wooden muscles benders flexers fingers gloved in fog
handwavers soughers and screamers thick-trunked doffers and donners
property markers
record keepers
windbreaks
landmarks
fenceliners
root runners
sidewalk tippers

IT HAPPENED SUDDENLY
(OVER A LONG PERIOD OF TIME)
A Clayoquot History

Just the other day (one of those exceedingly wet days we get out here) a past director of the Friends of Clayoquot Sound said, "I just realized it's been ten years since the Meares Easter Festival and the dedication of the Meares Island Tribal Park. I never thought then we would be where we are now." Where we are now is riding a kicking horse toward vast change in the perception of ecosystems. Building on the courageous steps of the early movement for Clayoquot Sound, we have shoved the government from stagnancy and recalcitrance to a reluctant but panicked effort to change forest policy and deal with First Nations' rights.

It poured during the sign raising and dedication of Meares Island as a Tribal Park by the Nuu-Chah-Nulth in July 1984. It poured on the 1,000 people who came up for the Meares Easter Festival, and it was glorious for the winter month blockades of 1985 on Meares Island which marked the beginning of the Friends of Clayoquot Sound's use of direct action in the struggle for the forests and justice for Natives. Sometimes it shines on the blockades and sometimes it rains for the festivals. Fifteen full seasonal cycles have passed since we began. The last cycle feels like we've been in the midst of a great storm and when the skies clear, forest policy in this region and perhaps around the province will be a changed landscape. We're dedicated to changing metaphorical landscapes, not the ones we live on.

The Friends of Clayoquot Sound have been in existence since 1979. They were, and continue to be, a grassroots environmental group based in the area they aspire to protect. We had an office in the basement of a two-story apartment building near enough to the bakery to be comfortable and technologically understated. For fourteen years, with one phone, a photocopier, and an incredible wealth of local knowledge and dedication, the Friends of Clayoquot Sound worked to change the world's attitudes toward ancient temperate rainforests. That dedication seems to be coming to fruition with Clayoquot Sound having become a symbol worldwide for our fears for the wild and natural areas and our hopes for their continuation.

The Friends of Clayoquot Sound have been working for the last fifteen years to protect the largest remaining costal lowland temperate rainforest in the world. This tract of forest is 260,000 hectares (624,000 acres) of deep valleys and fjords, islands, and mountains located on the west coast of Vancouver Island. It is home to marbled murrelets and has healthy populations of black bear, cougar, wolves, bald eagles, and myriad small mammals, birds and amphibians. It is an area full of salmon spawning streams on which the First Nations of the region have been dependent for thousands of years. Twenty-one percent of Clayoquot Sound has already been clearcut by multinational corporations.

The two major deforesters are MacMillan Bloedel and Interfor who, in conjunction with various governments, have tried to convince us all that in spite of all the "mistakes" (read devastation) of the past, their current plans to convert the majority of these irreplaceable forests to managed plantations is really the best thing since sliced bread. Prior to 1988 and the new improved Fish and Forestry guidelines they never said "we're sorry we made a mistake" when they destroyed a salmon stream, it was just part of doing business. Now saying "we're sorry we destroyed a salmon stream" is part of doing business in the new era of environmental sensitivity!

We have succeeded in protecting thirty-three percent of the land base, much of it the economically unviable coastal fringe forest and some interior forest. We have in fact been able to achieve protection for the 20,000 hectare Megin River watershed. It is a welcome honour to have the largest protected temperate rainforest watershed in North America, but a chilling reality when you consider there used to be ninety-one watersheds over 5,000 hectares (12,000 acres) on Vancouver Island and only six remain intact and only two of those are protected. In the rest of the temperate rainforest from southeastern Alaska to northern California the situation is even worse. The forest is in danger of becoming fragmented into small clumps, and the biodiversity sustained by the critical mass of forest cover is threatened. Fifteen years ago we didn't know any of this. We knew that big chunks of forest were coming down very quickly but we didn't know the scale of the destruction. It was a combination of local experience and a profound mistrust of corporate intentions which kept the Friends insisting that all was not well in the woods.

In 1982, the Friends of Clayoquot Sound became part of the two-year Meares Island Planning Committee negotiating with the unions, Natives, and MacMillan Bloedel over what, if any, logging could occur on Meares Island. After two years the negotiators came up with three options, none of which pleased MB, who pulled out of the process and loaded their loggers onto the crew boats to head for Meares. When they arrived, a flotilla of protesters, both Native and non-Native, blocked their way, preventing them from landing, and did so for most of the winter. The Island was dedicated as Meares Island Tribal Park by the Nuu-Chah-Nulth First Nations, and eventually Natives achieved an injunction barring logging, pending the settlement of their Native land title on Meares. At this time the Nuu-Cha-Nulth have spent almost $1.5 million on their court case and in the seven years that have passed there is still no settlement.

Basking in the apparent, however uncertain and temporary, success of Meares Island, the Friends set their sights on keeping the multinationals out of the Sound. By the end of 1988, the forest industry had set up the SHARE groups to fight their publicity battles for them (since industry had lost credibility and needed a front group that seemed less tied to their profits.) The Friends of Clayoquot blockaded a logging road being built by Fletcher Challenge for three months and were successful in stopping its construction, but the whole nature of environmental activism was about to change as the slick industry campaigns began. The industry successfully drove a wedge between the workers and the environmentalists, utilizing the SHARE groups to do the fear-mongering.

The Forest Alliance, Share the Clayoquot, and Share Our Resources, the Forest Forever TV ads all challenged us to become more sophisticated in our campaigns to protect Clayoquot Sound. While attempting to counter the assault of the anti-environment groups we entered into a local sustainable development strategy, which eventually was hijacked by government and became the four-year-long process which we dubbed the Task Farce, but the government called the Clayoquot Sound Sustainable Development Strategy Steering Committee, or CSSDSSC for short (!). We coined the term the NDP used in their election campaign ("We want an end to the valley-by-valley approach to decision making") to lobby for greater public control over the fate of our ancient forests, but everything we said was co-opted by either government or industry. All of a sudden industry was calling itself environmentalists and government was giving lip service to sustainable development while environmentalists were engaged in what we finally determined to be "talk and log" processes.

The advantage of being a non-hierarchical, radical, grassroots organization is that you do what you feel needs to be done as far as the locals see it. We've negotiated, we've educated, we've toured, media and politicians lobbied, and, when we felt it was necessary, we blockaded. It seems to be working. I feel there is something ultimately compelling about local people struggling to maintain the beauty that surrounds them; something inviting about people who are working hard for no pecuniary gain and who are peaceful in their nature. The backdrop for our struggle looms large, making it all the more visible. We have huge multinational timber companies gobbling up enormous volumes of forest for raw log export and telephone books, and we have the physical backdrop of one of the largest remaining tracts of glorious ancient temperate rainforest on planet earth.

We face incredible odds. The NDP government invested $50 million in one of the biggest logging companies in Canada, MacMillan Bloedel. Interfor is one of the largest timber corporations in B.C., and the timber lobby has millions more dollars to advertise their position than we have. The federal and provincial governments have also put $9 million into public relations for the companies, but somehow it isn't working for them. The movement for Clayoquot Sound has grown through the grassroots across Canada and into the U.S., and is looming large in Europe. With luck, dedication, the power of a vast group of individuals, and hope, it seems inevitable that Clayoquot Sound will be protected. We have begun to set the agenda for how we want to see our wild lands, everywhere respected. What happens in Clayoquot will empower people across Canada in their struggles to maintain the integrity of their local ecosystems, be they the boreal forests, the prairie grasses, or the Great Lakes.

Literally tens of thousands of people have participated in the Clayoquot Sound Campaign. Over 800 have been arrested in the largest civil disobedience action in Canadian history between July and October of 1993. MacMillan Bloedel has lost about $10 million in contracts in Europe and the United States, as companies there have decided to disassociate themselves from the destruction of these magnificent temperate rainforests. The forest corporations are on the defensive now. Their arrogance in the face of the public is turning to panic as they begin to comprehend that their days of controlling the forest agenda are numbered. This is a people's movement for natural ecosystems and Native justice. There are ninety-one endangered animal species and almost 200 endangered plant species in British Columbia, a province which is beyond the Treaty Frontier, and millions of people in this world have compassion for the indigenous people and indigenous species of this spectacular area.

The non-Native Canadian culture is a young one. We haven't a long history of art and literature, we don't have great cathedrals or pyramids. Our common heritage is in cathedral forest and vast expanses of wilderness. From Newfoundland to Vancouver Island we see ourselves as a people with a common thread, that of survivors in a harsh wild land. That sense of unity is being eroded by the corporate agenda to eliminate all, and the government agenda to eliminate eighty-eight percent of the natural productive forests in Canada. On Vancouver Island that agenda has been sixty percent fulfilled, and areas like Clayoquot have come to represent what we stand for and what we want to keep in our culture.

The wilderness and eco-forestry movements have coalesced, and social justice for First Nations has finally become an integral part of the movement's philosophy. Our vision for the future has matured to one which sees the need to integrate, not isolate. Our challenge is to change the forest policy landscape to one which reflects community stability and forest integrity and accepts an economy not based on greed and overproduction. With eco-forestry and secondary manufacturing we can cut at least one-quarter what we do now and employ as many people. Our campaign in Europe and the U.S. has linked with the campaigns for alternative paper fibers, recycling, and reduced paper consumption. It is the most outrageously reasonable campaign. There is no question that ancient forests should not be used for telephone directories or newspapers.

Our landscape is one which exists only as a fairy tale in most of the world. It is now our good fortune and our responsibility to ensure that the beasts and flora, large and small, and the indigenous culture do not become mythological creatures for the children of the future. The incarceration of peaceful and conscientious citizens has only spurred a successful international campaign. Jail is not a deterrent to civil disobedience; social and political change is. With Clayoquot as the symbol and the impetus, we will have justice, wilderness, and a much gentler forestry in British Columbia. This is not just idealism, it is the developing reality.

THE MAN FROM WILDWOOD

What is a logger doing getting arrested at the Kennedy Lake bridge? Shouldn't he be waiting in the trucks with the others, the revving diesel motors fuelling their impatience and blocking out the harmony of the wilderness? Doesn't he know that woodsmen aren't supposed to stop trees from coming down? Whatever the reason for his being here, you know it's not because he's still wet behind the ears. He's the oldest person on the road, and his wife, a Raging Granny, is beside him. Just as unlikely is the way he's welcomed and admired by his fellow protesters, few of whom would have thought they would find themselves allied with a man who makes his living cutting down trees. But this is Merve Wilkinson.

Eighty-one years old, the Nanaimo-born forester practises his own brand of forestry on his 137-acre Wildwood Tree Farm near Cedar which he bought in 1938. Wildwood is flush with wildlife and beauty—a side of logging rarely seen these days in British Columbia. Merve's sustainable approach has proven that there is a feasible alternative to the ecological destruction caused by clearcutting.

"I've contacted all the people involved in forestry over the years with proposals and suggestions that would have made the protest unnecessary," said Merve. "I've exhausted all the other approaches. The only thing left was to get out there and stand in the road." It was the first time Merve and his wife Anne had ever been arrested, but they both think it was worth it, and that the summer of protests have had an impact on the forest industry. He thinks the protests have encouraged other forms of logging, which are now being supported by the government. Even the corporations are showing more interest in alternate methods now that international market pressure has increased. The doors to these markets have been slamming shut to B.C. timber, and they aren't likely to open again until profound changes are made in the forest industry.

Merve and Anne decided to join the Clayoquot blockade after many years of trying to change logging practices through every legitimate means. Merve has taught courses, lectured, lobbied foresters, written letters, and hosted visitors to his tree farm. To schoolchildren, MLAs, IWA members, journalists, and scientists, Merve's message has always been the same: forestry is not the problem; it is the methods that are used.

Every year, students, ecologists, foresters, and scientists from around the world come to visit his productive forest on Yellow Point Road. They want to see for themselves how logging and wildlife can coexist and replace the "cut and run" approach to forestry. "It's a long-range view," says Merve, "it's looking at a future, not looking at finishing up and leaving town."

Sustainable, selective logging is currently practiced by only a few small forestry operators in B.C. and the western United States. It differs from clearcutting in that only a small proportion of the timber is harvested at any one time. Merve estimates that no more than fifteen percent of the timber should be cut during a harvest, otherwise the stand is susceptible to wind-throw. For his operation, this means one cut every five years, with occasional thinning in between. "I've made nine cuts since 1945. I've harvested more timber than was on it to begin with and I have more trees now than I had then."

The selection process Merve uses removes only those trees that fail to produce optimal growth, and that are also inappropriate as seed or habitat trees. "A healthy tree has at least sixty percent of its needles or leaves on it and still has its full growing capacity. When they start to thin, that's when I take them out, making way for trees that are still putting on their two percent (optimal growth) per year." Merve's operation could act as a model for change in the forest industry. "The best solution for Clayoquot is selective cutting based on annual growth rate. That way you're never out of business and you never have to clear more than one hectare, just enough to get in."

"With this system, you're always growing. When they clearcut, the land is out of production for four or five years before it's replanted, in some cases, and the damage done to the soil in that time is horrendous." Merve says agronomists tell him he has some of the best soil on the island, but that clearcutting would cause permanent damage to nutrient and micro-organism systems. "The part of the forest that lies below the surface we know the least about, and it's the most important. When that is destroyed, as happens in clearcutting, then the forest just will not grow."

You can learn a lot about Merve by letting him walk you through his operation. He's the embodiment of spry, and the first thing you notice is his energy and enthusiasm. After countless tours and hours of patient explanation, Merve can still see his forest through new eyes. He finds the forest intriguing and instructive. "I like to see some things just left to follow their course. Nature often tells me things that I have overlooked; I am always learning from it."

His ability to learn from the forest has made Merve as much a naturalist as a forester. "With this type of forestry you're going to consider aesthetics and habitat. Now, there's a tree there that a forester would tell you to take out," says Merve, indicating a gnarled fir. "Actually, that tree doesn't produce much seed, so if it's poor genetic quality, it's not going to reproduce anyway. That big limb with the broken end is frequently a home to a wood duck, and owls and ravens have nested there; it's a habitat tree.

You want to leave this in the forest because you need those species. That snag is an old tree that the woodpeckers use; I won't cut that either, I'll leave it for the birds."

In addition to aesthetics and ecology, there is a practical side to sustainable, selective logging. "I never have to plant, it's all natural seeding here and that's a big cost saver. I have to thin, periodically taking out the poorer trees, but it's less costly than planting. Nature shows you which are the best trees, so as you thin, you are gradually improving your stand, accelerating the natural selection process." Thinning creates openings in the forest canopy, forcing trees to shoot up straight to compete for the light. Trees don't branch out as much, resulting in first class timber.

Merve isn't speaking metaphorically when he talks about working with nature. "You have to leave some old stumps because squirrels will bury seed. They pick the best cones off the best trees and they always hide more than they use." Merve uses a wind map to pinpoint strategic places for seed dispersal, then leaves his best seed trees in these spots. "You look for seed trees with good cone crops. You can take the seeds and split them, or you can just watch the squirrels; if they're working on a tree early in the year, then it's a good seed tree, so you leave it."

At first, Merve was reluctant to leave things alone, picking up all the dead wood as he went. Then a fellow forester told him, "Merve, it's a

lovely show, but you're too tidy." "I've been less tidy since," says Merve, "leaving nurse logs which break down and feed the soil, while providing habitat for desirable insects and field mice, moles and voles that carry bacteria in their digestive systems and deposit them around. It's part of the balance of a natural area. As the logs break down, young trees start in them, and they take off. There is a purpose for the nurse logs in our forests." The red flash of a flicker darts through the tree tops, reminding Merve how birds help forestry, providing a natural defense system against insect pests. "In early spring they work up the bark of the trees, eating larvae. In some places, budworms and other pests become epidemics but I haven't seen a budworm here since 1939; I have a lot of birds."

Merve claims his forest is less susceptible to disease than clearcuts, which tend to contain even-age, or, in plantations, even-age, monoculture trees after the first cut. "The mixed forest (mixed heights, ages, and species) provides a natural immune system because what attacks the cedar tree won't attack the fir tree, or the balsam. Just make sure that you don't over-cut or let the stand get too dense; you can work with nature and it will work with you, but don't try to work against it."

Merve has never used chemicals in his forest. He's convinced that he'll never suffer an epidemic as long as he never sprays. "If you use chemicals then you wipe out your natural controls and defences. New Brunswick and Nova Scotia are in a mess because they use chemicals. The Germans tell us, 'keep the chemicals out of the woods,' don't even put fertilizer in there, forests don't like it. So much of forestry is common sense, and that's something the world is running out of."

Merve says that sustainable, selective logging would provide more jobs and more stability in the industry than clearcutting. He uses reforestation as an example, holding up what's left of some seedlings he collected that were planted in a clearcut several years ago. They are stunted, roots twisted and gnarled, branches sickly looking. "These come from land logged twelve years ago, planted eight years ago. Planting is done on a quota basis, and carelessness takes a heavy toll. Every year, these trees grew less and less. In another two years, that area will have to be replanted again. So, you've lost fourteen years of growth—about two million board feet of wood annually over that 2,000-acre clearcut. Using the industry figures, it takes 500,000 board feet to put one person to work full-time in the forest. In that small area alone, you've just lost fifty-six full-time jobs." The big companies generally offer two reasons why they don't use selective logging: it's too slow and it's too dangerous. Merve disagrees about the second point. "It's the safest kind of falling there is—all you do is step behind another tree and you're safe."

Merve thinks that another part of the problem in B.C. is that the "cut and run" approach undermines effective forestry management. Foresters, fallers, skidders, and haulers rarely log the same area twice, and as such, they are loosely connected with the land. Consider the knowledge farmers have of the qualities of their land, its resources, and their livestock or crops, knowledge essential for wise management and sustained productivity. "We don't have continuity with our foresters here, they're constantly shunted around and they don't get to know what the land is doing. When you go to Europe, you notice that foresters talk about 'their' forests. Of course, it's not theirs, the government owns it, but they call it their own because they'll be managing it for life."

In addition to losses through taking land out of production and failed re-forestation efforts, large operations result in a higher proportion of wasted wood. Merve claims that the portable mill that saws his wood yields a return of sixty-five to seventy percent usable timber from his cut. He says that larger operations are generally getting a return of fifty to fifty-five percent and that the proportion is lower because of the loss through destruction of unwanted trees. "They say they're planting two for every one they take, but they don't mention they destroyed fifteen others to get that one." The loss isn't only in terms of timber, says Merve. "The skidders that come here say their costs are sixty percent of what they are in the clearcut. Their ropes and chokers last longer, there's less wear and tear on their equipment and their fuel costs are down." The tangled litter of unsaleable timber throughout clearcuts creates higher fuel and equipment costs. Yet, when asked why Fletcher Challenge doesn't switch to sustainable, selective logging, company spokesman Tom Williams replied, "it takes more time. We need to clearcut to maintain production and economic levels; we have to maintain our volume."

It seems that big timber companies would still rather walk away from a forest than practise selective forestry. Four years ago, the public blockaded MacMillan Bloedel from clearcutting forests on Cortes Island. Logging was stopped and a meeting arranged. Merve was called in by the Cortes residents, and he and fellow forester Herb Hammond put together a proposed working plan for the area. According to Merve, when Charlie Burrell, then MacMillan Bloedel's Chief Forester at Powell River, saw that sustainable, selective logging was being proposed, he balked. "Instead," says Merve, "they haven't done anything on Cortes, and it's rumoured they just want to sell the land and move on."

Over forty-five years, Merve Wilkinson has proven that sustainable, selective logging works. He tells of similar success stories, scattered through B.C. and the western United States. For Merve, the choice to practise his brand of holistic forestry was a simple one. "It's like saying, 'I have so many dollars worth of timber here. I can have it all right now or I can have it a bit at a time over the next fifty years, and I won't be bothering somebody for unemployment insurance or welfare after I've spent all the money.' The difference between this and clearcutting is that you're keeping more people employed and you're using the forest better. You're keeping the forest intact so that you still have tourist appeal, you have fish and game, and a place for the photographer, for the poet. Aesthetically you've got something, and practically you've got something."

Aldo Leopold, the "Father of Conservation in America," would have liked Merve's approach to logging. Like Wilkinson, Leopold was also a forester, a naturalist, and a man of vision. Leopold foresaw the destruction of America's forests. In 1947, he pleaded for common sense and for action:

"I have no illusions about the speed or accuracy with which an ecological conscience can become functional. It has required nineteen centuries to define decent man-to-man conduct and the process is only half done; it may take as long to evolve a code of decency for man-to-land conduct. In such matters we should not worry about anything except the direction in which we travel. The direction is clear, and the first step is to throw your weight around on matters of right and wrong in land use. Cease being intimidated by the argument that a right action is impossible because it does not yield maximum profits, or that a wrong action is to be condoned because it pays. That philosophy is dead in human relations, and its funeral in land relations is overdue."

British Columbia Judge Lee Skipp called Merve "magnificently unrepentant" when he sentenced him and Anne to 100 hours community service. Merve was glad the trial provided an opportunity to "get it all into the books"; yet another place where his ideas for change in the forest industry have been heard. Merve offered to speak to schoolchildren as part of his community service, having addressed many classrooms in the past. "Oh no," said the John Howard Society administrator assigning tasks, "we can't have you talking about forestry."

LET US WORSHIP NATURE AGAIN

You have made enough progress.
You have advanced enough in science.
You have hoisted flags on the moon.
You have surpassed the previous glories.
You are flying in the heavens and the skies
And call yourself, the conqueror of space.
But, everyone on earth is ill and sick
And earth is affected with leprosy.

What worth is the progress, if coming generations,
Have to pay through their noses for past glories?
What worth is the progress, if coming generations,
Will be born without limbs, faces, or bodies?
Crawl like snails, worms, and reptiles
And probably have little fins or tails?

Just for a handful of jingling coins,
You are destroying living, breathing jungles.
Just for lust and seconds of pleasure,
You are molesting the virgin wilderness's beauty.
Not only are you making the earth's womb barren,
But you are also digging your grave or tomb.
Afraid I am, that you too like the lustful man
Who killed his mother to give her heart to his beloved,
Will lose both the loving mother and the beloved.

O Come, you still have time to repair
The damage you have done, to earth and to nature.
O Come, and listen to couplets of 'Nanak'
Learn and teach this lesson to children.
   "Nature is what you see, listen and touch.
   Nature is love, calmness and comfort.
   Nature is above, Nature is below,
   And Nature is the whole universe.
   Nature is earth and Nature is dust."
Let us worship nature again.

Notes:

Stanza 3. The last three lines refer to a story wherein a lustful man fell in love with a woman. The woman asked the man to prove his love by bringing his mother's heart to her. The man kills his mother, takes out her heart and runs to his woman. On his way, the man stumbles and falls. His mother's heart, full of motherly love, lying by his side, asks the man, "Son, are you hurt?" The man, ignoring his mother's sentiment, picks up the heart and runs to the woman. The woman rejects the man. "If you can kill your loving mother who gave birth to you and whose heart still worries about your well being, how can I trust you? How do I know that you won't kill me when you find someone more beautiful than me?"

Stanza 4, quote. These lines are from Sikh holy scripture which was written by the first Guru Nanak Dave.

ILLUSTRATION BY EDD ULUSCHAK

GLORIA, CREDO, SANCTUS
& OREAMNOS DEORUM

1

Knowing, not owning.
Praise of what is,
not of what flatters us
into mere pleasure.

Earth speaking earth,
singing water and air,
audible everywhere
there is no one to listen.

2

Knowing, not owning,
Being, not having
what knowledge we have.
Not owning the knowing.

Knowing the known
and not owning it means
embracing unknowing,
releasing the known

and becoming unknowing,
touching and being
knowing, unknowing,
known and unknown.

3

Sharpening, honing
pieces of knowledge,
pieces of earth,
and unearthing the knowledge

and planting the knowledge
again. Question
and answer together
inhabit the ground.

This is our offering:
hunger, not anger,
wonder, not terror,
desire, not greed.

Knowing, not owning
the touch of another,
the other's reluctance,
the incense of fear;

the smell of the horses
in darkness, the thread
of the story, the thread
of the thread of the story;

arrowhead, bowstring,
snare; the breath
going out, the breath
going all the way out,

and stopping. The breath
stopped. Waiting there.
Listening. Not
breathing. And then

breathing, the breath
breathing again.
The breath going out,
the breath coming in.

4

Killing and eating
the four-footed gods
and the winged and the rooted,
the footless and one-footed

gods: making flesh
of their flesh, thought
from the traces they leave,
words from their voices,

music and jewelry
out of their bones
to rekindle their lives
in our dreams and our dances,

begging forgiveness,
begging continuance,
begging continuance and forgiveness
from the stones.

FISH
for Vicky Husband

By day, carrying on with my fish body assembly work. By night, waking to find strangers in my bed. Last night, Mrs. Hanson and her three kids. A trial of a person.

Rip doesn't seem to mind the strangers. He just rolls over, grumbles about needing more covers, leaving me to contend.

By day, all is well. The important fish body assembly work continuing. But three nights ago, an elderly couple vacationing from Alberta. He bald and snoring, she in hairnet pondering. Maps and guidebooks spread out all over the quilt.

It's the nighttime crowds I can't stand. Whole families arguing. Some under the covers with Rip and me, others sitting on the bedside nattering.

It gets worse when I sweat because of too many people. Then I have to throw off the covers and everyone starts in on me then, complaining. Many of the strangers don't like our bedroom, for instance: no proper dresser, a doorless closet, the bed merely a double. I wish I wouldn't apologize so much. *Feel so responsible.*

"Perhaps if I cleaned up the room you'd feel better," I say. "Perhaps if I slept on the floor next to the dog."

More room for Mrs. Hanson and the three kids. Mrs. Hanson slithering naked next to Rip. Mrs. Hanson breathing lullabies into Rip's dozing face.

By day I'm a person of importance. Thank heavens. With my fish body assembly work. Nearly fifty thousand so far and the numbers keep climbing. The parts from Hong Kong, duty free. That was my doing. I found the rule about location making it permissible for a manufacturer to assemble a product on home turf thus avoiding import tax. The rule book was old but not forgotten. I take pride in that. Ferreter of antique rules.

The woman at Customs agreed, but not whole-heartedly.

"Right here on page fifteen of ENTRY REQUIREMENTS FOR PARTS FROM FOREIGN PARTS," I showed her.

She wasn't happy. They don't like to give anything away. They come to believe it's *their* rule you're tampering with.

"It's a nice rule," I told her. "One you should be proud of."

But she took it personally. That the government would be missing out on its due tax. That's dedication for you.

We all get on. Somehow. Me, I'm doing my part for the environment. Tax free. And I won't have to charge sales tax on the assembled fish bodies either because I won't be selling them. Because, in a sense, I'll be giving them away.

Rip was disappointed I didn't use my inheritance money for something more worthwhile. That's his opinion. A jazz trio, for example. I know he's always wanted one of those. Piano, bass, drums. Playing Bill Evans on demand. Actually he'd like to have Bill Evans as well. I've often hoped he'd visit us in bed but the dead can be very stubborn. So far, no show.

A Bill Evans tape wouldn't do. I suggested it.

"Too small," Rip said.

He wants to be wrapped in the live thing, ear to the electric bass speaker or to sit beside the piano player and stroke his fingers while he's playing. Or crouch beneath the piano player's leg and work the peddle. Involvement. That's what Rip wants.

But I only had enough inheritance money for one of us to be involved. And after all. It's important to me that I calm things down. Quit my job at the gas station just so I could take the time.

The fish bodies are all the same size. Ten inches. Just under the legal size limit. Plastic. Overall grey in colour, made up of three sections: head, shaft, tail. Flecks of pink and blue in the plastic. Could be mistaken for a trout, a cod, or a young salmon. That's not the important part, the type. It's just so *they can be seen to be there.*

I've always wanted to raise spirits.

Getting tired, though, with all these strangers turning up in our bed. I tell Rip about it but he just gets annoyed.

"Don't be so rigid," he says, "have a little flexibility. After all, they're not bothering you, are they? Not in any significant way? Beating you about the head or sitting on your back? Complaints about the bedroom furniture don't count. They're not actually hurting you, are they?"

Apart from Mrs. Hanson's gymnastics over Rip's body last night, I'd have to say, no, they're not.

"Well then," he says, "be like a rock in a stream, a tree in a storm. Let your turmoil flow around and away from you."

That's my Rip. He'd be a Zen Buddhist if he had the time. As it is, he's run off his feet. No wonder he sleeps through the nighttime visitors. By day, he's selling Bic pens, Eddy matches. He's got the whole territory from here to Burgoyne Bay and having the whole of anything is exhausting. So there's always someone in *his* bed. *In a manner of speaking.*

He's right though. I make too big a deal about everything. Always have. Still.

Seven members of the Golden Eagles Day Camp the night before last. Out on an adventure sleepover with their counsellor.

Children are far too active, especially in sleep. Why I've never gone for them. One of the campers tried to cuddle next to me, one even tried to climb into my arms. Rip just shoved them aside as if they were sleeping cats, heavy lumps. But me, I can't. I've always got to be taking charge. Half the night gone running back and forth to the fridge—juice for the campers. And then the nineteen-year-old counsellor having trouble with her boyfriend and wanting to talk. By morning I was a wreck from trying to keep everyone happy.

I can't leave well enough alone. Or in this case, bad enough alone. Doing my bit for the environmental movement. I can't stand it when people get upset. The depleting fish stocks. All the hue and cry.

My bit. Keeping the complainers happy. I have parts for one hundred and fifty thousand fish bodies. The boxes are stacked in the living room, hallway, kitchen, down the stairs to the basement. Thought of using Mini-Storage but the inheritance money is running low. If I were a midget, it would seem like a cardboard city inside our house. Towers of boxes, alleyways dark and spooky, no telling what goes on in there.

One of the campers got lost the other night on the way to the bathroom. Found her wandering terrified amongst the tail sections.

I'm especially happy about those tail sections. After all the faxes to Mr. Ni in Hong Kong.

"They've got to look like they're swimming," I faxed. "They've got to look like they're *moving in schools through the water.*"

Mr. Ni is a marvel. Even without an engineer he managed to come up with a propeller thingy that's connected to an elastic band. And he guarantees it. Either my assembled fish bodies self-propel or he'll take them back. That's business. So far, on my bathtub trials, success. Except for an occasional turn of swimming on their backs. You just pull this elastic band, the tails whirl and away they go.

I was trying to tell Mrs. Hanson about my plans last night in bed but she wasn't interested. Just wanted me to give the baby his bottle so she could get on with Rip's body rub.

The baby listened. "I will be delivering the first fifty thousand fish bodies by month's end," I told him. "I'm so excited. Rip has agreed to drive the hired truck. A dump truck. My plan is to back down the ramp at Anchor's Aweigh Marina about three in the morning. Only problem is, first I have to activate the tail sections. Otherwise, plunk, to the bottom of the deep blue sea."

Fifty thousand elastic bands snapping. I have to admit it's daunting. I'd have a nightmare about it, no doubt, if my nights weren't already so crowded. That's something. Too bad the strangers are always gone in the morning. I'm at the point where I could do with some help.

Right now what I picture before me is a string of busy, solitary days activating fish bodies. Their writhing grey forms mounting the cardboard box towers, scraping against the ceiling. Jiggling jelly. Maggot movement.

What keeps me going is *the thought*. All those upset people calmed down. Perhaps even happy. *Look, there's fish in the sea!* Again. After all. In spite of.

MESSAGE TO SOME MARTIANS

In the fall of 1994, Russia will launch a Mars lander carrying a CD-ROM disk entitled "Visions of Mars" addressed to future settlers on Mars. The disk contains an extensive anthology of fact and fiction prepared by the Planetary Society to comprise a history of terrestrial speculation about Mars. "Message" was written as an introduction to the anthology, which will also be published as an earthside CD-ROM album by Time-Warner.

We have always dreamed of heaven. This cannot be the same for you, whose consciousness as a culture began with your ancestors' flight through space.

Also—however you may have scattered and spread across your planet, you will have begun with some shared social and linguistic base. Human cultures and consciousness on Earth evolved in many languages from widely scattered and vastly varied enclaves: some broiling hot, some bitter cold; desert-dry or drenched with rain; on mountaintops, at the seaside.

But the earliest legends of each and every unique culture show that we were all, from the beginning, gazing in awe at the night skies, imagining ourselves somehow descended from those wondrous lights, looking to them for blessings, fearing their displeasure, hoping somehow, some day, to ascend once more to the brightness of the stars.

Long before there was any science of astronomy, we knew the difference between planets and stars. Pre-sciences of astrology everywhere endowed the planets with control of human life.

Great religions were shaped in the image of the constellations. We reached *up*; we built pyramids, towers, cathedrals, skyrockets, skyscrapers, aircraft. As I write, it is just over forty years, two terrestrial generations, since our first spacecraft broke free of Earth's gravity.

That venture—and this one, carrying messages to you who may someday inhabit the planet we call "Mars"—were made possible by a curious collaboration of science and romance. Scientists and social/political thinkers had for centuries made use of fables, "future fiction," and imaginary voyages to preach controversial or heretical ideas. As the advancing technology of astronomy refined our knowledge of the solar system, Earth's Moon became a prime destination for imaginary voyages. Then in 1877, Giovanni Schiaparelli observed what was mistranslated as the "canals" of Mars.

This apparent "proof" that Mars had water—and so probably air and, perhaps, life—inspired a new literary form, the tale of interplanetary adventure. The word "Mars" became synonymous with "space"—"Martian" with "extraterrestrial."

Most early spacefaring stories were patterned on the sad history of Earth's partisan warfares: Martians invading Earth were literally monsters: Terrestrials invading Mars were brave pioneers, civilizing colonists. But the dramatic growth of astronomical knowledge in this century, plus the ever-closer prospect of actual space flight, kept pushing the writers of these romances to more serious speculations.

How could Terrestrials best survive in space or in the different surface conditions on another planet?

Typically, each advance in astronomy or rocketry stimulated space fiction writers to new extrapolations. Typically, the thinking of astronomers and nascent spacecraft designers, was being inspired—and conditioned—by reading "science fiction."

Now the Earth sciences are making us frighteningly aware of the damage done to our native planet by our philosophies of conquest and domination.

Our stories of Mars are moving away from the old idea of the Conquest of Space.

We want to revise, not replay, the history of Earth. We have progressed from the idea of Martian-as-monster through Martian-as-mentor to Martian-as-just-"other."

We are beginning to rethink our old dream of "terraforming" Mars, and speculating instead on how best to adapt ourselves to suit the planet when we can, finally, reach there.

The stories we send you here, taken together, tell a larger story.

We who have lived and worked in this confluence of science and speculation send a message of hope:

When our descendants—your ancestors—come—came—to live on your planet, we pray they came seeking not to conquer a planet, but to find consonance with it.

POEM FOR THE ANCIENT TREES

I
am young and
I want to live
to be old
and I don't want to
outlive these trees—this forest.
When my last song is gone
I want these same trees
to be singing on—newer green songs
for generations to come
so let me be old let me grow
to be ancient
to come as an elder
before these same temple-green sentinels
with my aged limbs
and still know a wonder
that will outlast me
O I want long love long life
Give me
150 years
of luck
But don't
let me
outlive
these trees

CANADIAN ROULETTE

Canadians are not known to be great risk-takers. We often wait for others to take the initiative—especially when it comes to initiating acts of defiance. This has a positive side. We don't invade other people's countries, for instance, unless we are invited to by our allies. But during the summer of 1993 at Clayoquot Sound, we had a lot of Canadians taking initiatives—for their strong beliefs. They say one person with courage constitutes a majority, and I think each person who got themselves arrested represents how the majority of us feel. First of all, to the many who were arrested, I'd like to dedicate my poem. Secondly, it's for all those—myself included— who, for any number of reasons, have been unable to physically travel to Clayoquot Sound and get arrested, but were there in spirit. I think of the woman on the CBC who said, "First I have to find a babysitter. Then I'll change the world."

Let's not invent any more weapons.
Let's grope in the fog
wearing coarse wool underwear instead.
Let's be kind to one another
and let's not write any more hate poetry.

Let's pretend we're in love with one another.
You go first.

—Presented at the Writers for Clayoquot rally in Victoria October 11, 1993.

TALES FROM THE HOLOGRAPH WOODS

Where we walk, the immaculate
images of trees invent themselves—
pine, hemlock, phantom alder   apparitions
of bright air, coherent light.
Listen. There is wind and bird-song,
orchestrated insect murmur,
the sky cloud-patterned by day,
at night a zodiac glitter.

In the green shimmer of the photon forest
we celebrate the imperishable idea of trees—
arboreal icons mirrored to infinity,
each one discrete and unambiguous.
It is only at the edge of vision
when you turn your head too quickly
that you see the pattern
beginning to repeat itself.

Now imagine a forest
rooted in dark earth
where pale threads grow
knotted, nerve-tangled,
subtle and diffuse as hidden water:
the frail web that in an older physics
held the world together.

ORGANIZATIONS WORKING FOR THE
PRESERVATION OF CLAYOQUOT SOUND

In Tofino:

The Friends of Clayoquot Sound
Valerie Langer, Garth Lenz, Julie
Draper, Maryjka Mychajlowycz
Box 489, Tofino, B.C. VOR 2ZO
(604) 725-4218; Fax 725-2527

Clayoquot Sound Biosphere Project
Tofino, B.C.
Fax: (604) 725-2433

In Vancouver:

**Vancouver Temperate Rainforest
Action Coalition**
Ian Marcuse
P.O. Box 124, 1472 Commercial Dr.,
Vancouver, B.C. V5L 3X9
(604) 251-3190

**Western Canada Wilderness
Committee**
Paul George, Joe Foy, Mark Wareing
20 Water St.,
Vancouver, B.C. V6B 1A4
(604) 683-8220; Fax 683-8229

Greenpeace
Karen Mahon, Tzeporah Berman,
Karin Fritz
1726 Commercial Dr.,
Vancouver, B.C. V5N 4A3
(604) 253-7701; Fax 253-0114

The Media Foundation
Andrea Nemtin
1243 West 7th Ave.,
Vancouver, B.C. V6H 1B7
(604) 736-9401; Fax 737-6021
adbusters@mindlink.bc.ca

Environmental Youth Alliance
Doug Ragan
Box 34097, Station D,
Vancouver, B.C. V6J 4M1
(604) 737-2258; Fax 739-8064

Sierra Legal Defence Fund
Greg McDade
207 West Hastings St., Suite 201,
Vancouver, B.C. V6B 1H6
(604) 685-5618; Fax 685-7813

In Victoria:

Clayoquot Resource Centre
1314 Broad St.,
Victoria, B.C. V8W 2A9
(604) 383-7130 or
Arrestees' Hotline 381-2494

BC Wild
Dan Lewis, Peter Ronald
Victoria, B.C.
(604) 384-2686; Fax 384-2620

Ecoforestry Institute
Doug Patterson
P.O. Box 5783, Stn. B,
Victoria, B.C. V8R 6S8
Tel/Fax (604) 598-2363

Quakers
Clayoquot Co-ordinator:
Sheryl Harris
(604) 592-2080

Sierra Club of Western Canada
Vicky Husband
1525 Amelia St.,
Victoria, B.C. V8W 2K1
(604) 386-5255; Fax 386-4453
Clayoquot Tuesday Meetings
(604) 386-5255

Elsewhere in British Columbia:
Silva Ecosystems
Herb & Susan Hammond
R.R. 1,
Winlaw, B.C. V0G 2J0
(604) 226-7770; Fax 226-7446

**Vancouver Island Network for
the Environment (VINE)**
Bert Lamsa 727-6490,
Wk. 363-6625; Fax 363-6830
George Gibson 756-4614; Fax
756-9433
David White 385-0195; Fax 385-0068
Maureen Sager 724-2673; tel/Fax
724-4666
Sally Goldes 741-2688; Wk/Fax
741-2687
Kate Miller 748-4059; comp/Fax
748-1105
Jim Wight tel/Fax 360-1541

Sound Majority
c/o Susan Gage
(604) 386-6398

**Eco-Justice Alliance
(Inter-faith group)**
Mel Moilliet
(604) 382-9008

**Western Canada Wilderness
Committee**
201-19 Bastion Square
Victoria, B.C.
(604) 388-9292

Valhalla Wilderness Society
Colleen McCrory
Box 224,
New Denver, B.C. V0G 1S0
(604) 358-2333; Fax 358-7900

Nuu-Chah-Nulth Tribal Council
George Watts; Nelson Keitlah
Box 1383,
Port Alberni, B.C. V9Y 7M2
(604) 724-5757; Fax 723-0463

Friends of the Friends of Clayoquot Sound

British Columbia Groups:
Courtenay 338-9242
Denman Island 335-0964
Fanny Bay 335-1667
Nanaimo 741-1662/753-9117
Gabriola Island 247-7467
Saltspring Island 653-9406
Okanagan 766-4089
Errington/Coombs/Parksville/
Qualicum 248-3752

In the U.S.:
Rainforest Action Network
Camilla Fox
450 Sansone, Suite 700,
San Francisco, CA 94111
(514) 398-4404
EcoNet/APC:igclrainforest

Save America's Forests
Carl Ross
4 Library Court S.E.,
Washington, DC 2003
(202) 544-9219

In Ontario:
Ottawa Coalition to Save Clayoquot Sound
P.O. Box 1326, Station B,
Ottawa, Ontario K1P 5R4
1-800-567-1913

Toronto Clayoquot Action Network
c/o OPIRG (416) 978-7770

Media Island
Jimmy Mateson
Box 10041,
Olympia, WA 98502
Tel/Fax (206) 352-8526
mediaisl@peacenet

THE EDITORIAL COLLECTIVE'S
IDIOSYNCRATIC ANNOTATED BIBLIOGRAPHY

Atwood, Margaret. *Survival: A Thematic Guide To Canadian Literature*. Toronto: Anansi, 1972.
Twenty-two years later, her examination of survival themes in literature still holds up. "A curious thing starts happening in Canadian literature once man starts winning, once evidence of what (Northrop) Frye in *The Bush Garden* calls 'the conquest of nature by an intelligence that does not love it.' Sympathy begins to shift from the victorious hero to the defeated giantess, and the problem is no longer how to avoid being swallowed up by a cannibalistic nature but how to avoid destroying her" (p. 60). "This confrontation, individual against the impersonal 'grey towers' of the 'Administration,' the authentic people against imposed culture, attempted revolution foiled by the Mounties, is repeated over and over in Canadian history and the historical narratives based on it" (p. 169).

Banks, Lynne Reid. *The Indian in the Cupboard*. London: J.M. Dent & Sons, 1981.
A British boy is given a "secondhand plastic Red Indian" who comes alive. Very popular novel in upper elementary school (perhaps because the boy is bigger and so has power). Read to learn how attitudes of dominance are perpetuated.

Cooney, Robert and Helen Michalowski, eds. *The Power of the People*. Philadelphia: New Society Publishers, 1987.
Spanning anti-war, suffrage, labour, civil rights, and environmental movements, this book is a fascinating and comprehensive study of the non-violent revolution of our time.

Devall, Bill, ed. *Clearcut: The Tragedy of Industrial Forestry*. San Francisco: Sierra Club Books and Earth Island Press, 1993.
The colour plates of clearcuts from across North America have a tremendous impact. "Multiply the landscapes you have just seen by a factor of several thousand and you will approximate the destruction wrought by industrial forestry across North America." Also contains essays by writers including Herb Hammond, Alan Drengson, Jim Cooperman, and Colleen McCrory.

Dickason, Olive Patricia. *Canada's First Nations: A History of Founding Peoples from Earliest Times*. Toronto: McClelland & Stewart, 1992.
Everything they never told us in school. Dickason has done a wonderful job

of filling in the large holes in history texts. She contributes Native histories prior to white contact and balances Native and white perspectives after contact.

Druska, Ken, Bob Nixon, and Ray Travers, eds. *Touch Wood: BC Forests at the Crossroads*. Madeira Park: Harbour, 1993.
A very important book. Seven knowledgeable people, not directly involved in industry, government, or environmental organizations, discuss the issues raised by Clayoquot.

Gandhi, M.K. *Collected Writings on Nonviolent Resistance*. New York: Schocken Books, 1951.
Gandhi's writings clearly demonstrate that active non-violent resistance is something much more than a mere tactic to be employed; it is a soul-force to truth and justice rather than power.

Gould, Stephen Jay. *Bully for Brontosaurus*. New York: W.W. Norton & Co., 1992.
His latest essays on natural history put human time in planetary perspective. Gould doubts we can, in any real sense, harm the planet, but we can certainly harm ourselves and other species. He recommends we apply the golden rule—do unto others as you would have done unto you—to the earth.

Hammond, Herb. *Seeing the Forest among the Trees: The Case for Wholistic Forest Use*. Winlaw: Polestar, 1991.
A registered professional forester outlines specifically what needs to happen so that we can have more productive economic development while protecting our forests: "Change should no longer be human-centered, but should be ecosystem-centered. Let's stop talking about changing the forest, and start talking about changing ourselves." Another book that convinced us we didn't have to presume solutions.

Hardin, Garrett. *Exploring New Ethics for Survival: The Voyage of the Spaceship Beagle*. Toronto: Penguin, 1972.
Explores the problem of human over-population within the concept of Earth as spaceship. Most relevant is his appended 1968 essay on "The Tragedy of The Commons": "tragedy" in the sense of remorseless destruction, and "the Commons" where private and public rights collide. Uses the ocean as example, but easily transcribed to forests. A useful working metaphor.

Hutchison, Bruce. *The Unknown Country*. Toronto: Longmans Green, 1948.
A book we can return to for the quintessential expression of Canada as

wilderness. "All about us lies Canada, forever untouched, unknown, beyond our grasp, breathing deep in the darkness and we hear its breath and are afraid."

Inglehart, Ronald. *Culture Shift in Advanced Industrial Society* Princeton: Princeton University Press, 1990.
Academic longitudinal politico-sociological (but still readable) treatise on European and American cultural changes over twenty years. Postulates materialist (survival, security) versus postmaterialist (quality of life, environment) value dichotomy within the Hegelian dialectic. Sheds light on why long time New Democrats are deserting for Green and Reform Parties.

Jacobs, Jane. *The Death and Life of Great American Cities*. Toronto: Vintage/Random House, 1992.
Reissue of 1961 classic by a clear and important thinker. Relevant to considerations of human communities. Has had immense impact on urban planners.

_____. *Systems of Survival*. Toronto: Vintage/Random House, 1992.
Very readable dialogue in the Socratic style. Identifies two moral syndromes, one for business and one for politics, and explores what happens when they collide. Important.

Kimmins, Hamish. *Balancing Act: Environmental Issues in Forestry*. Vancouver: University of British Columbia Press, 1992.
Emphasizes the need for a balanced stance, and calls for a commitment to sustainable development, a long-term outlook, and a recognition of the inextricable linkage between people and forests.

Kuhn, Thomas S. *The Structure of Scientific Revolutions*. Chicago: University of Chicago Press, 1962.
Not an easily-read style but useful information on paradigm shifts.

Marshack, Patricia. *Green Gold*. Vancouver: University of British Columbia Press, 1983.
A good examination of logging, with recommendations for change.

McCrory, Colleen, et al, eds. "Brazil of the North." *Canada's Future Forest Alliance*. New Denver, B.C.: January 1993.
Considers the state of forests across the country. "In Canada, one acre of forest is clearcut every twelve seconds. In Brazil, one acre is cut or burned every nine seconds."

McPhee, John. *Encounters with the Archdruid*. New York: Farrar, Strauss & Giroux, 1971.
Good for those who want an "objective" account of the environmental/developmental discourse without authorial intrusion; frustrating for those who don't believe in "author objectivity." A balanced presentation of complex questions. Don't expect answers.

Merton, Thomas. *The Nonviolent Alternative*. New York: Farrar, Strauss, Giroux, 1980 .
An insightful collection of essays exploring non-violent solutions to war, racism, and exploitation of every kind.

Moses, Daniel David and Terry Goldie, eds. *An Anthology of Canadian Native Literature in English*. Toronto: Oxford University Press, 1992.
Contains a wide range of writing by Natives, from transcriptions of "orature" (oral literature) to the present. Important for everyone.

Musgrave, Susan, ed. *Clear-Cut Words*. Victoria: Reference West, 1993.
Limited-edition chapbook containing the writing read at the Writers for Clayoquot Sound rally, in front of the Legislative Assembly in Victoria on October 11, 1993.

Nelson, Joyce. "Burson-Martsteller, Pax Trilateral, and the Brundtland Gang vs. The Environment." *The New Catalyst*. No. 26, Summer 1993.
Excellent, well-documented account of a large public relations firm hired to, it would seem, scoot dirt under carpets. MacMillan Bloedel is one of Burson-Marsteller's recent clients. Read anything by Nelson. (Read *The New Catalyst*: P.O. Box 189, Gabriola, B.C. V0R 1X0.)

Pearse, Peter H. *Timber Rights and Forest Policy in British Columbia*. Victoria: The Report of the Royal Commission on Forest Resources, 1976.
For all its shortcomings, the Report takes a step towards recognition of the issues, calling for a revision of our concept of "progress." Important in remembering how we got here.

Pollen, Michael. *Second Nature: A Gardener's Education*. New York: Atlantic Monthly, 1991.
A delightful read. Contains two brilliant chapters on changing the way we view trees and wilderness.

Rogers, Linda and Jill Thomas, eds. *Clayoquot Diary 1994*. Victoria: The

Clayoquot Resource Centre, 1993.
Contains quotes, statements, poems, photos, and graphics arranged thematically by month. Printed on 100-percent tree-free paper.

Sharp, Gene. *The Politics of Nonviolent Action.* 3 vols. Boston: Porter Sargent, 1973.
Sharp offers the social change activist an encyclopedic treatment of the theory and practise of non-violence.

Thomas, Lewis. *The Fragile Species.* Toronto: Collier Macmillan, 1992.
More of his excellent essays on natural phenomena. "If the ecologists are right in their predictions, we are confronted by something new for humanity, a set of puzzles requiring close attention by everyone." Thomas considers it hubris to think that humans have the ability to destroy the planet. We are, however, wreaking too much havoc. "Getting along in nature is an art, not a combat by brute force."

Vance, Joan E. *Tree Planning: A Guide to Public Involvement in Forest Stewardship.* Vancouver: B.C. Public Interest Advocacy Group, 1990.
Explains how the Ministry of Forests actually makes decisions. The guide was developed as an instruction manual for members of the public who wish to use the system and to change it where it is deficient. (BCPIAG: 701-744 W. Hastings St., Vancouver, B.C. V6C 1A5.)

Also noteworthy:
Vancouver Island at the Crossroads is a joint project of *BC Wild,* the Conservation Alliance of British Columbia, and the Sierra Club of Western Canada, in support of the Vancouver Island Conservation Sector table team who gave their time and dedication to planning a sustainable future for Vancouver Island. This publication was printed as a special supplement to *Monday Magazine* and *Sierra Report.* It covers the conservationist response to the CORE report of February 9, 1994.

Strait Arrow is a monthly newspaper started by Randy Fred in September 1993. Covers issues from a Native point of view. Well worth $15 subscription from 55 Victoria Rd., Unit L1A, Nanaimo, B.C. V9R 5N9.

The International Journal of Ecoforestry is a quarterly edited by Alan Drengson. It is dedicated to philosophies and practises of ecologically-responsible forest use. Individual annual subscriptions are $25 from Ecoforestry Institute, P.O. Box 5783, Station B, Victoria, B.C. V8R 6S8.

p. x:	Gek Bee Siow.
p. xii:	Mark Hobson.
p. 4-5:	Thumbprints Art & Design.
p. 12:	Mark Hobson.
p. 15-16:	Garth Lenz.
p. 25, 27:	Mark Hobson.
p. 30, 32:	Hilary Stewart.
p. 36:	Heide Brown.
p. 40:	Blaise MacMullin.
p. 45, 48:	Mark Hobson.
p. 58:	John Dafoe.
p. 62:	Jim Demler.
p. 64:	Heide Brown.
p. 73:	Mark Hobson.
p. 78:	Lynn Thompson.
p. 81, 86, 88:	Mark Hobson.
p. 90:	Blaise MacMullin.
p. 95, 101, 113, 118:	Mark Hobson.
p. 138:	Adrian Dorst.
p. 147:	Carole Itter.
p. 161:	Darlene Mace-Harvey.
p. 166:	Helen MacMullin.
p. 176:	Blaise MacMullin.
p. 181:	Julie Draper.
p. 194:	Helen MacMullin.
p. 203:	Joan Best.
p. 211:	Mark Hobson.
p. 219:	David Neel.
p. 223, 235, 237:	Adrian Dorst.
p. 258-259:	Blaise MacMullin.
p. 263:	Adrian Dorst.
p. 265:	Edd Uluschak.

Alison Acker is a writer, retired academic (denied tenure because of "an unprofessional attitude to authority"), and songwriter with the Victoria Raging Grannies. Arrested August 19, 1993, she served two weeks in Nanaimo Correctional Centre, and is still unrepentant.

Lillian Allen grew up in Jamaica and now lives in Toronto, where she is a dub poet. "Dub poetry is not just an art form. It is a declaration that the voice of a people, once unmuzzled, will not submit to censorship of form." "The Subversives" is from her latest book, *Women Do This Everyday* (Women's Press, 1993).

Anneliese Anderer is a translator/interpreter and lecturer in Italian at the University of British Columbia, and writes fiction, children's books, and screenplays. She plans to teach Montessori pre-school and, with her son, Max, is interested in ceremony and the spiritual.

Shannon e. Ash: "Born in 1967 of Celtic/French/English descent, an activist for over ten years, I have lived in Ontario, Alberta, and Newfoundland and am currently living in Vancouver." "Turning the Tide" first appeared in the September 1993 issue of *Kinesis.*

Winona Baker has published four collections of poetry. In 1989 she was the International Grand Prize winner of the Japanese Foreign Minister's Prize in the Basho haiku contest. "Endangered Species" was published in *CVII* in 1984.

Louise Bell lives on Denman Island. Her article "Getting Arrested" first appeared in the *Comox District Free Press,* August 25, 1993.

Jessica Elaine Bentley is eight years old. She lives in Abbotsford, B.C. and enjoys Brownies, choir, the running club, and writing. "Sometimes I think about Clayoquot Sound. Do all those trees have to come down? To me nature is a park. I don't want my kids to miss this park of nature. I am glad you are doing a book about Clayoquot Sound because it will make more people aware of the problem."

Tzeporah Berman works with Greenpeace. "Spirit Rising" first appeared in *Clayoquot Diary 1994* (Clayoquot Resource Centre).

Joan Best is a retired printer. She is the Outings Chair and a member of the Sierra Club's Cowichan Group. She has two daughters and has lived on Gabriola Island for fifteen years where she gardens, paints, and does photography.

Denise Birklein-Lagassé is a preschool teacher and mother of three young children. Denise is an avid gardener and lives in a house made mostly of recycled materials. She is active in peace and environmental issues on B.C.'s Sunshine Coast.

Frank Bond stopped counting trees several years ago after he'd planted a million. He still hopes that some will grow to the size of the stumps he's planted around. He lives on Gabriola Island and is a writing student at Malaspina University College.

Bob Bossin is a folksinger and songwriter. He wrote and performed the play,

"Bossin's Home Remedy For Nuclear War." "Sulphur Passage" is on his album, *GABRIOLA V0R1X0*.

Marilyn Bowering's poem "Calling All the World" was published by Press Porcépic in 1989, and also appeared in the chapbook *Clear-Cut Words: Writers for Clayoquot* (Reference West, 1993). Her latest collection is *Love as It Is* (Beach Holme, 1994).

Howard Breen-Needham is a survivor of many years of direct-action campaigns and is busy raising daughters Heather and Sky—a new generation of eco-defenders from Gabriola Island. He hopes to soon begin a novel.

Brian Brett's books include *Poems: New and Selected, Allegories of Love and Disaster, The Fungus Garden,* and *Tanganyika.* He lives on Salt Spring Island, where he cultivates his garden, writes, and creates ceramic forms. He first discovered Clayoquot and Long Beach in the acid days of 1968, and still returns, although with some sadness—now a witness to the years of destruction.

Robert Bringhurst is the author of *The Beauty of the Weapons: Selected Poems 1972-82* (McClelland & Stewart), *Pieces of the Map, Pieces of Music* (McClelland & Stewart), *The Black Canoe* (Douglas & McIntyre), and other books. He lives on Bowen Island.

Heidë Brown is a Gabriola Raging Granny who is mad as hell.

Terry L. Brown has long been a lover of the earth and enjoys exploring it through sea kayaking, travelling, and scuba diving. His passion for the Creation finds expression in writing, photography, and public speaking.

Todd Butler is a musician, songwriter, and humorist from Onoway, Alberta who has been performing for fifteen years. He has lived in Banff and Victoria, and currently calls Vancouver home.

Carole Chambers lives on a small island in Georgia Strait. She has published two books of her poetry, *Still Life under the Occupation* (Quadrant, 1988) and *From the Gulf,* a 1992 fund-raiser for the Save Georgia Strait Alliance.

Don Coles was born in Woodstock, Ontario, studied at Cambridge, and lived in Europe for a number of years. He currently teaches at York University, Toronto. The poem which appears here is from his book *Forests of the Medieval World* (Porcupine's Quill), winner of the Governor-General's Award for poetry in 1993.

Susan Crean grew up in Toronto and lives in Vancouver and on Gabriola Island. She is the author of four books and the editor of *Twist and Shout,* an anthology of feminist writings from *This Magazine* (Second Story Press, 1992).

Lorna Crozier has published eight books of poetry. Her most recent, *Inventing the Hawk* (McClelland & Stewart), received the Governor-General's Award for Poetry in 1992, the Canadian Authors Association Award, and the Pat Lowther Award. She presently teaches at the University of Victoria.

Iain Cuthbert is a biologist and writer living in Nanaimo.

John Dafoe lives on his sailboat in False Creek and works out of his studio on

Granville Island in Vancouver. He is a freelance photographer whose work has appeared in many yachting magazines.

Guy Dauncey is the author of *After the Crash: The Emergence of the Rainbow Economy* (Greenprint, 1988) and editor of *Greater Victoria EcoNews*. Since 1991, he has been working as environmental consultant for the proposed environmentally responsible town at Bamberton, B.C. "Bewitched, Bothered, and Bewildernessed" first appeared in *Greater Victoria EcoNews*, August 1993.

Jim Demler lives on Gabriola Island, and is a kayaker and photographer.

Adrian Dorst is best known for his photographic portrayal of wilderness, wildlife, and scenics on the B.C. coast. His work has appeared in numerous magazines, books, posters, and calendars. His most notable book, *Clayoquot, on the Wild Side*, depicts the beauty and grandeur of Clayoquot Sound. He lives in Tofino.

Wild Iris Dragonwomon is a feminist, environmentalist, writer, and wiccan. She spent several years doing selective horse logging in the Cariboo. She is currently writing a book, *Psychosis: The Power to Heal*, and lives on an organic herb farm in Coombs, B.C.

Julie Draper is an artist and activist living in Clayoquot Sound, working towards the protection of the rainforest and the creatures trying to live out their wild lives.

Kirsten Duncan has a B.A. from the University of Victoria. She has been tree-planting around B.C. for five years. When she has a fixed address, it is usually in Victoria.

Sandy Frances Duncan has delighted in editing this anthology, even though the others made her remove her favourite paragraph on millenialism from the introduction and she threatens to write an article called, "So you want to do an anthology, eh?" She supports any movement to popularize the *snippet* as the genre for *a thought in process*. She has published seven novels for Young and (Old) Adults. Her work-in-progress is *Motherlode*, a long snippet.

Laurie Edwards has published work in *Geist, Toronto Life,* and *This Magazine*. He currently lives in Vancouver.

Deb Ellis is a Toronto-based activist and writer responsible for organizing and training people in civil resistance for feminist, Native, disarmament, and environmental campaigns.

M.A.C. Farrant has published two collections of short fiction: *Sick Pigeon* (Thistledown, 1991), and *Raw Material* (Arsenal Pulp, 1993), the latter of which includes "Fish."

Deborah Ferens is a '50s boomer. Schooled in the idealism of the '60s, she somehow missed the disco craze of the '70s and found herself amidst babies, bottles, and diapers in the '80s. So far the '90s means struggling to get to work on time, the kids to school, and meals on the table. A treasured quiet moment is spent daydreaming about living on a farm.

Mona Fertig has published eight books of poetry and edited *A Labour of Love*, a poetry anthology on pregnancy and childbirth (Polestar). She also publishes *(m)othêr Tøñgués*, a literary magazine, and is working on a collection of prose poems. She lives with her husband and two children on Salt Spring Island.

Patricia Fraser was arrested on the Kennedy Lake bridge on September 23, 1993. She is a writer for radio, and has broadcast a number of pieces on CBC.

Sue Frazer. "Librarian. Served W.R.C.N.S., married Glen, R.N.Z.A.F., children Colin and Marion. Befriended by Ruth Masters, conservationalist, and by valued enviro-peace groups." She lives in Port Alberni, B.C.

Randy Fred is the founder of Theytus Books and currently the editor of the newspaper *Strait Arrow*; his piece is from a *Strait Arrow* editorial in the March/April 1994 issue. He lives in Nanaimo.

Joe Garner, born in 1909 on Salt Spring Island, was a hunter and a trapper when knee-high, a logger at ten, and has been involved in his province's forest industry for over seventy years. He has seen and done it all—has known the big and the small, the good and the bad. He has seen the province by tramping the backwoods, by jeep and truck in remote areas, and by air from his float plane. He is the author of four books. "Sammy Craig" is from *Never Under the Table*; "Tom and Joe Learn About Logging" is from *Never Fly Over an Eagle's Nest*; and "Thelma Godkin, Logger" is from *Never Chop Your Rope*.

Kim Goldberg is a journalist, author, and photographer in Nanaimo, B.C. She is a columnist for *Canadian Dimension* and the *Nanaimo Times*. Her books include *The Barefoot Channel: Community Television as a Tool for Social Change; Vox Populi: Getting Your Ethnic Group on Community TV;* and *Submarine Dead Ahead: Waging Peace in America's Nuclear Colony*. "Axed" was nominated for Project Censored Canada's Top Ten list of the most underreported stories of 1993.

Patrick Guntensperger is the author of numerous articles, film criticism, screenplays, and novels. Having worked in various fields, from movie stunt work to teaching philosophy, he now lives on Gabriola Island.

Mark Hobson has been active in many campaigns to protect wilderness on Vancouver Island. His latest book is *Vancouver Island: In Search of the Dream*. His photographs have appeared in magazines including *Nature Canada, National Geographic, Outdoor Canada,* and *Canadian Geographic*, and in *Clearcut: The Tragedy of Industrial Forestry* (Sierra Club/Earth Island Press, 1993).

Margaret Hollingsworth has been teaching and writing in Canada since 1968, when she emigrated from England. Her plays have received stage, TV, and radio productions in Europe, Canada, Australia, and New Zealand. Her plays have been published in *Willful Acts* (Coach House, 1986) and *Endangered Species* (Act One, 1988). She has also published a short story collection, *Smiling*

Under Water (Lazara, 1989). "The House That Jack Built" is included in *Endangered Species*.

Cori Howard is currently co-editor of *The Sound* newspaper in Tofino. She is also a freelance journalist and documentary filmmaker.

Angela Hryniuk is a poet and author of *no visual scars* (Polestar, 1993) and *walking inside circles* (Ragweed, 1989). She lives in Vancouver. Along with Brian Brett and William Deverell, she organized the Great Clayoquot Writers' Reading and Literary Auction in Vancouver.

Peter Huston was born in England and came to Canada in 1959. Much of his poetry is on nature themes. A frequent visitor to the Coast, he is now retired and living on Gabriola Island. "Shore Pines" first appeared in *To an Inland Sea*, edited by Tim Lander.

Carole Itter is an artist and writer who has lived for over half a century in British Columbia's largest clearcut, the Lower Mainland. Her recent assemblage, *Desolate Combination of Objects with Long Assemblage*, was exhibited at the Pitt Gallery in Vancouver in 1994.

Mavis Jones is a founding member of Friends of Caren, which addresses many of the Clayoquot issues. Her poems have appeared in various journals and anthologies, and her short stories have been broadcast on the BBC.

Kami Kanetsuka is a Vancouver freelance photojournalist who has travelled extensively and observed devastation from tree cutting in other parts of the world. She is currently working on a book about her almost thirty-year relationship with Nepal.

Audrey Keating grew up in Manitoba and recently moved from Nanaimo to Gabriola.

Des Kennedy is an award-winning writer and author of two books, a twenty-year environmentalist, travelling eco-satirist, broadcast journalist, and passionate gardener. He lives on Denman Island and was arrested at Clayoquot along with his companion and a large contingent of Islanders, in September 1993.

Eileen Kernaghan lives in New Westminster, B.C. Her poems and short stories, mostly on speculative themes, have appeared in many Canadian and U.S. publications. She is also the author of three fantasy novels set in bronze-age England.

Joy Kogawa divides her time between Toronto and Vancouver. Her latest book, *Itsuka*, was published by Penguin.

Wendy Kotilla has ten years experience working with salmon, including commercial fishing, salmon enhancement, and as a fish and forestry consultant. She is committed to salmon stock conservation through education and volunteering for fish habitat projects in Clayoquot Sound.

Patrick Lane turned fifty-five on March 26, 1994. As a birthday surprise, poets from across Canada contributed poems about Lane, or inspired by him, for a book entitled *Because You Loved Being a Stranger: 55 Poets Celebrate Patrick Lane*, edited by Susan Musgrave and published by Harbour.

Valerie Langer is one of the directors of the Friends of Clayoquot Sound, an environmental organization based in Tofino, and on the board of directors of the Tofino Recycling Society. Her writing on environmental issues has been published in *The Globe & Mail*. She is being sued by MacMillan Bloedel for her environmental activities in Clayoquot Sound.

Stuart Lee was born in Wetaskiwin, Alberta and spent the next few years of his life travelling the world. He has studied molecular biology, hockey, Jungian psychology, Zen, and astrology, among other subjects. He is currently working to bring forestry and environmental points of view closer together on Vancouver Island.

John Lent lives in Vernon, B.C., where he teaches Literature and Creative Writing at Okanagan University College. He has published four books, most recently a novel, *The Face in the Garden* (Thistledown Press, 1990). He has just completed a volume of short stories entitled *Bright Fields*.

Garth Lenz is a photographer and forest activist whose photos have appeared in the *New York Times* and *International Wildlife*, among other publications. He has toured extensively trying to bring international attention to the plight of Canada's temperate and boreal forests. His photos also appear in *Clearcut: The Tragedy of Industrial Forestry* (Sierra Club/Earth Island Press, 1993).

Peter Light has been involved in many Clayoquot issues, and co-edits *Not Guilty*, a newsletter for Clayoquot arrestees.

Charles Lillard was born and raised on the northwest coast, and is the author or editor of more than thirty books. He lives with his family in Victoria.

Peter Lucas is an Anglican priest, formerly of the Diocese of Qu'Appelle in Saskatchewan, now retired and living in Victoria.

Patricia Ludwick grew up on Vancouver Island, where she spent a lot of time climbing trees. Since 1969, she has worked in Canadian professional theatre as actor, playwright, dramaturge, and instructor. She now lives on Gabriola Island. *Coming of Age* was first presented at the Women in View Festival in Vancouver in 1994.

Darlene Mace-Harvey is a Gabriola photographer and stained glass artist.

Don Malcolm has had a wide variety of employment including the Canadian Navy, logging, crane operating, investment sales, and truck driving. In 1984, concern over rampant consumerism and its impact on finite planetary resources drove him out of the regular work force and into the environmental movement. He now lives on Cortes Island where he is associate editor of *The Watershed Sentinel*. "Loggers: The Glory Days" first appeared there in a longer form as a five-part series, Fall 1993/Winter 1994.

Jean McLaren spent three months teaching non-violence in the Clayoquot Peace

Camp in 1993. She has been an activist for forty-five years, and has been arrested nine times for civil disobedience. She lives, weaves, and writes on Gabriola Island, and sings with the Raging Grannies. Her book *Spirits Rising: the Story of the Clayoquot Peace Camp* is soon to be published.

Blaise and Helen McMullen live in Nanaimo and work together as freelance photographers and part-time gardeners. They enjoy pizza, pasta, perogies, pruning, photography, and preservation.

Florence McNeil was born and raised in Vancouver, and her work is full of west coast themes, especially of how the landscape shapes the people who live there. She has published nine books of poetry, four novels, and several works in other genres. She presently lives in Delta and writes full-time. "Discoveries II" is from *Emily* (Clark Irwin, 1975).

George McWhirter's "A Little Something in the Mail about Election Time" is from his current poetry project. His most recent book is *A Staircase for All Souls* (Oolichan, 1993).

Logan Medland is a writer and pianist living in Niagara-on-the-Lake, Ontario with his wife and two friendly cats. His work has been published in Toronto magazines and regional anthologies. Currently, he is working on a book of irreverent short stories about human beings.

Mary Meigs is a painter and writer who lives in Quebec. She has written four autobiographical books, published by Talonbooks, and is currently at work on a new one.

Heather Menzies is an Ottawa-based writer and activist in various movements concerned with peace, justice, and equality. She is the author of five books, most recently *By the Labour of Their Hands: The Story of Ontario Cheddar* (Quarry, 1994).

Judith Merril is an un- and dis-organized crone, a great-grandmother with a half-century history as science fiction writer and editor, broadcaster, anti-war activist, and general shit disturber. "Message to Some Martians" © 1994 by Judith Merril and the Planetary Society. All rights reserved.

Glenn Milbury is a former waste-management professional who now co-owns Coastal Connections: Interpretive Nature Hikes in Victoria.

Mavor Moore's article "Writers for Clayoquot" appeared in *Clear-Cut Words: Writers for Clayoquot*. He recently published his autobiography, *Reinventing Myself* (Stoddart, 1994).

Rona Murray was born in England and spent her early childhood in India where poor farmers were the first people to hug trees—their land was being swept away by deforestation. She has published many books, most recently *Journey Back to Peshawar* (Sono Nis, 1993), and has taught English in various colleges and universities.

Susan Musgrave's great-grandfather settled on Salt Spring Island in the 1800s.

Her most recent books are *Musgrave Landing* (Stoddart, 1994) and *Forcing the Narcissus* (McClelland & Stewart, 1994). She is working on her third novel, *Cover Girl*. "Canadian Roulette" was published by Exile Editions in 1991, and also appeared in *Clear-Cut Words: Writers for Clayoquot*.

David Neel is a photographer, artist, and author whose work has been exhibited internationally. He is a member of the Kwagiutl Nation of Fort Rupert, B.C. and lives in Campbell River with his wife and five children. His book *Our Chiefs and Elders* was published by UBC Press in 1992.

Joyce Nelson is the author of six books, including *Sultans of Sleaze: PR & the Media* (Between the Lines, 1989). She lives in Victoria. "Technology, not environmentalism, cuts forest jobs" first appeared in the *Victoria Times-Colonist*, July 30, 1993.

Peter C. Newman's latest book is *Canada 1892: A Portrait of a Promised Land* (McClelland & Stewart, 1992). "Trees are renewable, but forests are not" first appeared in the Business Watch column of *Maclean's*, August 16, 1993.

Norman Newton is a retired producer of music, drama, and documentary with CBC Radio, and has published seven books in the United Kingdom and Canada. He now lives on Gabriola Island.

P.K. Page's poem "Planet Earth" first appeared in *Clear-Cut Words: Writers for Clayoquot*.

Kalwant Singh (Nadeem) Parmar is retired and writes full-time. He started writing at the age of twelve in Urdu and Punjabi. His first book of Urdu, *Azal*, was published in 1992.

John Pass lives near Sakinaw Lake, B.C., where he runs High Ground Press with his wife, Theresa Kishkan. They have three children. His tenth book of poetry, *The Hour's Acropolis* (Harbour, 1991), was shortlisted for the B.C. Book Prize.

Michael Passoff is a Ph.D. student in the Department of Forest Science at the University of Alberta.

David John Paul is a teacher of high school English living in London, Ontario with his wife and two sons. He has had poems published in *Quarry*, *The Antigonish Review*, and *The Fiddlehead*.

Robert Priest's selected poems, *Scream Blue Living*, was published by the Mercury Press. "The Ancient Tree" comes from his new book *A Terrible Case of the Stars*, published by Puffin. He also writes songs.

Al Purdy's poem "The Nurselog" was published by McClelland & Stewart in 1986, and also appeared in *Clear-Cut Words: Writers for Clayoquot*. His most recent book is his autobiography, *Reaching for the Beaufort Sea* (Harbour, 1993).

Adrian Raeside was born in New Zealand in 1957 and came to Canada in 1972. His editorial cartoons appear in over 250 newspapers and magazines worldwide. His latest book, *Raeside's Canada* (Doubleday Canada), will be published in the Fall of 1994. The cartoons which appear here first appeared in the *Victoria Times-Colonist*.

Phyllis Reeve is an ex-academic who co-owns a gathering place on Gabriola Island. She has lived in Fiji, Montreal, Los Angeles, and Vancouver, authored three books and co-authored five children. For the first quarter of 1994 she lived inside this anthology.

Linda Rogers is a poet, reviewer, novelist, children's writer, and entertainer. She was the poetry editor of *The Clayoquot Diary*. Her new titles include *Hard Candy* (poems), *The Half Life of Radium* (novella), and *Frankie Zappa and the Disappearing Teacher* (juvenile novel).

Joe Rosenblatt's poem "Alligator Song" was published by McClelland & Stewart in 1975, and also appeared in *Clear-Cut Words: Writers for Clayoquot*.

Emily St. John Fairbanks: "I was born in 1979 on Vancouver Island and in 1993, witnessed my mother's arrest at the blockades of Clayoquot Sound and the court process that followed early the next year. I wrote this poem when I was fourteen years old and I reside on Denman Island, B.C."

Stephen Scobie's poem "Forest" was published in 1990 by Wolsak and Wynn, and also appeared in *Clear-Cut Words: Writers for Clayoquot*. His most recent book is *Gospel* (Red Deer College Press, 1994).

Robin Skelton has lived and taught in Victoria since 1963. Co-founder of the *Malahat Review*, and founding Chair of the University of Victoria's Creative Writing Department, he is author or compiler of over ninety books of poetry, fiction, history, criticism, drama, art criticism, and the occult.

Joan Skogan grew up in Vancouver and has spent most of her adult life in small communities up and down the coast. When she is not travelling or teaching English in eastern Europe, she lives on Gabriola. Her most recent book is *Voyages: At Sea with Strangers* (HarperCollins, 1992).

Eileen Sowerby (Clayoquot arrestee #473) has three children. She worked as a physician in Zambia and Papua New Guinea and currently studies and teaches philosophy at Malaspina College in Nanaimo, B.C.

Linda Spalding is the editor of *Brick, A Literary Journal*, and the author of the novels *Daughters of Captain Cook* (Lester & Orpen Dennys) and *The Paper Wife* (Knopf Canada).

George Stanley lived in Terrace, B.C. for fifteen years, and now lives in Vancouver. His recent work is included in *Four Realities* (Caitlin, 1993), an anthology of northern B.C. poets.

Hilary Stewart is a writer and artist living on Quadra Island, B.C. Three of her eight books on early Native cultures have won awards, including *Cedar: Tree of Life to the Northwest Indians* (Douglas & McIntyre).

George Szanto has been Director of the Comparative Literature program at

McGill University in Montreal. His latest book is *Friends and Marriages* (Véhicule, 1994). He divides his time between Montreal and Mexico.

Alice Brydon Thomas lives in Toronto where she attends the Claude Watson School for the Arts. She spends every summer with her grandparents in Nanaimo. Her interests include the arts and computers.

Lynn Thompson is a freelance photographer living on Denman Island.

Peter Trower was born in England and emigrated to Canada in 1940. He was a logger for twenty-two years. He is the author of ten books of poetry, a novel (*Grogan's Café*), and a local history (*Rough & Ready Times*). His second novel, *Frankie's Ticket*, and a new poetry collection, *Upwind from Yesterday*, are in progress.

Edd Uluschak's cartoons have earned him the National Newspaper Award twice, the Basil Dean Award for Outstanding Contribution to Journalism three times, and a nomination for the Pulitzer Prize. He lives on Gabriola Island.

Ed Varney has published six books of poetry. He lives in Vancouver where he refuses to worship at the Church of Money.

Baka Washi (Psycho Eagle), was born in 1945. Thirty years poems, prominent personality, goofball grandparent, salutes the sun, and damns the bomb. All who lives, loves, or dies.

Richard Weatherill is a jack of (almost) all trades; according to one acquaintance, an iconoclast with an anarchist bent; Aquarian, with a repressed desire to be Zorro, Robin Hood, and Martin Luther.

Phyllis Webb lives on Salt Spring Island where she writes, paints, and makes photo collages. The author of ten books of poetry, she won the Governor-General's Award in 1982 for *The Vision Tree: Selected Poems*. Her most recent book is *Hanging Fire*.

Joanna M. Weston was born in England and is married with three sons. She has been published in several anthologies and in the chapbooks *One of These Little Ones* (1987), *Cuernavaca Diary* (1990), and *Seasons* (1993).

Sue Wheeler has lived on Lasqueti Island since 1972. Her poems have been widely published. She was arrested at the Kennedy Lake bridge on September 15, 1993.

Gail D. Whitter's poetry, visuals, and haiku have been widely published in Canada and the U.S. Her second book of poems, *Her Name Was Johnny*, will be published by Trabarni Productions.

George and Ingeborg Woodcock have been committed anarchists and pacifists for sixty years. "But man can be liberated only in an earth freed from exploitation. Hence we stand firm on Clayoquot Sound as on all environmental issues. Incidentally, we did, after months, receive letters from Premier Harcourt, carefully answering the questions we had not asked!"

Aki Yamamoto has spent most of her life attending various educational institutions in B.C. She has travelled a fair bit. She appreciates trees.

Susan Yates has been active in environmental and peace organizations for fifteen years. She is a single mother with two young daughters, and has worked as a librarian for eight years. A resident of Gabriola Island, she is serving a third term as an elected Islands Trustee.

Cameron Young teaches writing at the University of Victoria. Over the past two decades he has written numerous articles and two books about the forests of British Columbia. Clayoquot Sound is in his blood.

Patricia Young's poem "Murals" appeared in *Clear-Cut Words: Writers for Clayoquot.*

Annette Yourk is a freelance writer who lives on Quadra Island, B.C. She often experiences *writus interruptus* but continues, by the light of the midnight oil, to write for local and Vancouver Island publications and has a lot of great ideas with excellent intentions.

SELECTED TITLES FROM
ARSENAL PULP PRESS

Hey, Monias! / *Stewart Dickson*
The story of Raphael Ironstand, a Métis man caught between two cultures who recounts life growing up on a reserve in Manitoba. *$13.95*

The Imaginary Indian / *Daniel Francis*
A history of the "Indian" image mythologized by Canadian culture since 1850, propagating stereotypes of the "Noble Savage" that exist to this day. *$15.95*

Imagining Ourselves / *Selected by Daniel Francis*
A gathering of selections from classic Canadian non-fiction books that in some way have had a major impact on how Canadians view themselves. *$19.95*

The Little Green Book / *Edited by Luinenburg & Osborne*
A charming and often bizarre collection of quotations on the environment. "Eighty percent of pollution is caused by plants and trees." —RONALD REAGAN *$4.95*

Resistance and Renewal / *Celia Haig-Brown*
A frank and disturbing history of the Indian residential school in Kamloops, B.C. Winner of the Roderick Haig-Brown Regional Prize. *$11.95*

Stoney Creek Woman / *Bridget Moran*
The bestselling biography of Mary John, a Carrier Native elder and mother of twelve. A slice of Native history from a unique woman's perspective. *$11.95*

Available through your local bookstore, or directly from:
ARSENAL PULP PRESS
100-1062 Homer St., Vancouver, B.C. V6B 2W9
Please add $2.50 per title for shipping, plus 7% GST (in Canada only).